IMAGES
of America

PEARCE AND SUNSITES

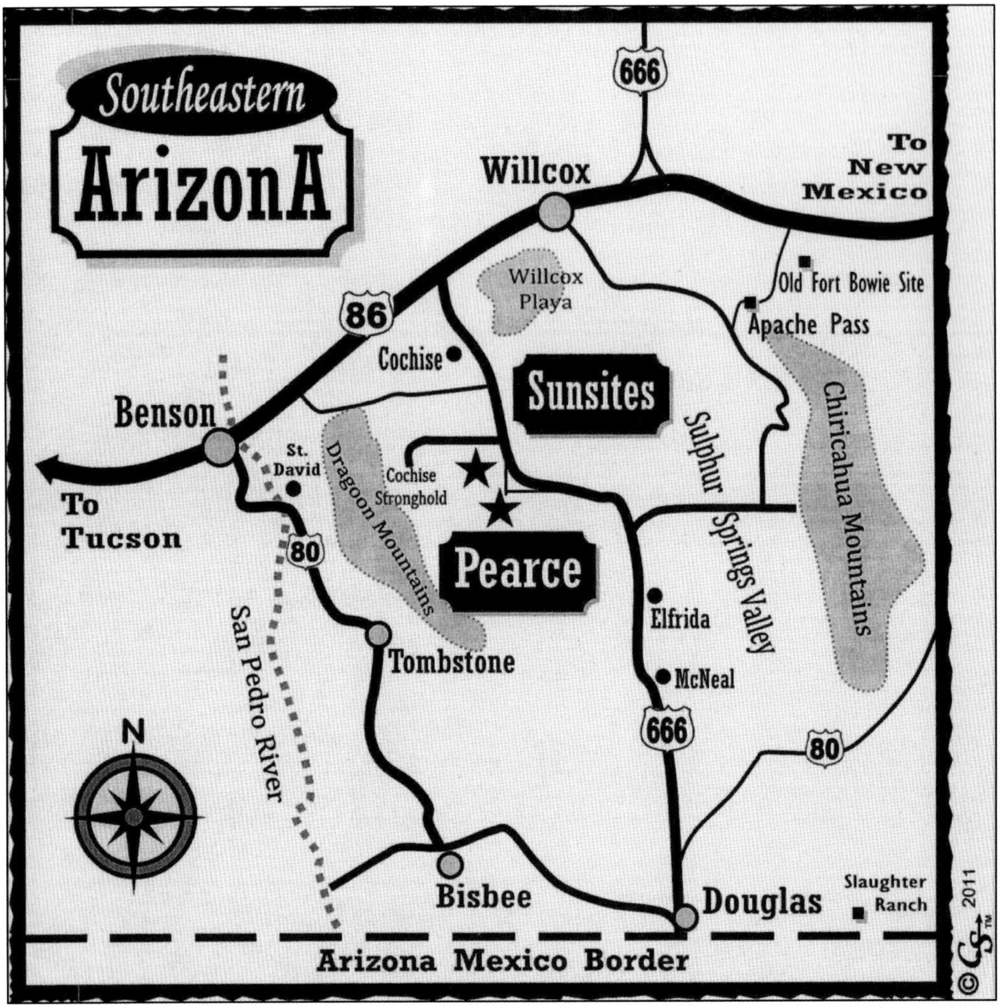

Vintage maps were used to design this representation of the Sulphur Springs Valley and the surrounding area. (Roma Payne.)

On the Cover: A group of friends pose in front of the Bucket of Blood saloon in Pearce in 1897. The Bucket of Blood was one of the earliest saloons in town, and by all accounts, one of the roughest. And with a name like *Bucket of Blood*, not much else could be expected. (Bisbee Mining and Historical Museum.)

IMAGES
of America

PEARCE AND SUNSITES

S.M. Ballard, Anna Nickell, Naaman Nickell, and the
Sulphur Springs Valley Historical Society

ARCADIA
PUBLISHING

ISBN 978-0-7385-8473-7

Published by Arcadia Publishing
Charleston, South Carolina

Printed in the United States of America

Library of Congress Control Number: 2011929765

For all general information, please contact Arcadia Publishing:
Telephone 843-853-2070
Fax 843-853-0044
E-mail sales@arcadiapublishing.com
For customer service and orders:
Toll-Free 1-888-313-2665

Visit us on the Internet at www.arcadiapublishing.com

To the pioneering spirit of the people who came before us.

CONTENTS

ACKNOWLEDGMENTS

To research and assemble a volume of this nature requires the work of many hands and of many hearts. S.M. Ballard would like to thank the following individuals for their contributions to the Pearce section of this book: Joyce Aros, for permission to use her exceptional rendition of Cochise, of whom there is no known photograph; Brian C. Ballard, of the Old Pearce Preservation Association (OPPA), for his technical expertise, computer know-how, and patience; Kathy Klump, of the Sulphur Springs Valley Historical Society, for her willingness to search out information and pass it along to her fellow historians; Charlotte Cushman, at the Postal History Foundation, for her ability to ferret out the most elusive bits of trivia; Antique Automobile Club of America member keiser31, for his car knowledge; Ruth Wilcoxson, for her hard work and fervor; Mary Appel, for sharing her family photographs and memories; Steven Carlson, a friend from afar, eagerly searching out family information and willing to share the same; Patti and Michael Burris, for their unlimited knowledge and contagious enthusiasm of all things Pearce; Rebecca Orozco, John Magoffin, and Jane Eppinga, for unselfishly allowing their photographs to be used; and Keith Davis, not only for his photographs, but his assistance in all things computer-related. Sunsites librarian Louise Sirois organized a group, which included Gary Horton, Harry O'Neil, and Anna Nickell, to research and to preserve the history of Sunsites. The chamber of commerce, the Sunsites Community Library, and Great Western Bank provided drop-off locations to collect Sunsites memorabilia. Evelyn and Jim Olson loaned Our Lady of Victory Catholic Church for a storage and work space. Wendy Gilchrist contributed images of early-1960s Sunsites, taken by John Pearce. The *Arizona Range News* generously allowed us access to back issues of their papers to research the Sunsites photographs from the Sulphur Springs Valley Historical Society. The *Sunsiter*, the *Ghost Town Trail News*, and Sunsites Community Association minutes provided some of the inspiration for this overview of Sunsites from its beginning. In addition to thanking our present Arcadia editor, Stacia Bannerman, we would also like to thank our original editor, Jared Jackson, for recognizing our vision. Many images in this volume appear courtesy of the Sulphur Springs Valley Historical Society (SSVHS) and the Sunsites Community Library (Library Archives).

INTRODUCTION

Before there was Pearce, there were the mountains and valleys, the canyons and arroyos, and the stark beauty of southeastern Arizona. This area had experienced skirmishes between Apaches and Europeans since the appearance of the Spaniards in the 15th century. However, in the beginning of his leadership, the Chiricahua Apache chief known as Cochise and his people were peaceful. The Bascomb Affair, in which a young boy was kidnapped by Coyotero Apaches and the Chiricahuas falsely accused of the crime, changed everything. Following numerous bloody skirmishes with the US military, Cochise and his men were driven into the Dragoon Mountains, where they utilized the rugged peaks and twisting canyons as a stronghold, a base from which to continue their form of guerrilla warfare, and as a place of shelter. With intervention by Cochise's white friend Thomas Jefferson Jeffords, Cochise brokered a peace treaty with Gen. Oliver O. Howard in October 1872. A reservation was established. It comprised the land around Fort Bowie, the Chiricahua Mountains, the Dragoons, and the Sulphur Springs Valley. Just two and a half years after the 1874 death of Cochise, the Chiricahua Reservation was divided and opened up to settlers. The first to enter the former reservation were miners. Next came the ranchers, among them John Chisum, William Fourr, Charles Helm, Patrick Doyle, Michael Noonan, and John A. Rockfellow and his partners. Although large ranching concerns dotted the Dragoons and the valley below, renegade Apache continued to be a threat up to about 1890, when the raids subsided and the area settled down permanently.

While searching for strays, a local cattleman stumbled across the largest gold strike seen in the Arizona Territory. On February 18, 1895, John James "Jimmie" Pearce filed his first claim, the Common-Wealth. The next weeks would find him filing 10 more, including the One and All, the Silver Crown, the North Bell, and the Silver Wave. Word leaked out that Jimmie Pearce had struck not only gold, but also silver, and a horde of would-be millionaires flooded the valley. It was said that within four hours of the assay, news of the rich strike hit Tombstone and the town emptied of inhabitants. To put matters into perspective, Ed Schieffelin's first Tombstone claim, Lucky Cuss, assayed at between \$12,000 and \$15,000 a ton in silver, and between \$1,200 and \$1,500 to the ton in gold. Jimmie Pearce's samples assayed out at \$22,000 a ton in silver and \$5,000 in gold. Claims were filed for miles around Pearce Hill, and a town sprang up from the valley floor. Entrepreneurs took advantage of the human flood and made money not from the mines, but from the miners. Water haulers, wood haulers, saloon owners, shopkeepers, brothel owners, restaurateurs, purveyors of all things necessary to sustain a mine or a miner, leapt into being. Entire buildings from Tombstone were dismantled, placed into wagons, and hauled the long, dusty way to Pearce, where they were reassembled. Of these structures, one still stands today—the Prickly Pear Emporium building, at the southern edge of town. For nearly a year, the boomtown had no official name, though local residents called it "Pearceville." It was not until Thomas Chattman took on the job as the first postmaster on March 6, 1896, that the name *Pearce* was chosen as the settlement's permanent moniker. In 1898, investors John Brockman, Daniel

Barringer, and Richard Penrose bought out the Pearces for a paltry $250,000 and moved quickly to incorporate their property, calling it the Common-Wealth Mining and Milling Company. A 60-stamp mill with an initial capacity of 30 tons a day was built soon after. This eliminated the need to haul crude ore to Cochise for transport to a smelter. The mill's capacity soon increased to 200 tons with the addition of sixty 1,000-pound stamps. Fire destroyed the mill in June 1900, but a new 80-stamp mill was built soon after and began operations early in 1901. Wagons hauled the ore 18 miles to Cochise, where it was loaded onto Southern Pacific freight cars for its trip to out-of-state smelters. Not until 1903 did the Arizona & Colorado Railroad complete a spur from Cochise to Pearce. This line eventually connected to Gleeson, and tracks were laid toward Naco. This line was never completed, nor was a proposed branch to Douglas. In the latter months of 1924, the Southern Pacific assumed operations of the Cochise-to-Pearce railroad. Ore of less and less quality and quantity continued to be removed from the mines, until it finally grew too costly for the results achieved. Mining virtually ceased after 1927, though a final mine continued on a small scale until 1940. The United States fell into the depths of the Great Depression. In July 1933, the Southern Pacific ceased all its train operations to Pearce. World War II loomed on the horizon. The population dwindled as residents moved to the larger cities for work. Yet some people remained, too obstinate, too attached to their homes to let go and move on. They worked where they could and kept the school open; the post office and the mercantile remained the spots to gather and enjoy the company of friends and neighbors. Pearce stubbornly hung on.

In the late 1950s, retired New York lawyer and real estate investor Joseph Timan looked over the dusty ranch lands of southeast Cochise County and envisioned, of all things, thousands of people eager to buy into the dream of sunshine, inexpensive lots, and rural living. In 1959, he founded Horizon Land Corporation with $300,000, according to a 1971 story in the *Tucson Daily Citizen*. Convinced that his dream would someday be realized, Timan, as president of Horizon, quickly began buying huge chunks of land in the vicinity of Pearce. The company eventually amassed about 50,000 acres and began selling lots through a widespread advertising campaign. Timan further underscored his confidence in the American Dream of home ownership as the wave of the future by purchasing additional land in Arizona, plus making investments in New Mexico and Texas. That Timan had such an expansive vision was no surprise. His rise from an 11-year-old Polish immigrant to noted real estate lawyer and investor demonstrated an intelligence and drive that seemed up to any challenge—even building a community in such an unlikely environment as the arid Southwestern desert. However, Horizon battled the Federal Trade Commission (FTC) for years over charges of improper sales practices, before settling in 1981 and agreeing to, among other requirements, "establish . . . a $14.5 million trust fund to be distributed to eligible past purchasers." Also, the FTC opinion required the firm to spend $45 million over 20 years "to improve certain properties." The stringent financial requirements weakened the company, but Horizon remained alive into the 21st century. However, in 2004, the remaining holdings of Horizon Corporation were merged into MCO Properties Inc., according to a spokesperson for that company. Although Horizon Corporation is no longer around, there would not be a Sunsites story if it were not for Joseph Timan's willingness to gamble on his dream becoming a reality.

One

Before Pearce

The Dragoon Mountains and the Sulphur Springs Valley have been home to humankind for thousands of years, but it is the Apaches' existence with which the Dragoons are closely tied, and to one Apache in particular—Cochise. With the death of Cochise in 1874, the reservation system he helped establish broke down. Settlers coveted the land for ranching and farming. The Chiricahua Reservation was broken up and opened to settlers. The first to enter the former reservation were miners. Silver was discovered at Goose Flats, later named Tombstone; at Dos Cabezas, gold-bearing quartz was found. Miners flooded the area. Ranchers followed, among them New Mexico cattle baron John Chisum. Chisum drove his longhorns into the Sulphur Springs Valley from Point of Mountain, on the east side of the Winchesters, southward to where Pearce now stands, and from the Dragoons to the Chiricahua Mountains. Other ranchers followed, one of the first being William Fourr. Fourr was followed by William and Robert Woolf and Robert Pursley. Next to arrive was Charles Helm with partner Alfred Shultz and Shultz's brother Hugh. To the South Pass came Patrick Doyle, and near what would become known as Grapevine Canyon, Michael Noonan. About a year after Mike Noonan, W. Augustus Fiege established his C-Bar Ranch in Dragoon Pass. The most famous man to pursue ranching in the Sulphur Springs Valley was New Yorker John A. Rockfellow. In 1877, Rockfellow, a civil engineer, set out with boyhood friend Bill Hartt for the West. In Nogales, the men met up with Walter Servoss. Along with Servoss, Rockfellow and Hartt invested in a Dragoon Mountain ranch. In addition to their Cochise Stronghold acres, they acquired property eight miles into the valley. They christened their new headquarters Esperanza, later changing the name to the New York Ranch, as their brand was *NY*. In 1894, a local cattleman searching for strays stumbled across the largest strike seen in the Arizona Territory. John James "Jimmie" Pearce had made his way from Tombstone to set up a homestead in the shadow of the Dragoons. His lucky discovery rocked the territory. Gold!

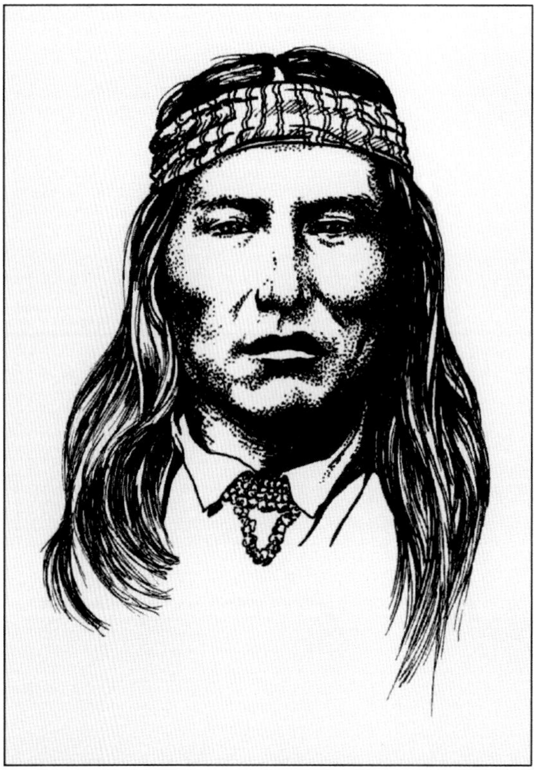

Cochise was a chief of the Chiricahua Apaches, the tribe that lived in and around the Dragoon and Chiricahua Mountains, southwestern New Mexico, and northern Sonora, Mexico. Accounts give the year of Cochise's birth as 1812. Cochise's peace treaty with Gen. Oliver O. Howard in October 1872, brokered by Thomas Jeffords, resulted in the establishment of a reservation and was a pledge of faith between opposing leaders. (Drawing by Joyce Aros.)

Council Rocks, on the western side of the Dragoon Mountains, forms a natural amphitheater, and as a gathering place, it was ideal. Ancient pictographs, believed to be 1,000 years old, decorate the surrounding rocks. Some of the drawings may have been enhanced by the Apache people, who came later. Purportedly, Council Rocks is where Cochise made his peace with General Howard in 1872. (Old Pearce Preservation Association.)

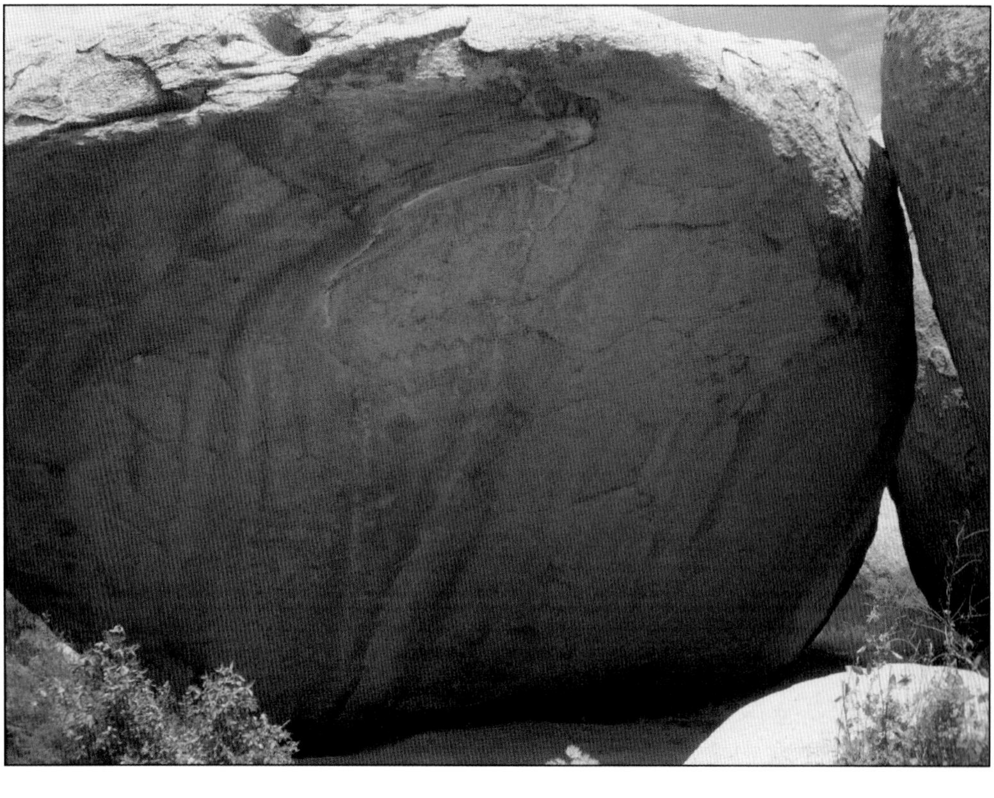

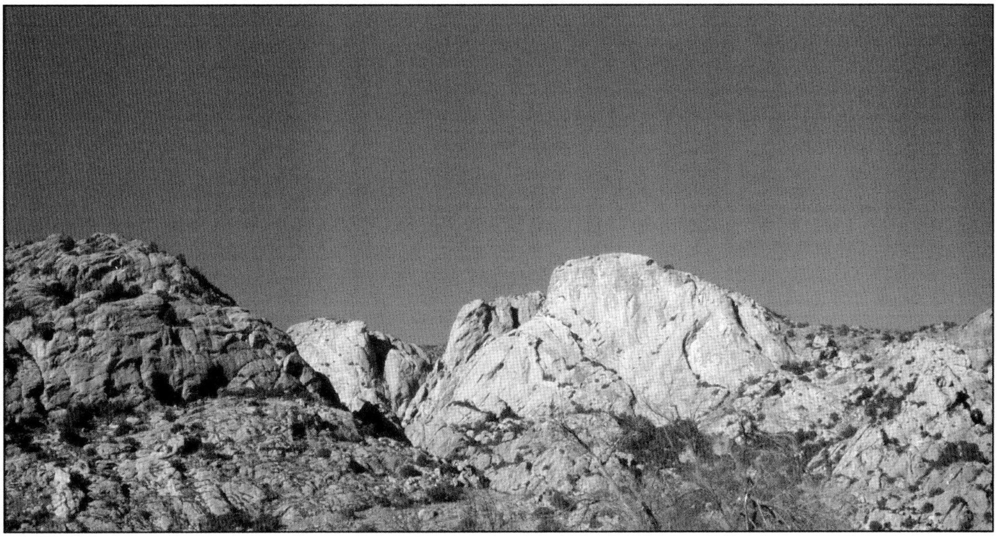

Cochise died of natural causes on June 8, 1874. His body was given a secret burial in the Dragoon Mountains. It has yet to be found. He left behind two sons, Taza and Naiche, neither of whom proved to be the caliber of leader their father was. After Cochise's death, the reservation system broke down, and the remaining Chiricahua Apaches were herded onto the San Carlos Indian Reservation. (Ballard collection.)

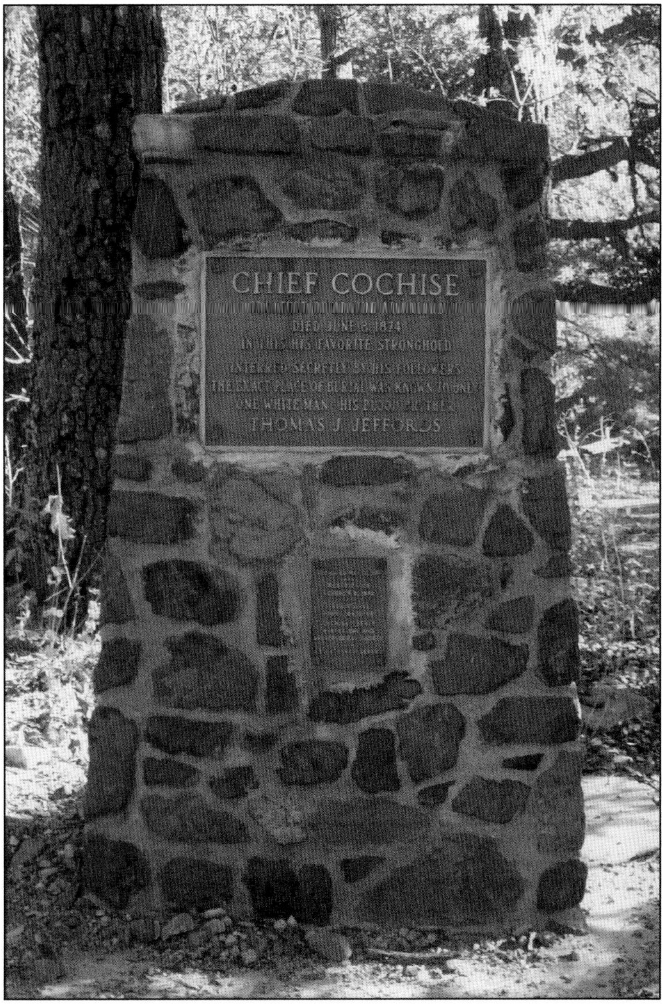

This marker honoring Cochise was originally dedicated on May 13, 1934. The Dragoon Mountains were incorporated into the Chiricahua National Forest in 1910, and in 1917, they became part of the Coronado National Forest. (Old Pearce Preservation Association.)

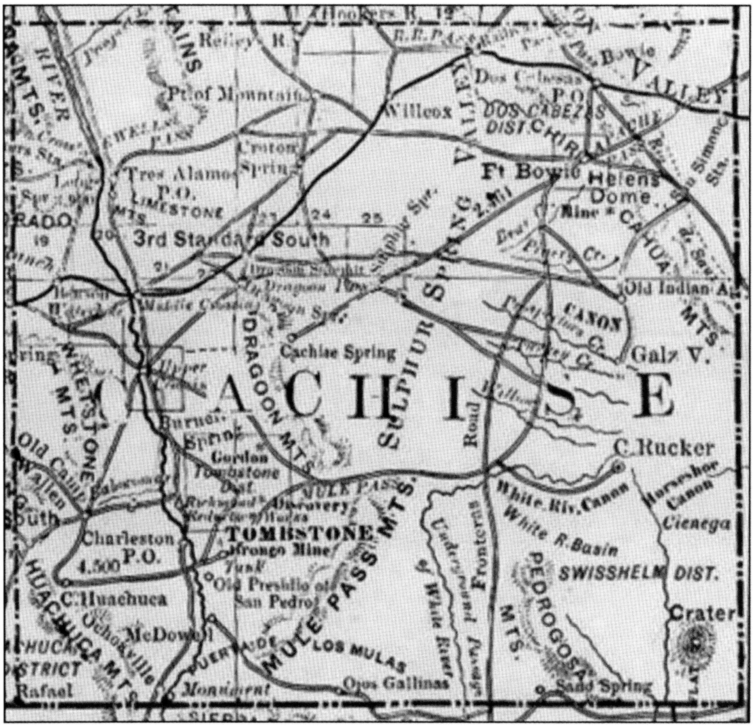

Originally spelled "Cachise," Cochise County was formed on February 1, 1881, from a portion of eastern Pima County, and named after the Chiricahua Apache chief. Tombstone acted in the capacity of county seat until 1929, when power transferred to Bisbee. Cochise County takes up an area of 6,219 square miles. The 1890 census showed a population of 6,938. By 2010, that number had escalated to 131,346. (Ballard collection.)

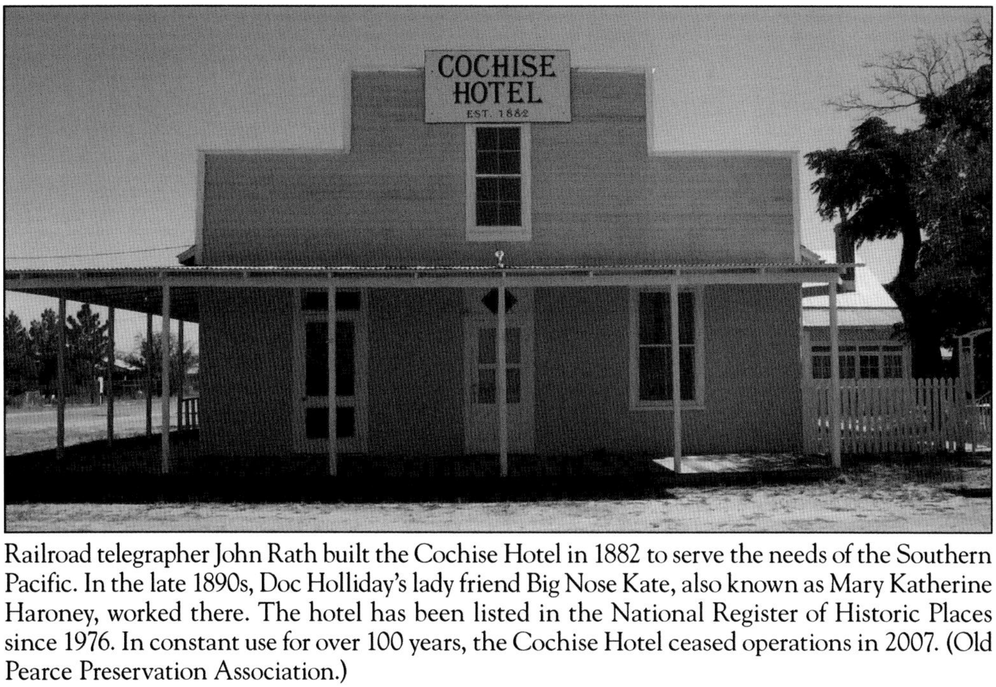

Railroad telegrapher John Rath built the Cochise Hotel in 1882 to serve the needs of the Southern Pacific. In the late 1890s, Doc Holliday's lady friend Big Nose Kate, also known as Mary Katherine Haroney, worked there. The hotel has been listed in the National Register of Historic Places since 1976. In constant use for over 100 years, the Cochise Hotel ceased operations in 2007. (Old Pearce Preservation Association.)

Johnny Ringo died July 13, 1882, in West Turkey Creek Canyon. Found sitting at the base of several clustered oaks, Ringo died from a bullet wound to the head. He was bootless, his torn undershirt wrapped around his feet. He wore two gun belts, one fastened around his waist upside down. Although the coroner ruled suicide, to this day speculation as to the cause of death continues. (Ballard collection.)

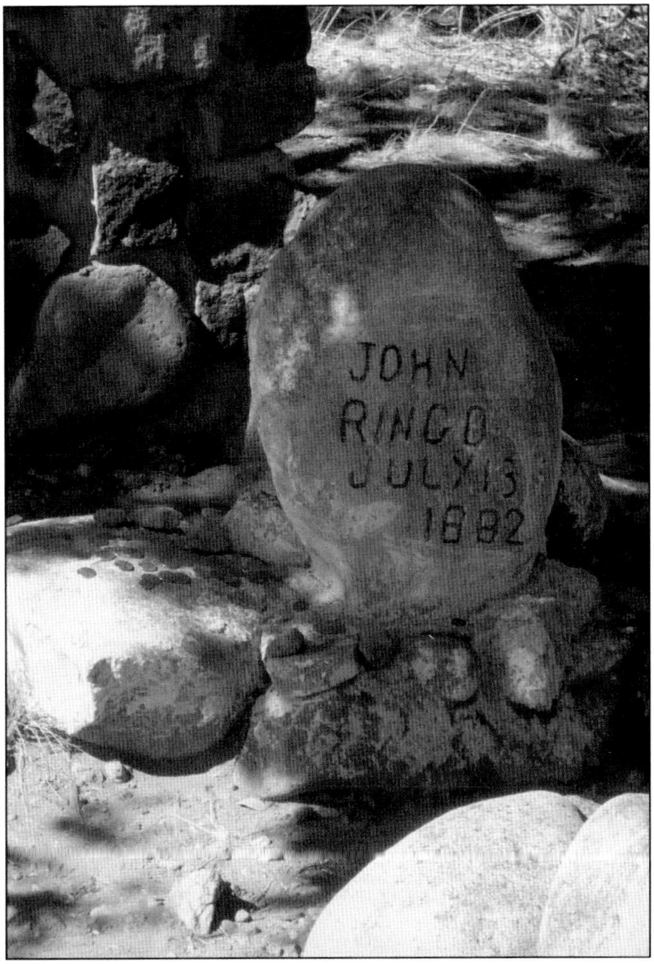

West Turkey Creek Canyon is a lovely spot; no doubt it was just as beautiful the day Johnny Ringo met his death there in 1882. In 10 years, the population of the area was great enough to justify the county school district's establishment of the Wilgus School. The remains of the town of Wilgus are visible across the road and down a bit from the site of Johnny Ringo's grave. (Old Pearce Preservation Association.)

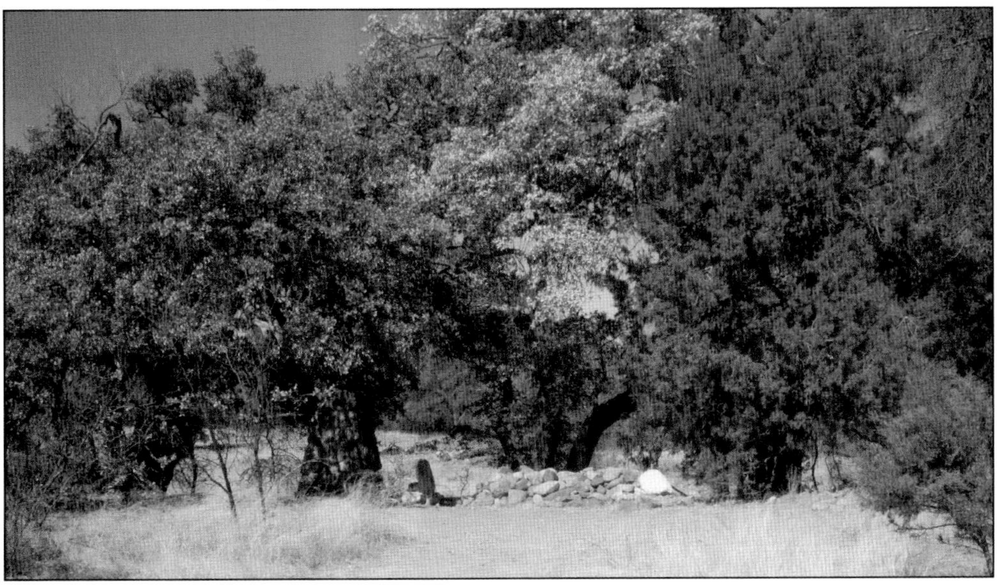

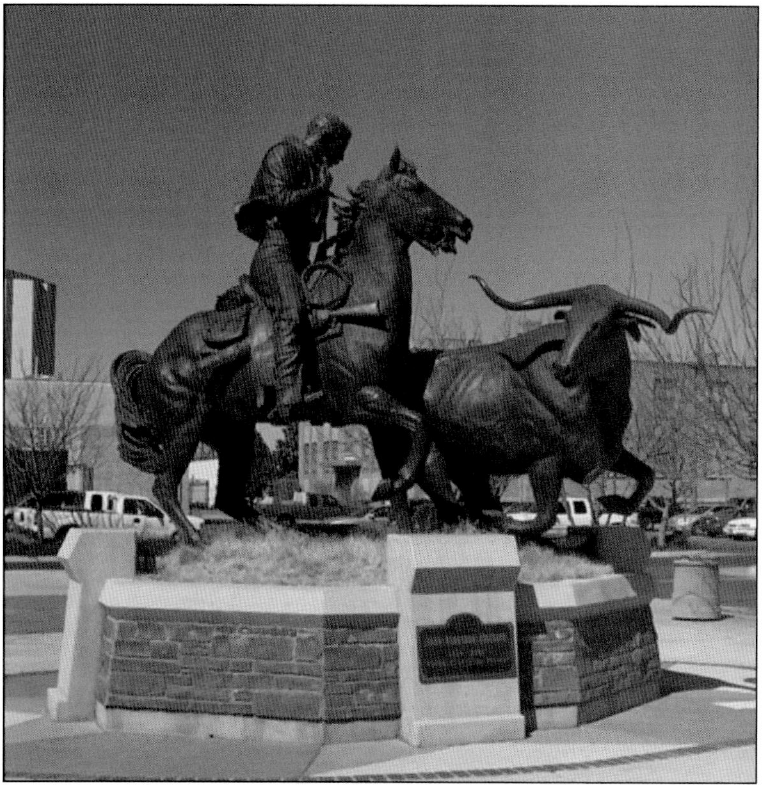

In 1876, trailblazer John Chisum headed 1,500 longhorns west into the Sulphur Springs Valley. Croton Springs, also called Chisum Springs, south and west of Willcox, was the site of one of the cattleman's base camps. This bronze of John Simpson Chisum with his lead steer, Ruidoso, is located in Roswell, New Mexico. (Ballard collection.)

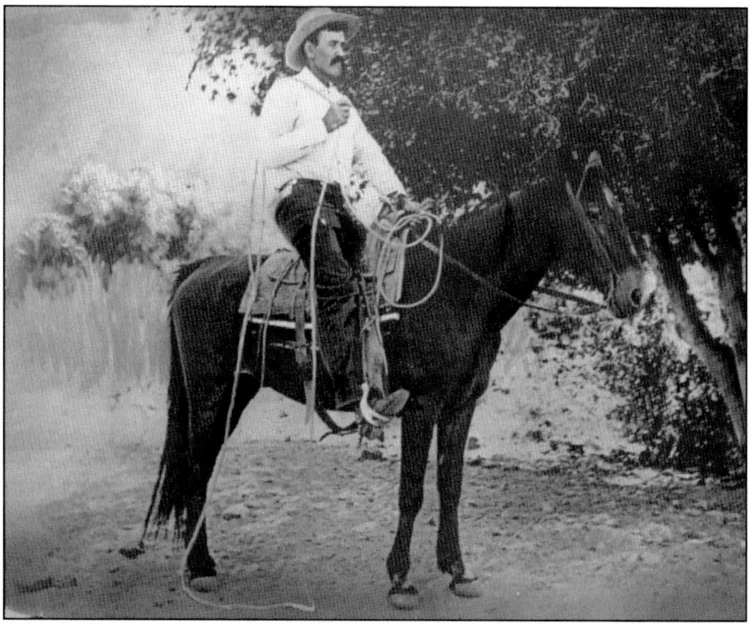

Jackson Busenbark was born in 1875 in Texas. The family moved to Cochise County sometime in 1893. By age 11, he was already working as a cowhand, and by age 26, he was foreman for the Chiricahua Cattle Company. Taken later in life, this photograph shows him on his horse, Rifon. (Mary Appel.)

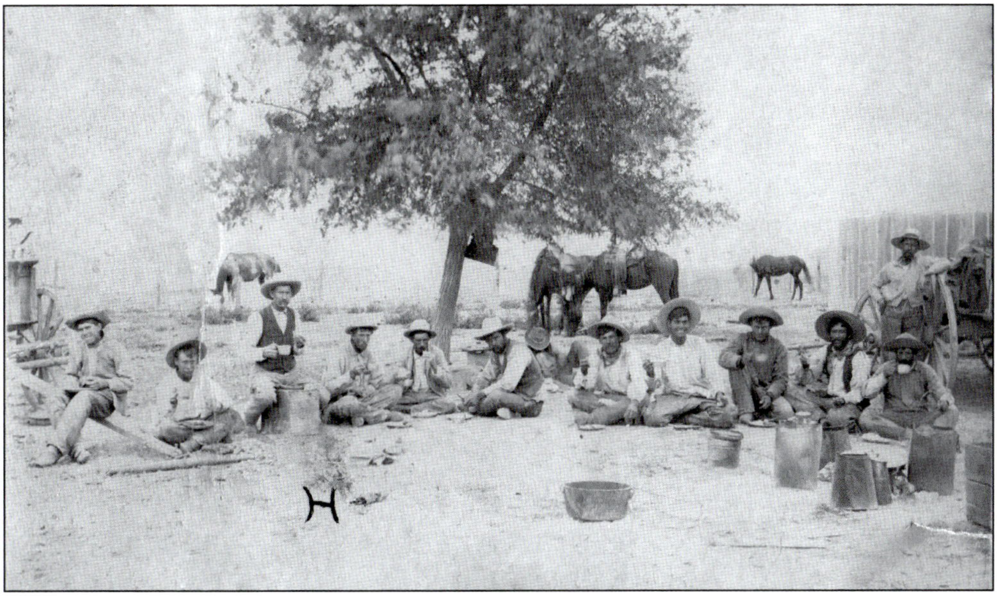

Pictured are ranch hands of Henry Hooker's Sierra Bonita. David Stuart Drew, later of Pearce, acted as foreman for Hooker, serving the Monk Ranch in the same capacity. Cattle ranching spanned the Sulphur Springs Valley and included the New York Ranch, the Chiricahua Cattle Company, the Sierra Bonita, Rucker Ranch, and Monk Ranch, to name a handful. In the beginning, cattle was king. In the Sulphur Springs Valley of today, that saying remains true. (SSVHS.)

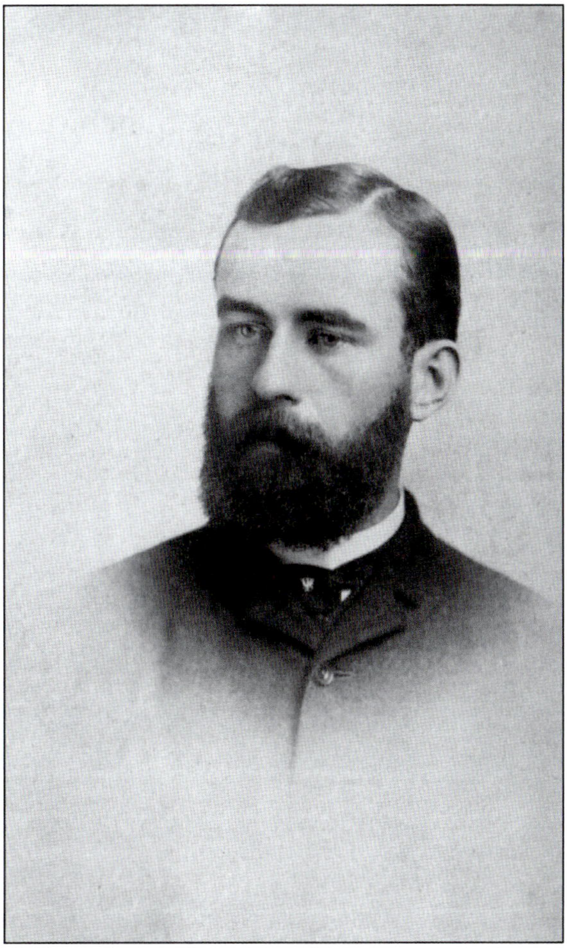

Walter Servoss joined his friend John Rockfellow in many endeavors in and around the Sulphur Springs Valley, including mining and ranching, partnering in the New York Ranch in August 1883. Servoss eventually left for a mining venture in Colombia, South America; he was gone seven years. Returning to the valley, he again took up residence at the ranch. Servoss acted as postmaster of Cochise in 1905–1906. He died in 1908. (*Log of an Arizona Trail Blazer.*)

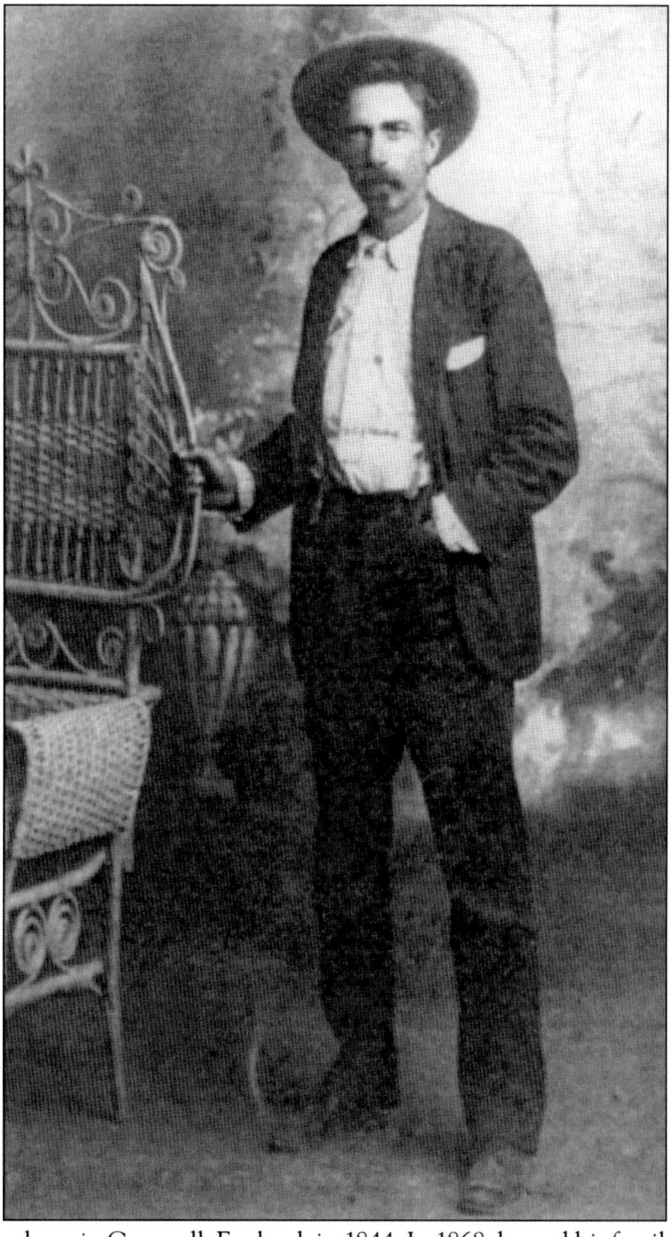

James Pearce was born in Cornwall, England, in 1844. In 1868, he and his family immigrated to the United States and by 1881, were in Tombstone. He worked there as a miner for many years. In 1894, the Pearces moved east over the Dragoons to the Sulphur Springs Valley and began cattle ranching. One day, riding out to check on cattle, James stopped for lunch. Up on the hill to get a better view of the valley, he sat on a rock ledge and ate. He picked up stones, broke one open, and saw a glint of color. There are a couple of different stories about who actually discovered the gold, but all that matters is that the Pearces made the discovery that set into motion a rush that would change the area forever. By 1896, the family sold the claims that would become the Common-Wealth Mine and split the money. James and Maria Pearce soon moved from the valley. On September 16, 1910, James Pearce died in his home in Oakland, California. (Cochise County Historical Society.)

Two

The Growth of Pearce

Jimmie Pearce's discovery of gold in 1894 and his subsequent filing on his claims in early 1895 started the stampede into the Sulphur Springs Valley. The Common-Wealth Mine was born. Men uprooted their families lock, stock, and barrel—and often even their homes or businesses—and moved. Tombstone, in decline since the flooding of its silver mines, was especially hard hit, losing many of its residents to the new town known collectively as Pearceville, Pearce Town, or just plain Pearce, as it became known with the establishment of the first post office in 1896. Investors came from all over the country, vying for the opportunity to obtain wealth beyond a man's dreams. However, The Common-Wealth brought not only gold and silver to its investors, but also provided good livings for the townspeople. Businesses flourished. Families grew and prospered. The year 1907 saw a population upwards of 500. According to the business directory of the time, the main occupations were mining and stock raising. Other businesses included restaurants, a blacksmith, butcher, livery, hotels, saloons, attorneys, and general merchandisers; whatever a population required was available. Pearce thrived.

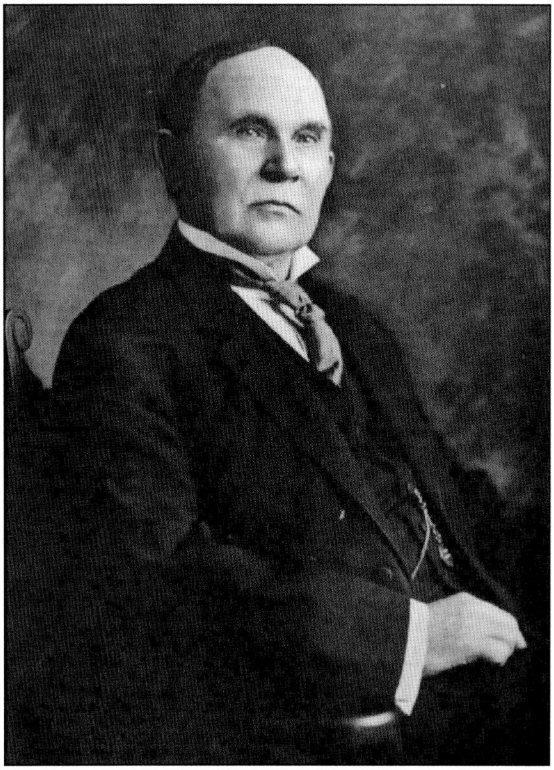

In the 1880s, John Brockman was established as a successful businessman in New Mexico. Upon hearing of the Pearce strike, he made an offer of $250,000. The Pearces accepted. Now all he had to do was raise the money. He gathered a group of four men as initial investors: Daniel Moreau Barringer, Lewis Barringer, Count Pourtales, and Richard Allen Fullerton Penrose Jr. (Ballard collection.)

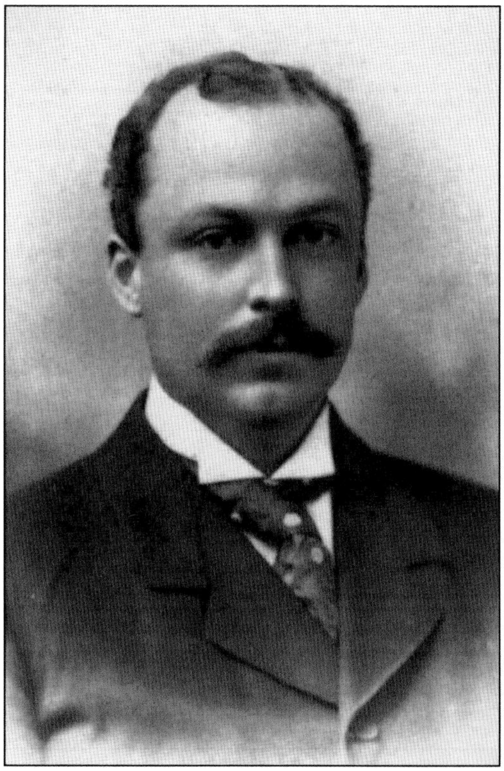

Richard Allen Fullerton Penrose Jr., born in 1863, was from a famous Philadelphia family. A Harvard graduate with a doctorate in geology, by 1895, he was a professor at the University of Chicago. John Brockman approached him about the Pearce property. After the two visited the mine site late in 1895, he was in. He would enlist his friend Daniel Moreau Barringer, also a Philadelphian, as another investor. (Ballard collection.)

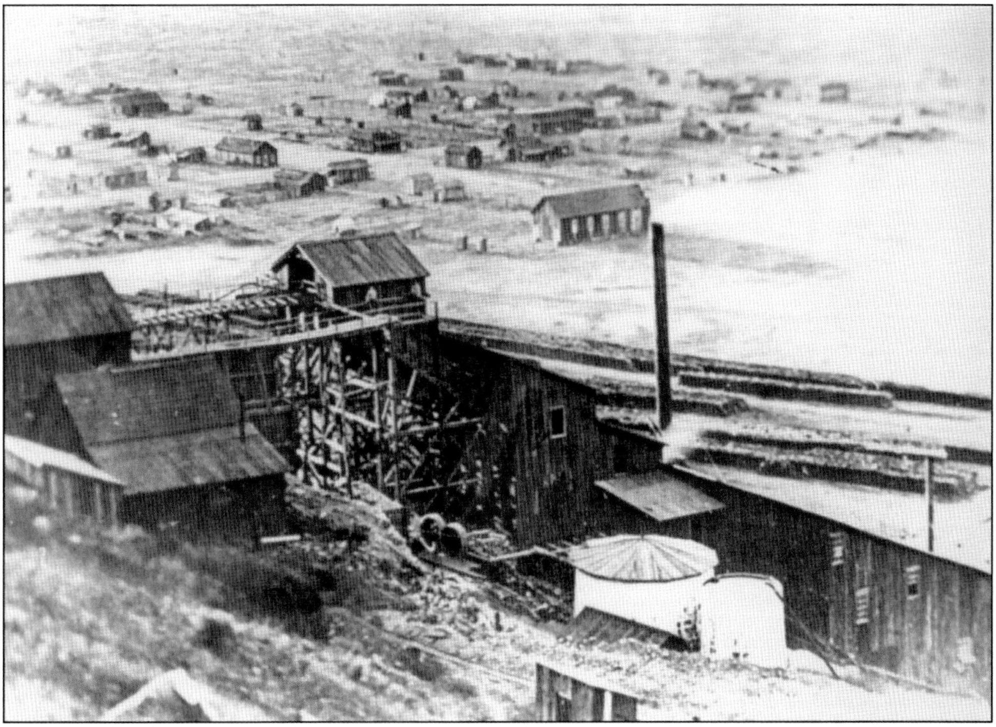

In 1896, the Common-Wealth Mining and Milling Company was formed. Richard Allen Fullerton Penrose Jr. was president, Daniel Moreau Barringer was treasurer-secretary, John Brockman was manager, and Lewis Barringer and Count Pourtales were directors. By 1897, the Common-Wealth had paid off its bond to the Pearces. (Cochise County Historical Society.)

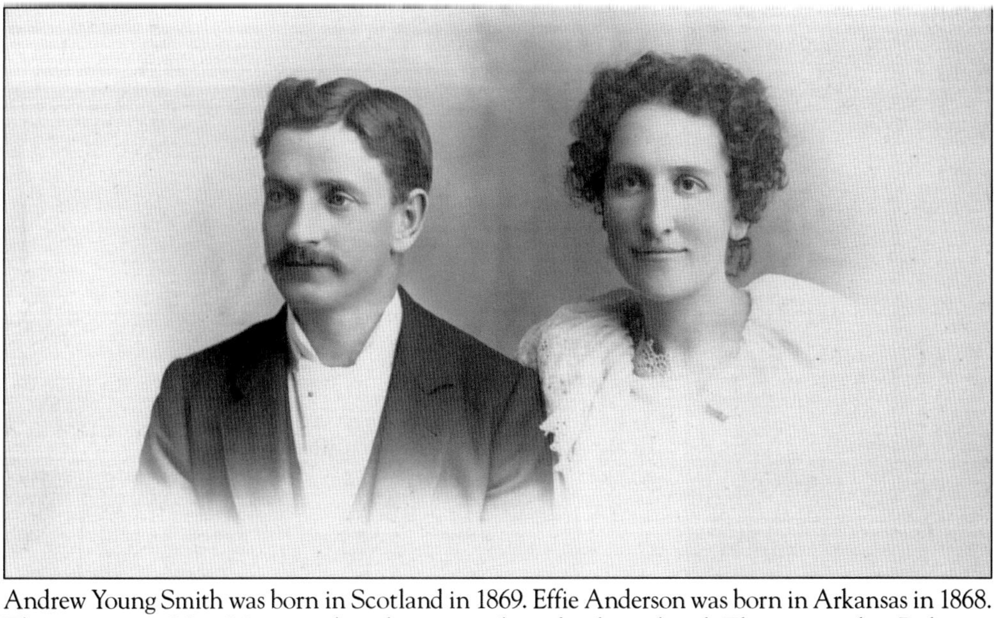

Andrew Young Smith was born in Scotland in 1869. Effie Anderson was born in Arkansas in 1868. The two met in New Mexico, where he was working for the railroad. They married in Bisbee in 1895 and lived in Benson a short time before moving to Pearce. Andrew Young Smith was employed by the Common-Wealth Mine as a head of the accounting department. (Steven Carlson.)

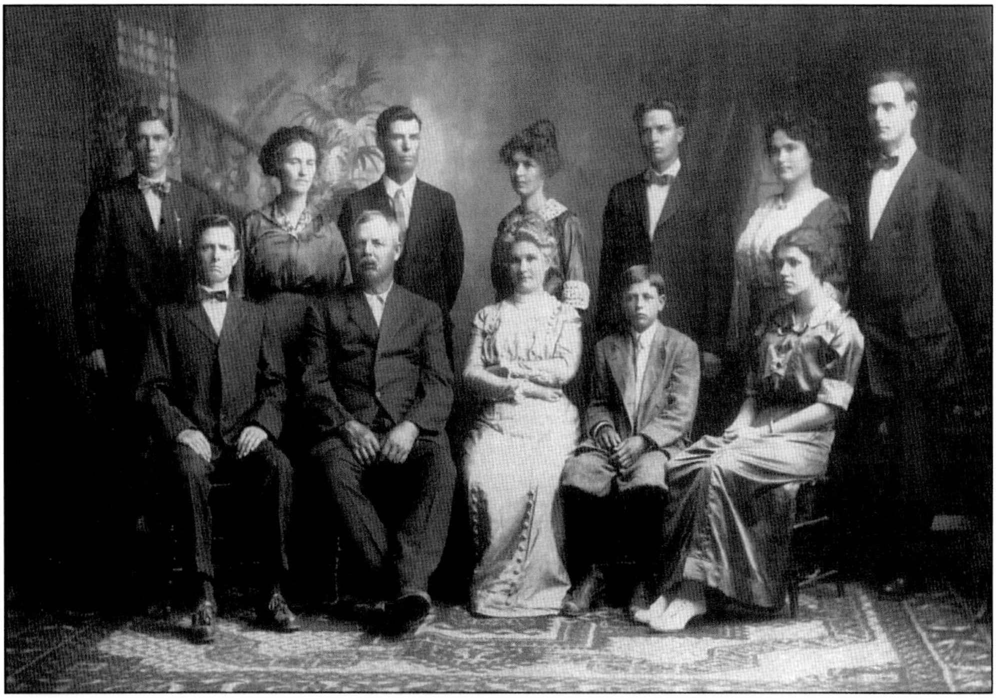

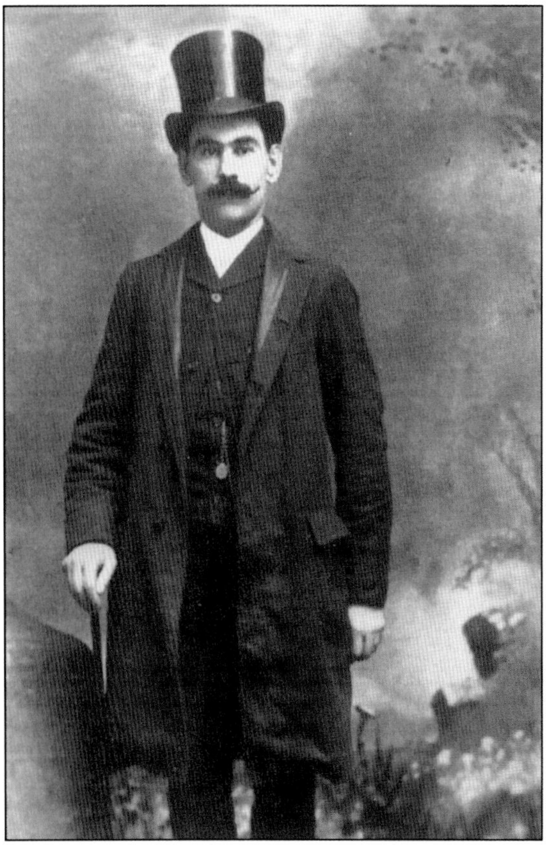

The Clifford family was in St. David when word of the Pearce strike spread. Henry Clifford, being in the freighting business, saw an opportunity and moved to Pearce. The Clifford family stayed in Pearce until the mid-teens, when Henry and his wife, Eliza, moved to Safford. (Henry Clifford collection, SSVHS.)

Upon news of the gold strike in Pearce, Joe Bignon literally pulled up stakes. He disassembled his home, loaded it aboard a freight wagon, and moved it through South Pass, reassembling the structure at the foot of Six Mile Hill. Ever the entrepreneur, Joe Bignon established the first saloon in Pearce. The lavish Pioneer opened its doors in March 1896, offering faro, roulette, and the finest spirits. (Jane Eppinga.)

At six feet tall and topping the scales at 200-plus pounds, Minnie Bignon was first an entertainer, dazzling audiences by performing in pink tights, then an entrepreneur. With husband, Joe Bignon, she owned the Bird Cage Theater in Tombstone and later, the Crystal Palace. With the decline of Tombstone's mining industry, the couple moved across the Dragoon Mountains to Pearce. Big Minnie found her final resting place in the Pearce Cemetery. (Jane Eppinga.)

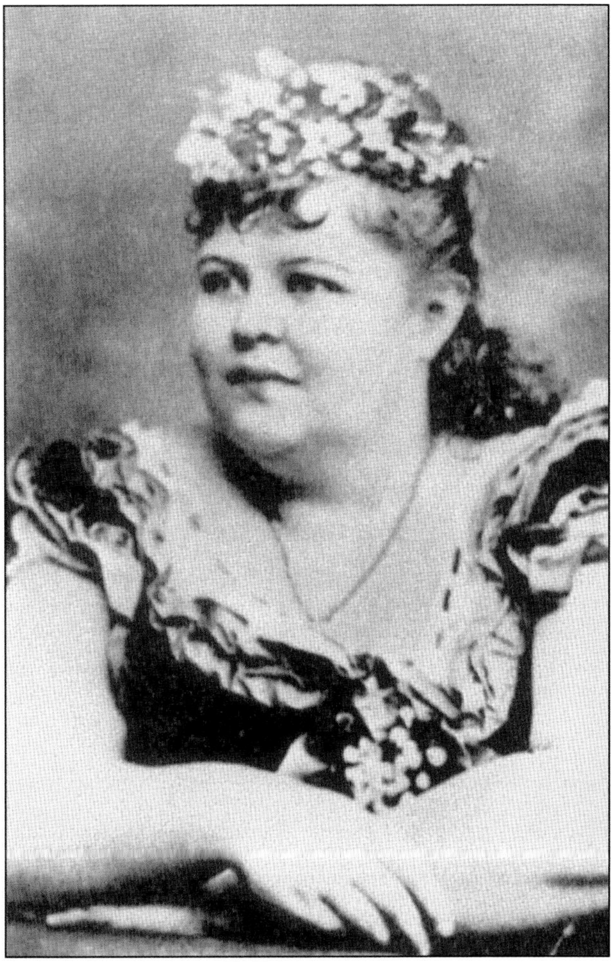

News of the strike caused people to pack up their belongings and move. In some cases, they disassembled their homes and carted them to their new location for reassembly. The Prindiville home, two small cabins put together, shows how easily this was accomplished. (Mary Appel.)

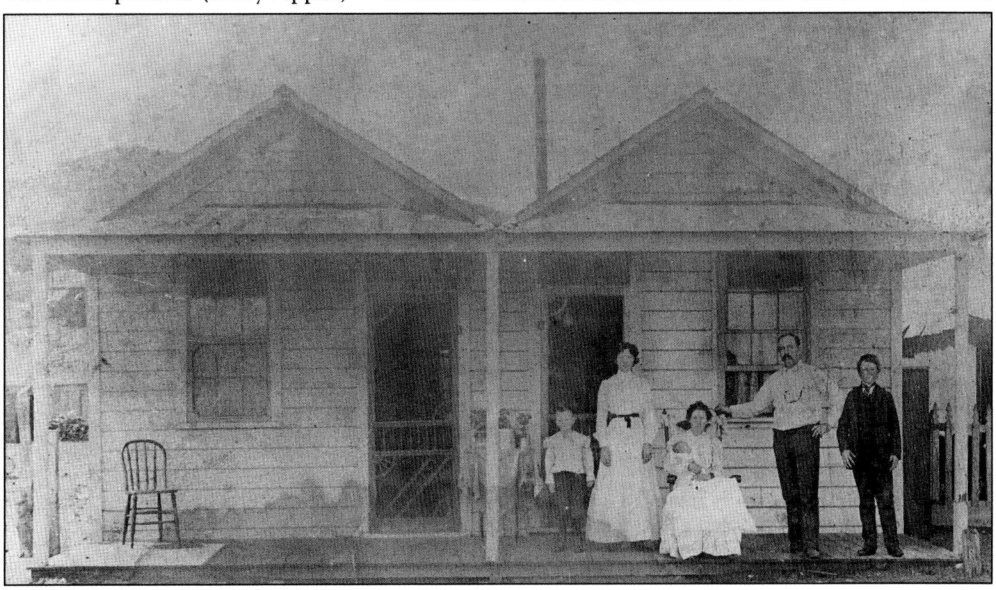

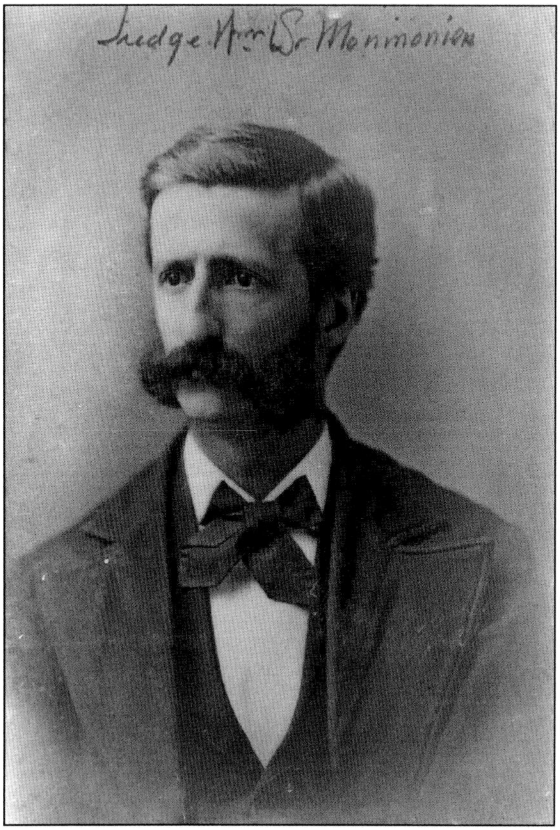

William D. Monmonier worked as Cochise County recorder and school superintendent between 1880 and 1890. May 1890 found him employed as Tombstone's interim mayor. He moved his family to Pearce in 1896, where he ranched and speculated in mining. After Charles Cinder finished his term as Pearce's first duly elected justice of the peace, Monmonier took over, working in that capacity for many years. (Rebecca Orozco.)

Already successful in Willcox, the Soto Brothers and Thomas Chattman rushed to Pearce to set up their general store. In 1896, there were enough people in camp to warrant a post office. It was then that a name was chosen, and the camp became the town of Pearce. Chattman, standing in the doorway, was selected as the first postmaster. He stayed at the job for about a year. (Arizona Historical Society/Tucson 1782.)

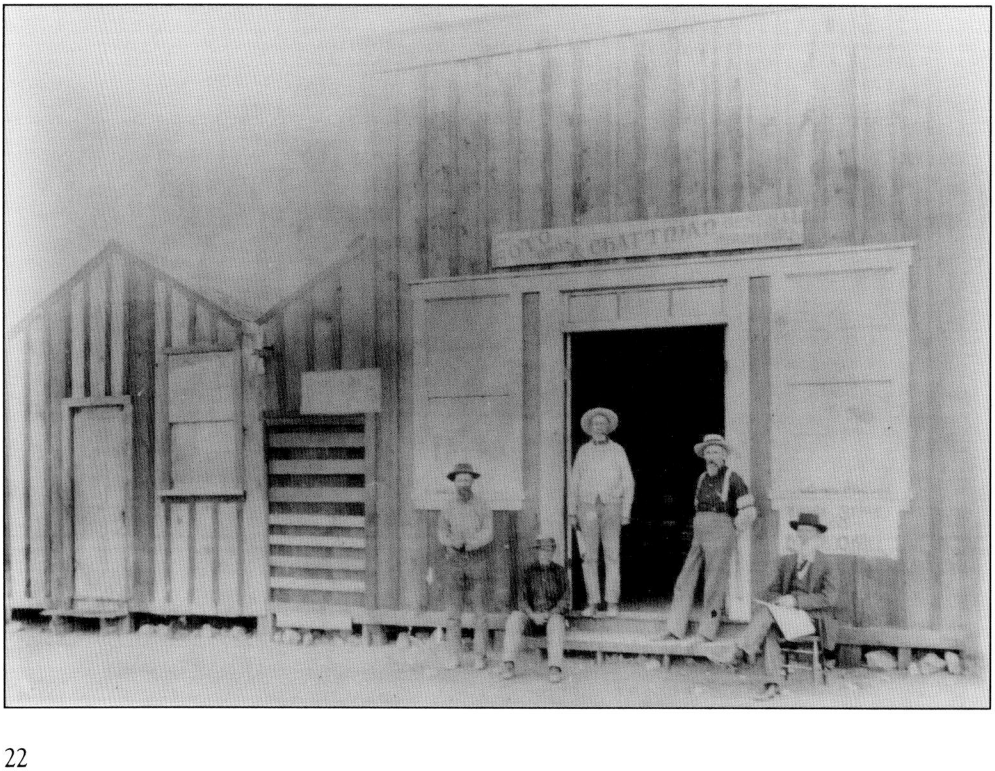

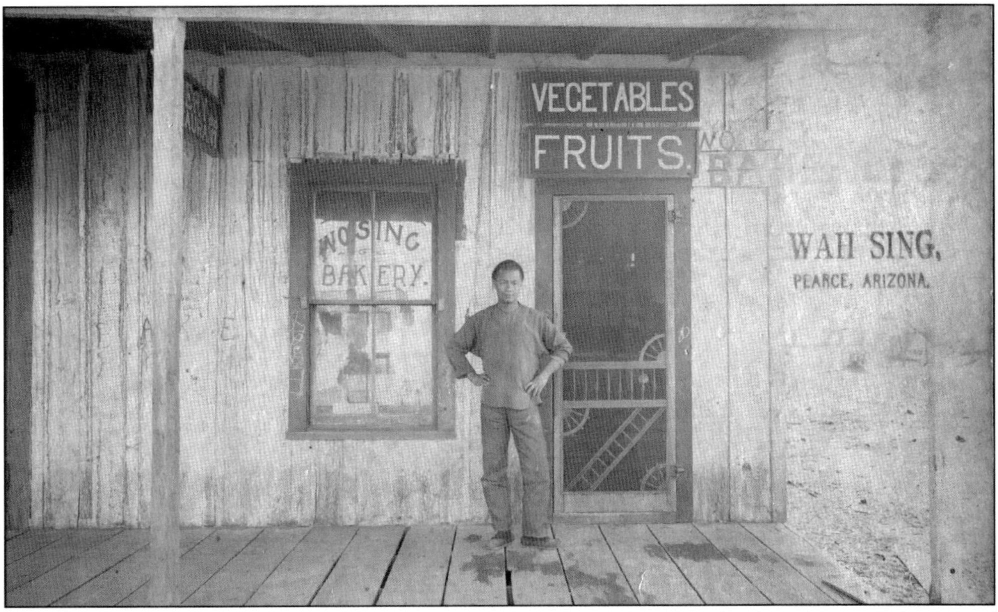

Wah Sing, or Wo Sing, is shown standing in front of his bakery, which also advertises fruits and vegetables. He looks proud, and well he should. The Chinese in early America were hardworking, fastidious people, providing many needed services to boomtown residents. The 1900 Pearce census gives the names of at least 20 Chinese residents. (Drew family collection, SSVHS.)

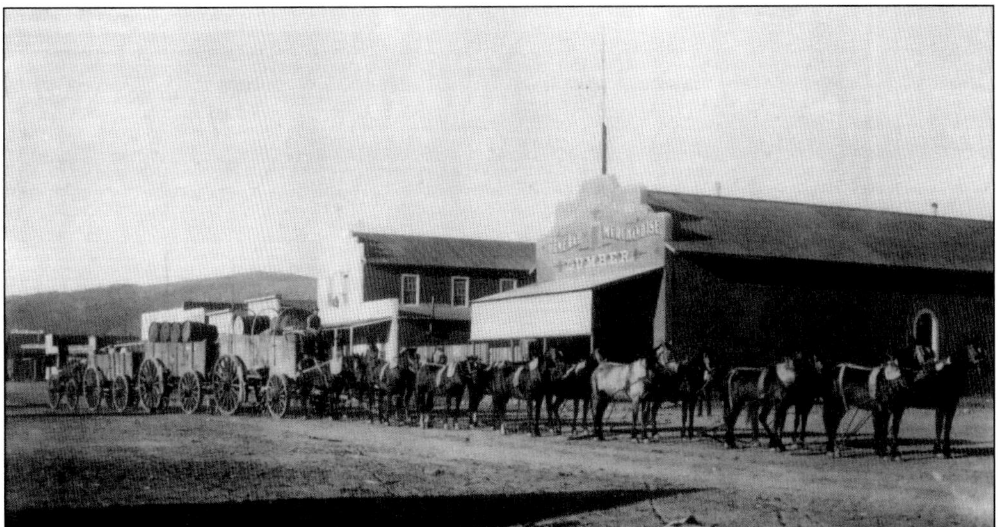

Standing in front of the Soto Bros & Renaud store, this 14-horse team was the typical way to move goods in or out of town. Horse teams like this were also used to haul ore from the mine to the railhead, located 16 miles north in the town of Cochise. (Postal History Foundation.)

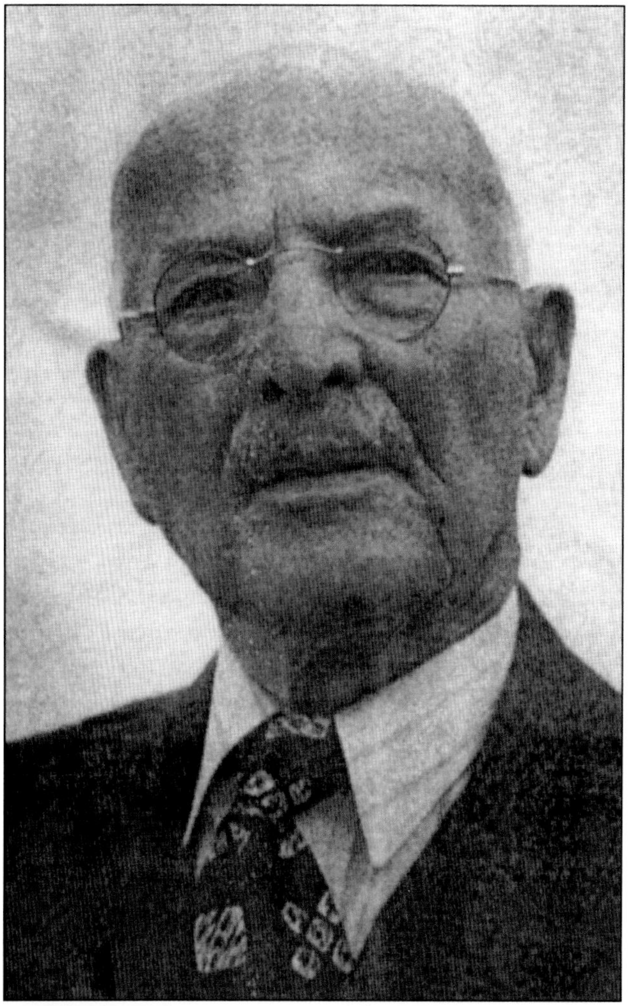

Born in Iowa in 1859, Charles Moses Renaud was a shipping agent in Willcox in 1890. He came to Pearce as an employee of the Soto Bros. and Chattman Store. When Thomas Chattman left, Charles Renaud became a partner and, eventually, sole owner. When the Renauds left Pearce, the store was sold to Albert Rothe. In 1940, Charles Moses Renaud died in California. (Old Pearce Mercantile collection.)

On June 1, 1900, John Gray set out to take the first federal census of Pearce. It would be the first look at the makeup of the townspeople and their occupations. It reveals people from almost every state and many far-flung countries, including China, Italy, Germany, France, Japan, the United Kingdom, and Mexico. The majority of residents were employed in mining. (Ballard collection.)

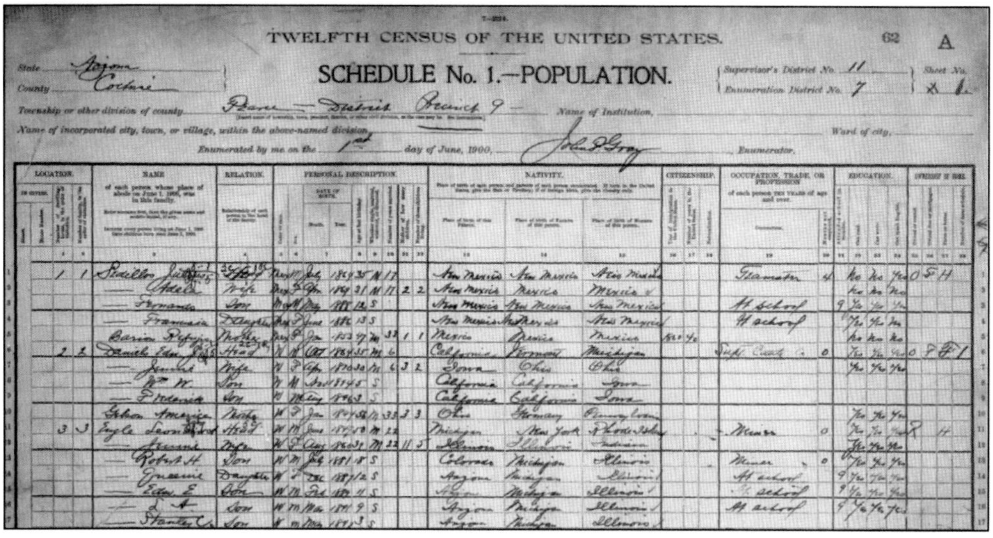

TWELFTH CENSUS OF THE UNITED STATES. 62 A

SCHEDULE No. 1.—POPULATION.

State: Arizona
County: Cochise
Supervisor's District No. 11
Enumeration District No. 7
Township or other division of county: Pearce District Precinct 9
Enumerated by me on the 1st day of June, 1900, John S. Gray, Enumerator.

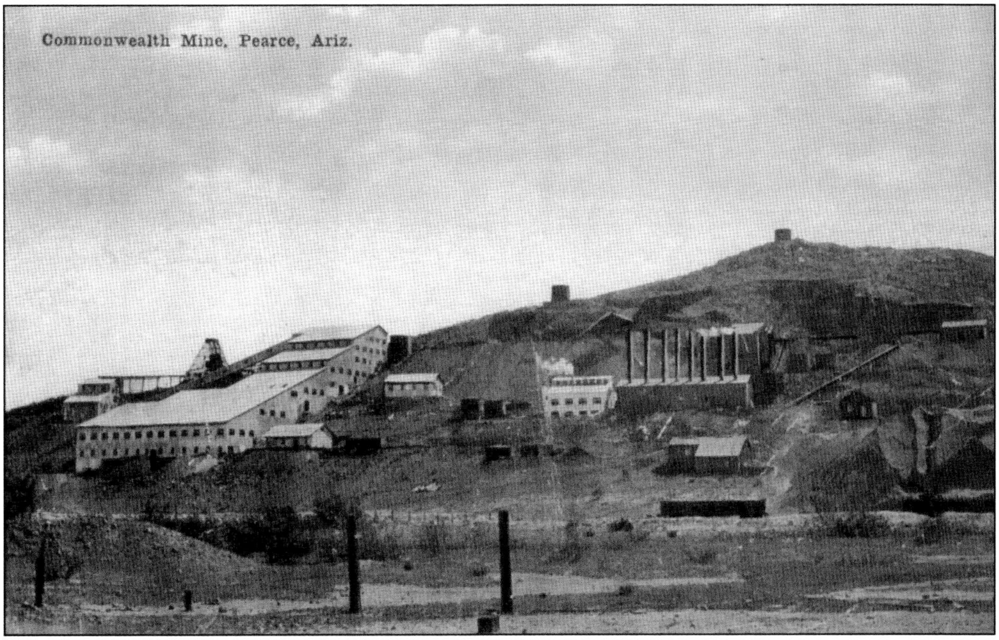

By the turn of the century, the Common-Wealth Mine produced more than $100,000 a month in gold and silver bullion. In 1900, a fire destroyed many of the buildings. The blaze was attributed to a change in fuel used to run the mill. Company losses were placed at $200,000. Insurance claims were paid, and by the third week of August, Richard Allen Fullerton Penrose Jr. placed orders in Denver for machinery to continue the work. The mill was equipped with 80 stamps. Power for the mill, hoist engines, and dynamo were supplied by steam generated by seven water-tube boilers. Crude oil remained the fuel of choice. The operation employed 130 men. A year later, the payroll exceeded 200, with shifts going day and night. (Above, Henry Clifford collection, SSVHS; below, Orville Mickens.)

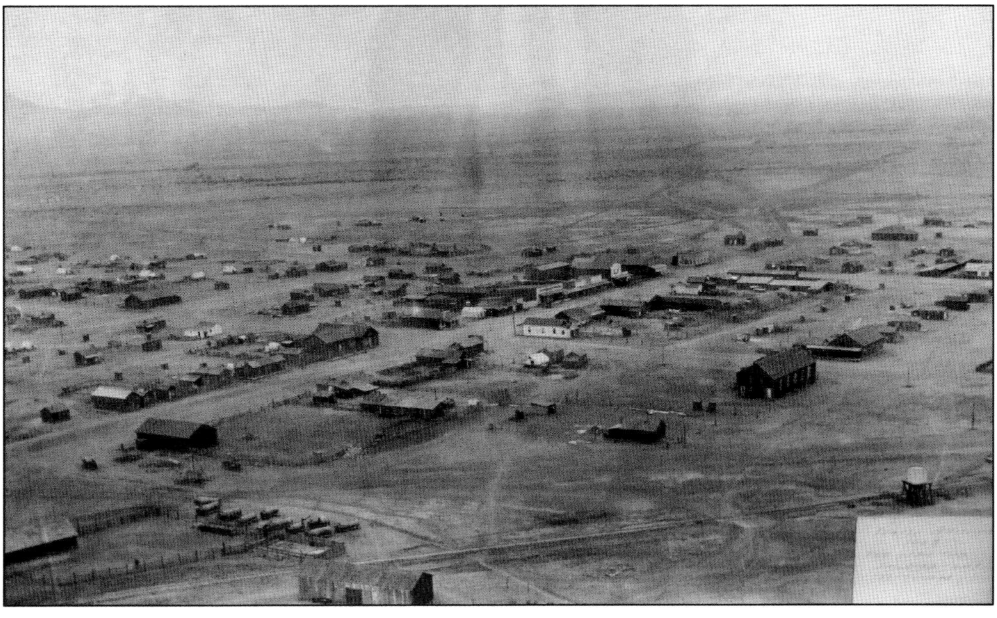

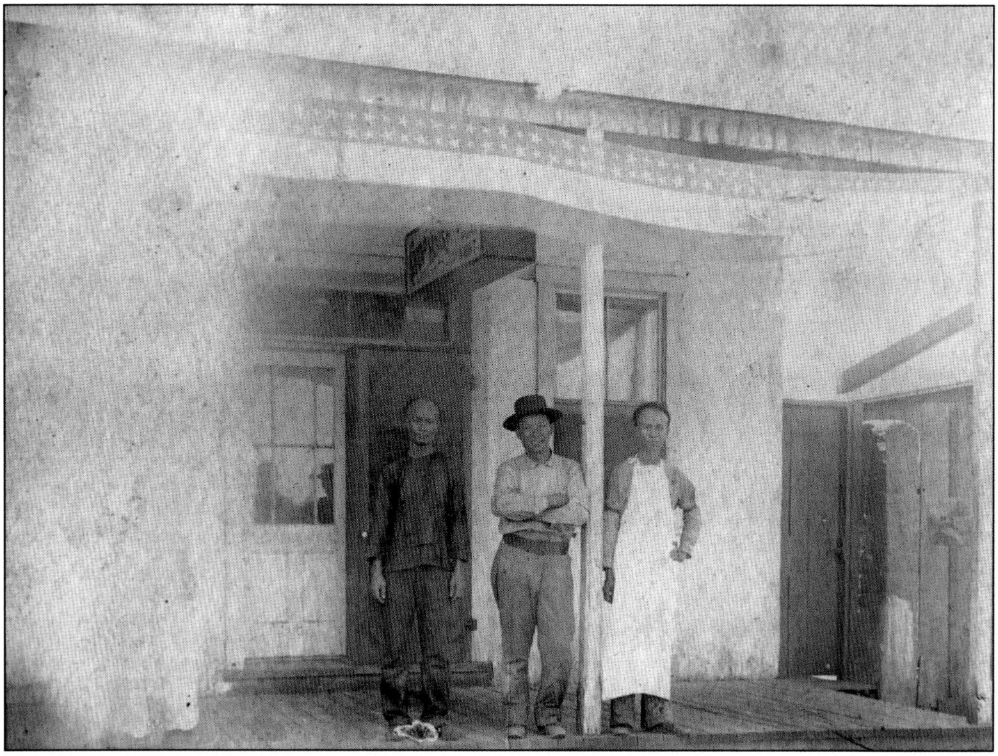

Sporting the obligatory pigtail, or queue, three Chinese men lounge in front of their "chop shop," or restaurant. Some Chinese, to make a quick boomtown buck, operated beneath the law. One such fellow, Quong Hing, was arrested in July 1897 for running an opium "joint." Tried in front of Pearce's Judge Monmonier, he was convicted and fined $45. (Drew family collection, SSVHS.)

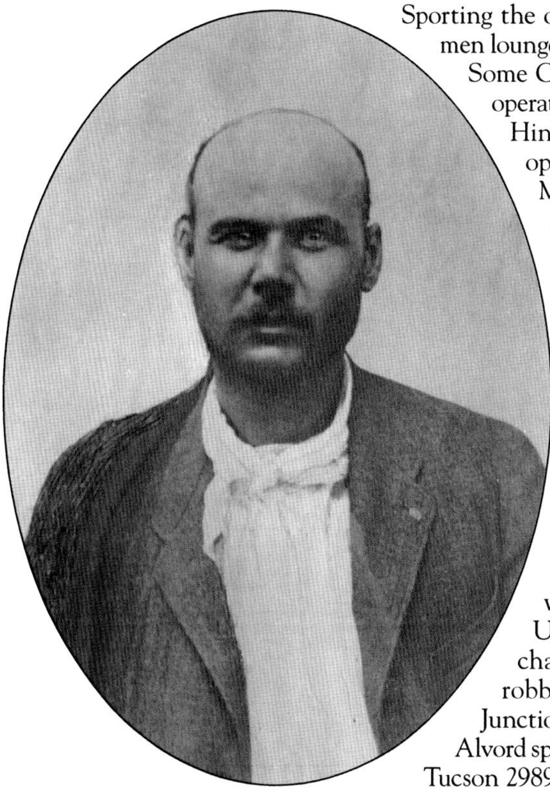

As one of Sheriff John Slaughter's deputies, Albert "Burt" Alvord proved his mettle as a lawman. In 1896, he married Lola Ochoa and moved to Pearce, where he was a deputy to Constable George Bravin. Unfortunately, Alvord decided on a career change. In September 1899, he planned the robbery of the Southern Pacific at Cochise Junction. A subsequent robbery went wrong, and Alvord spent time in jail. (Arizona Historical Society/ Tucson 29897.)

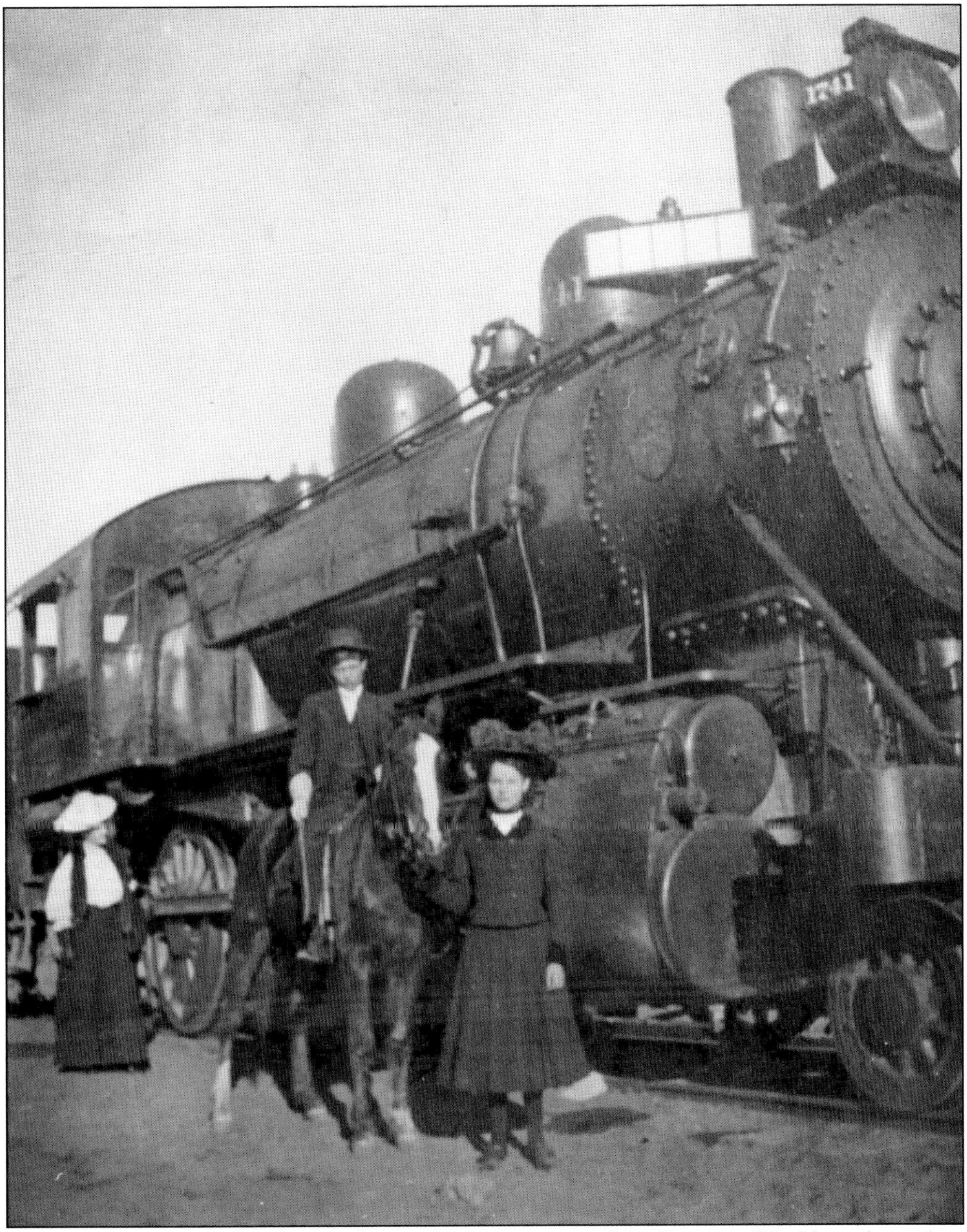

The decision was made by John Brockman, the first manager of the Common-Wealth, and president Richard Allen Fullerton Penrose Jr. to approach the Southern Pacific Railroad and ask that a spur be built between Cochise Station and Pearce. Epes Randolph, head of the Southern Pacific, agreed. The first six miles of track were laid by February, 1, 1903, and the last spike driven the third week of May. On May 28, the first train pulled into Pearce. (Old Pearce Mercantile collection.)

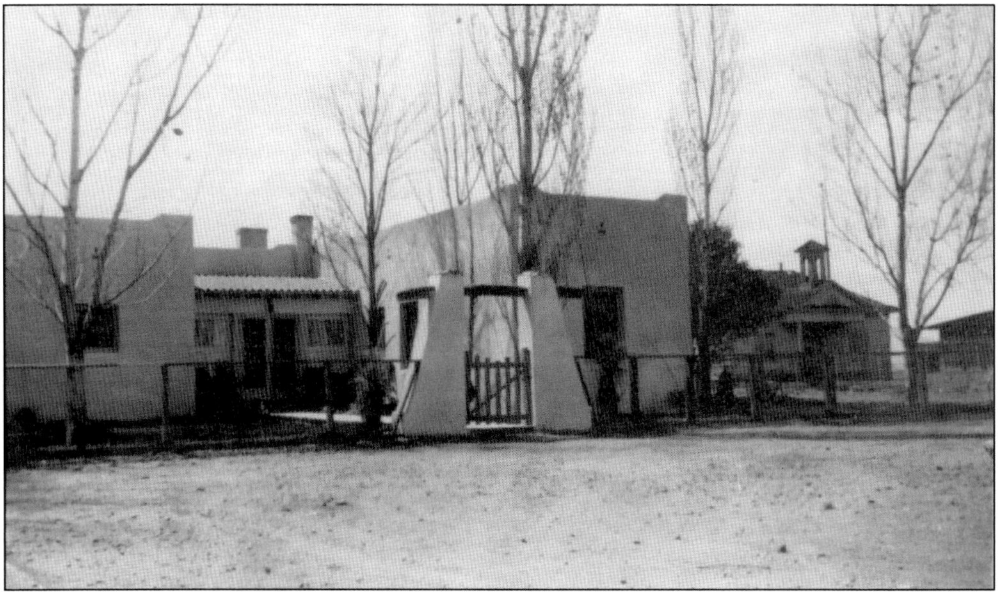

Built on Common-Wealth Mine property, this house acted as the mine manager's home. This large adobe structure was one of the fancier looking houses in Pearce. It became the home of Andrew Young Smith and was known in the family as Smith Home No. 3. In the background, both the first schoolhouse and a bit of the newer schoolhouse are visible. (Steven Carlson.)

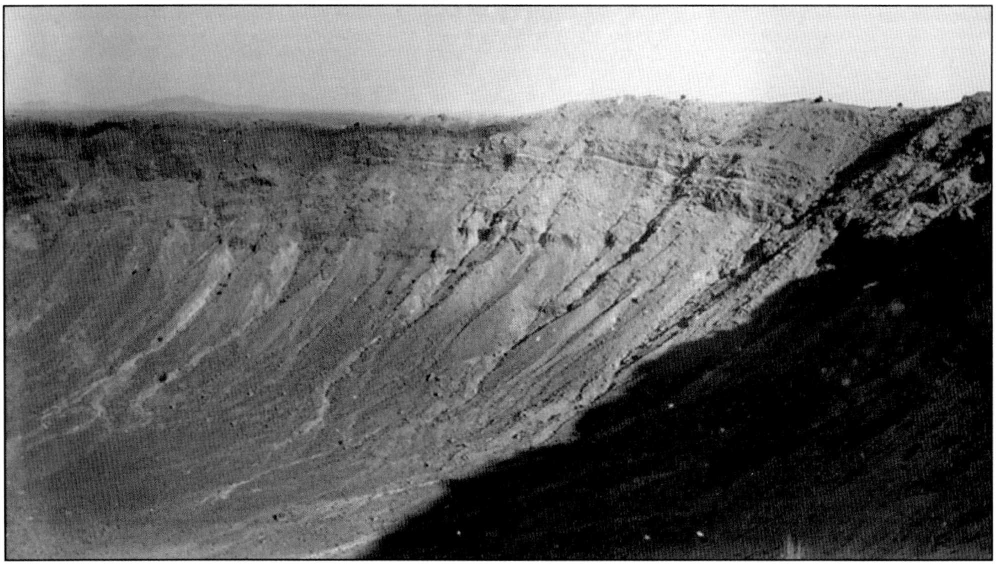

Daniel Moreau Barringer used his profits from the Common-Wealth Mine to buy Coon Butte in northern Arizona. He spent the rest of his life and money trying to prove that a meteorite had created the crater. Unfortunately, Barringer passed away before his theory was accepted as the truth. Today, we know it as Meteor Crater. (US Geologic Survey.)

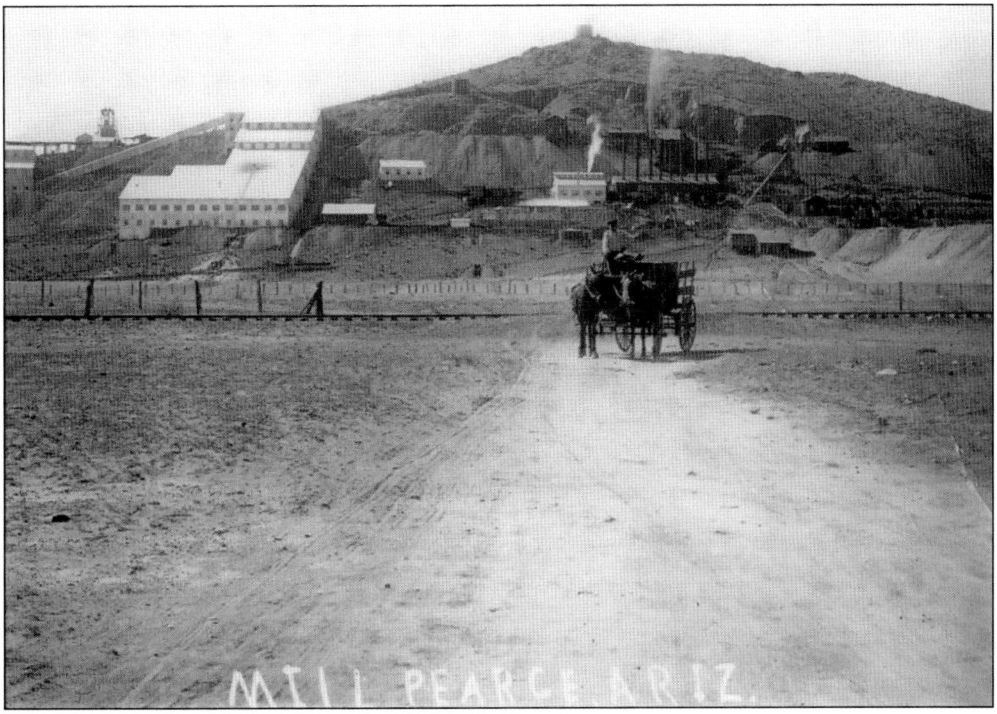

A freight hauler returns to town after making a delivery to the Common-Wealth Mine. Even with the train running to Pearce, horse and wagon were still used for moving goods. (Keith Davis photograph collection.)

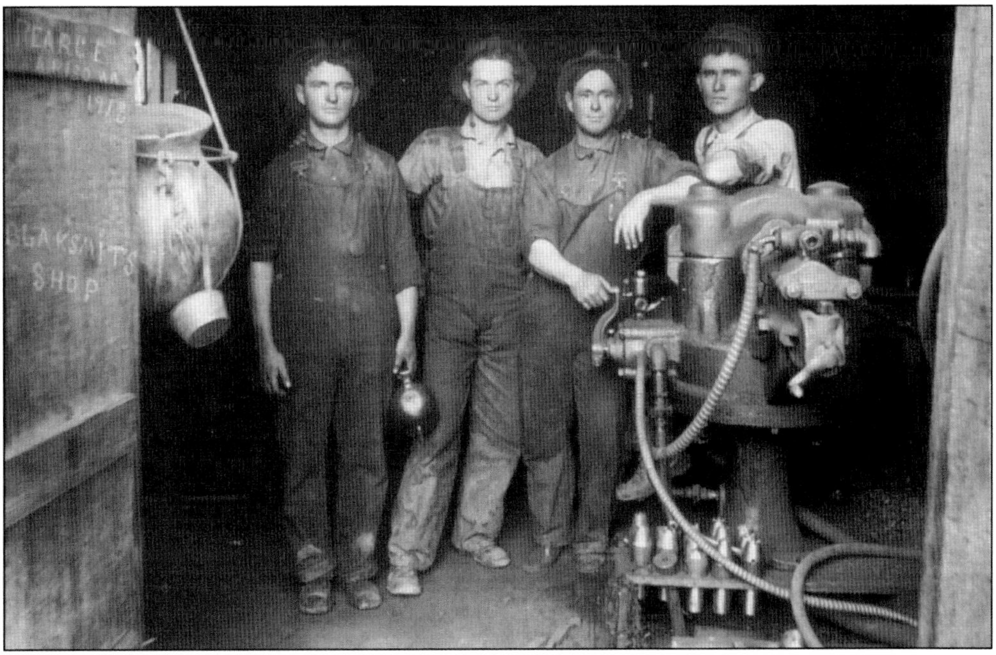

In 1913, four mine workers take a break to have their photograph made. From left to right are Eustes Monmonier, Fred Clifford, Charles Monmonier, and George Waln. (Henry Clifford collection, SSVHS.)

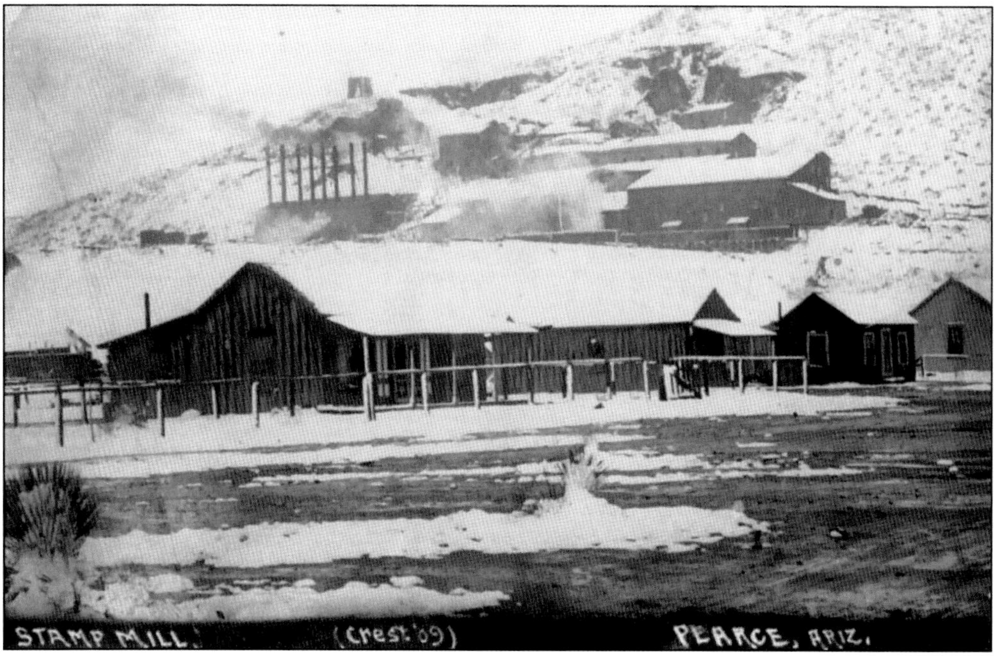

Snowstorms, though rare in some parts of Arizona, occur several times a year in Pearce, where the above-4,200-feet elevation lends itself to four seasons. This 1909 snowfall left the Common-Wealth Mine and the streets of Pearce blanketed in the white stuff. (Both, Orville Mickens.)

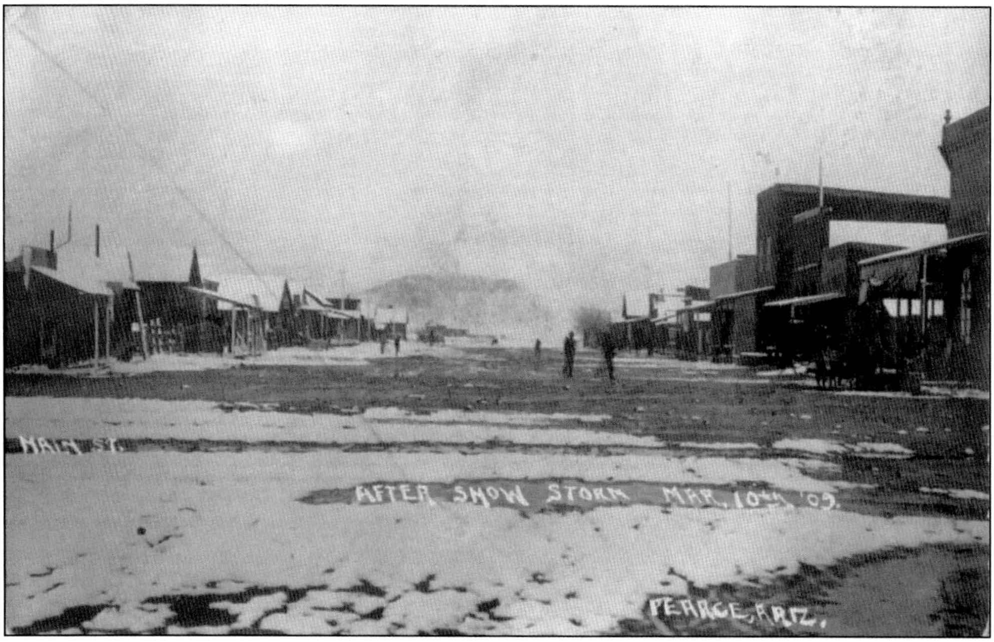

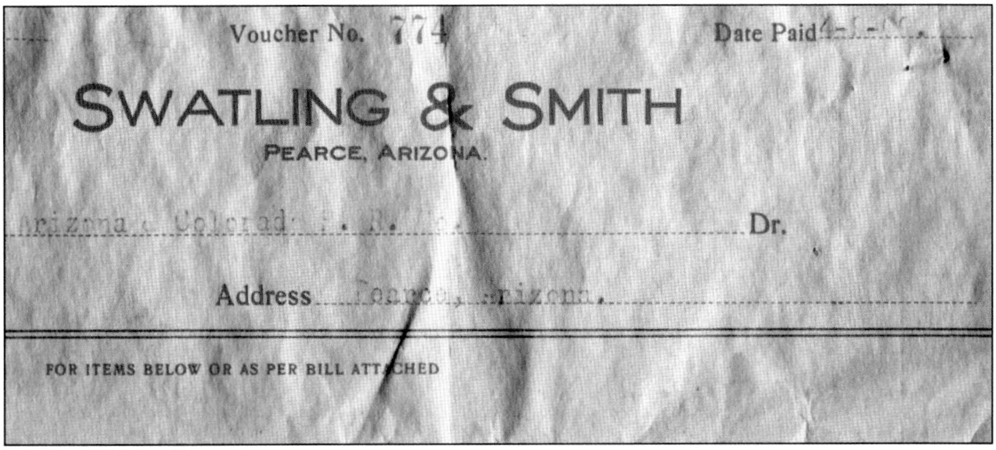

Voucher No. 774 Date Paid

SWATLING & SMITH

PEARCE, ARIZONA.

Dr.

Address

FOR ITEMS BELOW OR AS PER BILL ATTACHED

David Swatling and Andrew Young Smith teamed up in many endeavors, from investing in a local store to a telephone company. But their biggest was the taking over of the Common-Wealth Mine. As original investors started to sell, Swatling began buying until he owned enough stock to have a majority interest. In 1910, Swatling became president of the company, while Smith became mine manager. (SSVHS.)

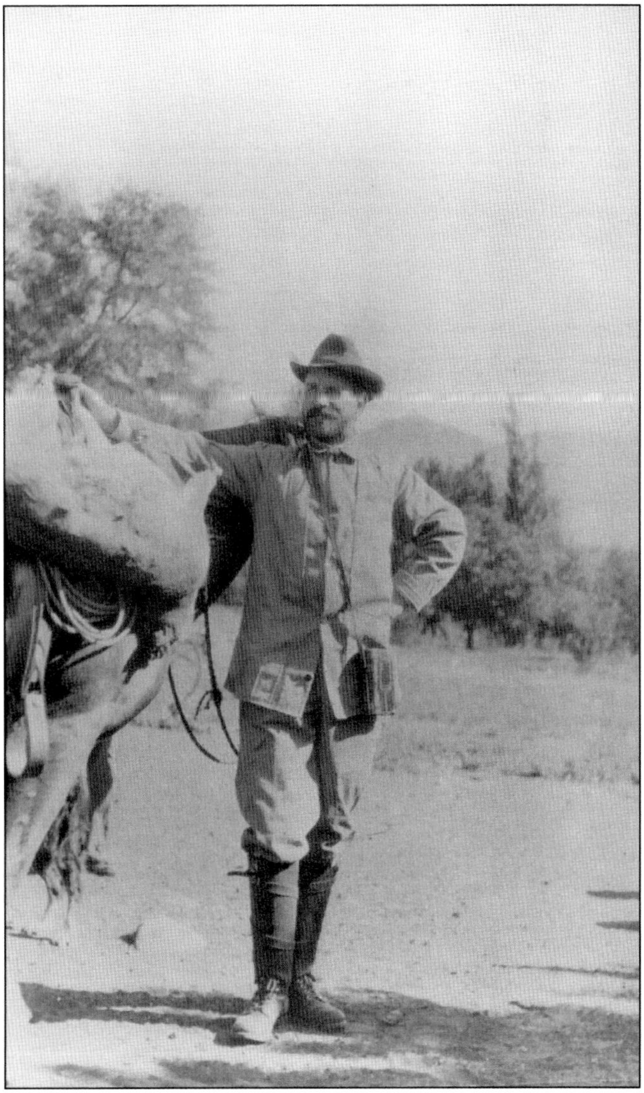

Under David Swatling and Andrew Young Smith, seen here, the Common-Wealth mill was completely remodeled, and its capacity increased to 120 stamps. Adding a new process, they would be able to deal with lower grade ore. On March 24, 1910, on the first run-through, a fire broke out and destroyed the mill. On April 4, 1910, David Swatling died in California of complications from diabetes. (Steven Carlson.)

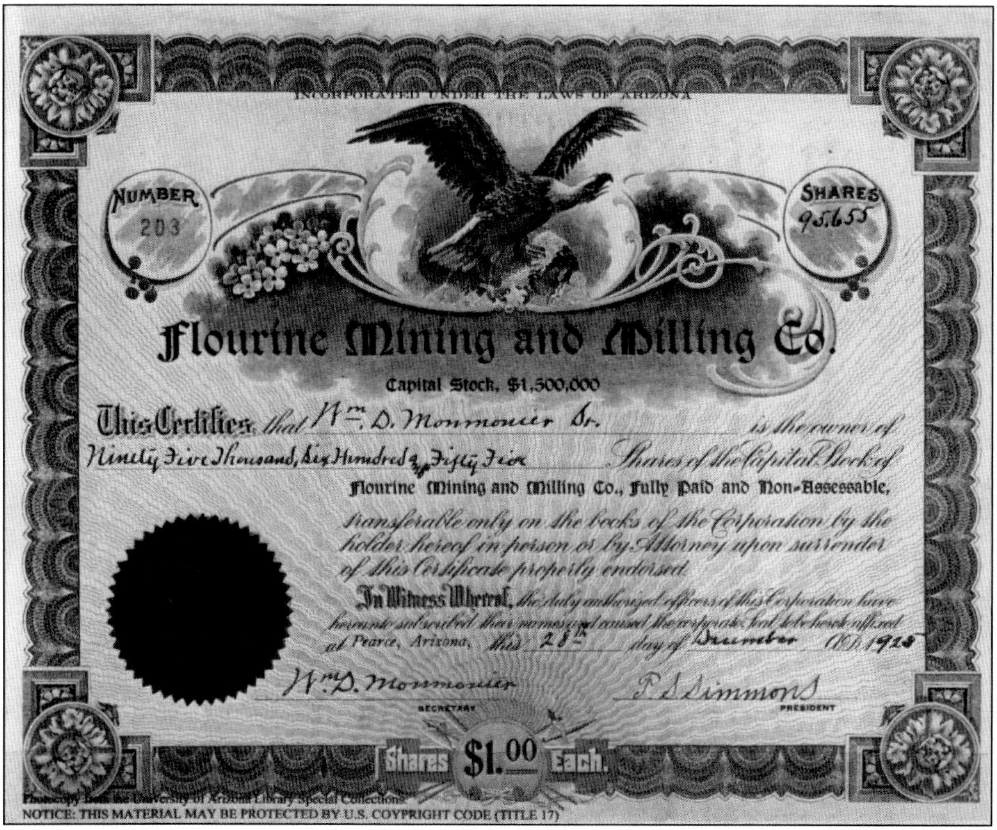

The Flourine Mine, just east of Pearce, was originally established by W.D. Monmonier, Julius Monmonier, and John Peterson. Around 1909, it was incorporated with Peter Simmons as president, W.D. Monmonier as secretary, and Charles Monmonier as treasurer. Over the decades, other mines would be developed in the area, including the Black Diamond Mine, Middlemarch Mine, and Gold Cliff Mine, to name a few. But none of these had the impact of the Common-Wealth. (University of Arizona Special Collections, Monmonier Papers.)

Three

THE HEYDAYS OF PEARCE

The Common-Wealth Mine continued to add new jobs to the town, despite the setback of two mill fires within a decade. Investors flocked to the site. Pearce grew in leaps and bounds. The population peaked around 1918, with the number of residents hovering around 1,500. Businesses kept up with advancing technology. The listing of F.J. Gallagher, blacksmith, now included automobile repair. Pearce had its share of raucous behavior, but lagged far behind other so-called boomtowns in the amount of violence on its streets. This was because the town owed its existence to a single large concern, the Common-Wealth Mine. Whereas other towns survived because of many mining ventures backed by many investors, Pearce remained a stable family town, thanks to its one major employer. A school, churches, fraternal organizations (such as the Knights of Pythias and the Red Cross), a baseball club, a gun club, a golf course, and dances, gave Pearce residents cohesiveness and kept them entertained. How long would it last?

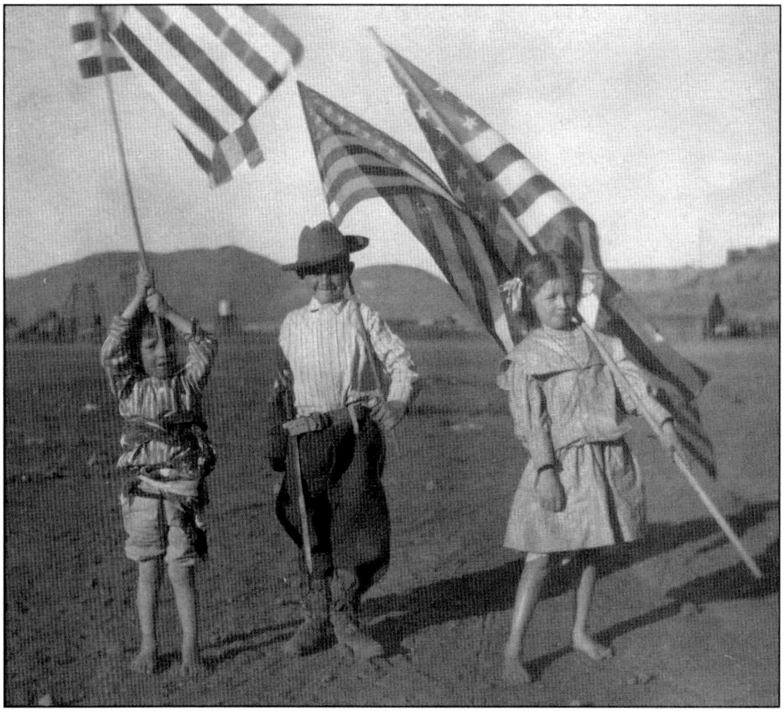

The people of Pearce loved hosting activities in their town so they could show it off. Families from all over the Sulphur Springs Valley, and even some from over the Dragoons, came to all kinds of events, including fairs, dances, horse races, and baseball games. Here, three Pearce children get ready to celebrate the Fourth of July. (Steven Carlson.)

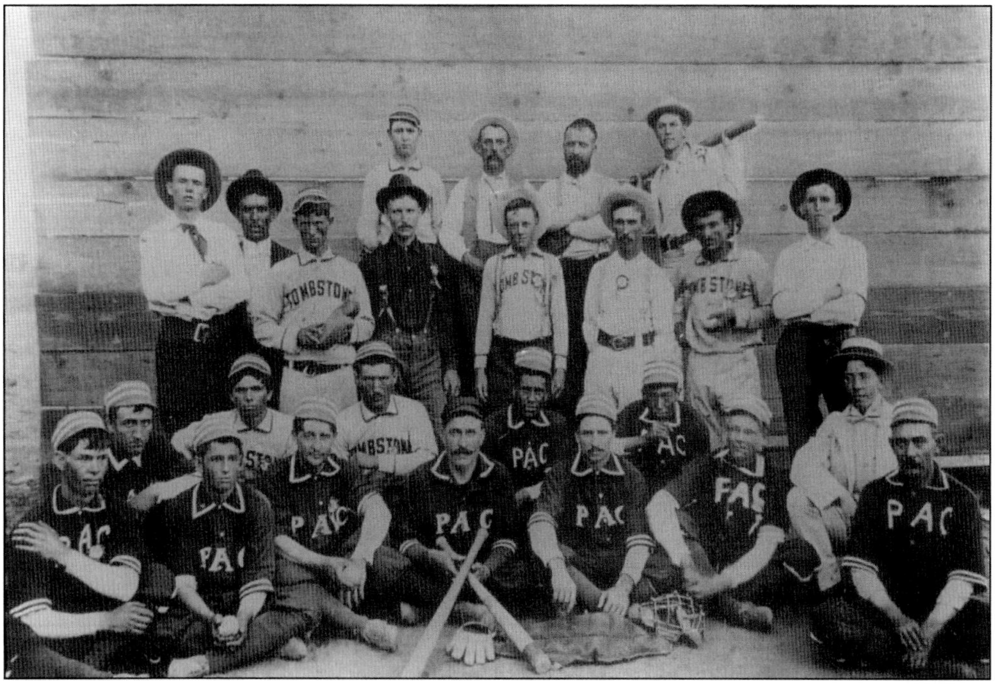

The 1907 Pearce Athletic Club baseball team poses for a photograph after playing the team from Tombstone. Pearce players are, from left to right, Henry Clifford, Roy Powell, Charles Monmonier, John Smith, Walt Cummings, King Chief, Dick Smith, Frank Gonzales, Ole Walker, manager Frank Moreno, and William "Billy" Curlew. (Henry Clifford collection, SSVHS.)

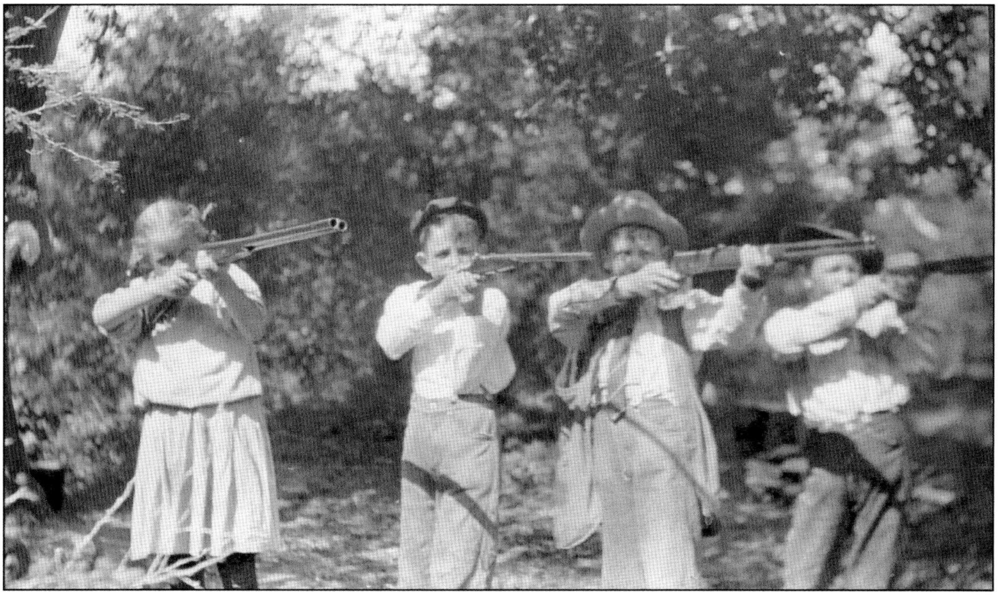

Cochise Stronghold was a favorite place for Pearce residents to escape the summer heat. Pictured from left to right are Henrietta Rockfellow, Lewis Smith, Charlie Renaud, and Phil Rockfellow. (Steven Carlson.)

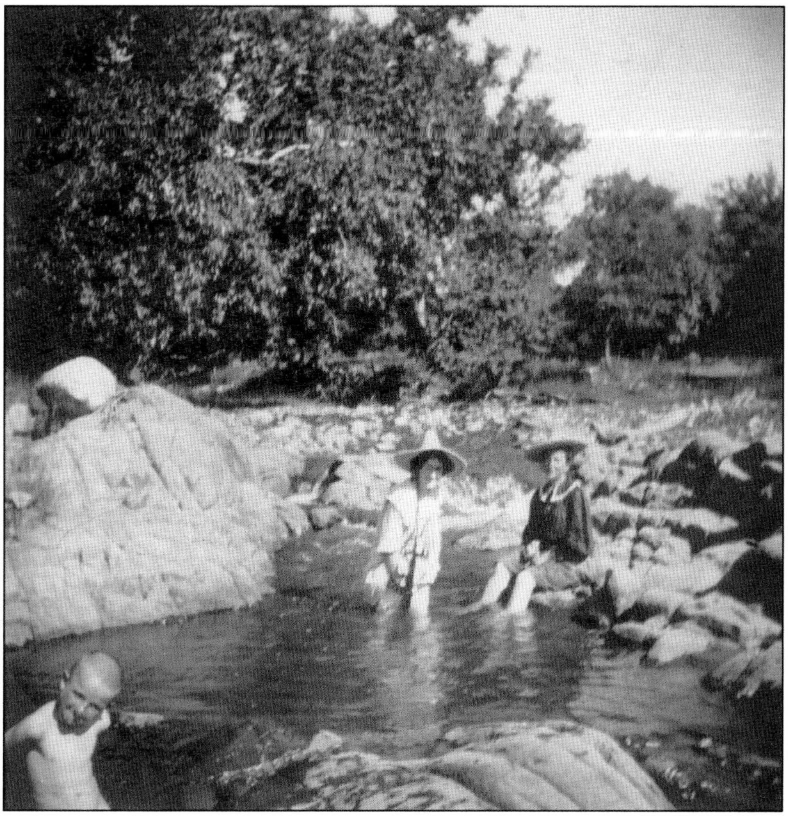

Another place Pearce residents visited often was the Chiricahua Mountains and the Turkey Creek area, east of Pearce. Many a hunting trip was taken in the Chiricahuas, and many a hot summer day was spent cooling off in Turkey Creek. Seen here from left to right are Pearce residents Lewis Smith, Effie Anderson Smith, and Mrs. Charles McKean. (Steven Carlson.)

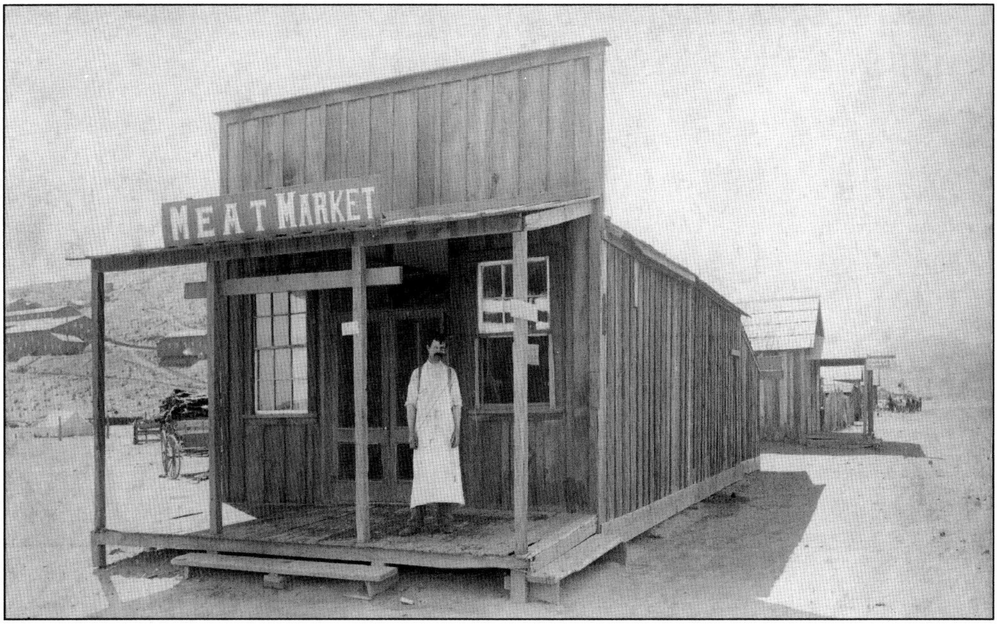

David Stuart Drew was born in 1858, one of four sons and a daughter born to Georgiana "Anna" Stuart Drew and William Henry Harrison Drew, a former San Pedro postmaster. The Drew family ranched in the Dragoon Mountains and also worked as teamsters. David S. Drew opened a butcher shop in Courtland, eventually moving the business to Pearce, where he settled down, built a fine home, and raised his family. David's brother Edward, a Pinal County deputy sheriff, was shot and killed in the line of duty during a May 1911 botched robbery attempt in Sonoratown, just outside the city of Ray, Arizona. Ed Drew is buried in the Pearce Cemetery. (Both, Drew family collection, SSVHS.)

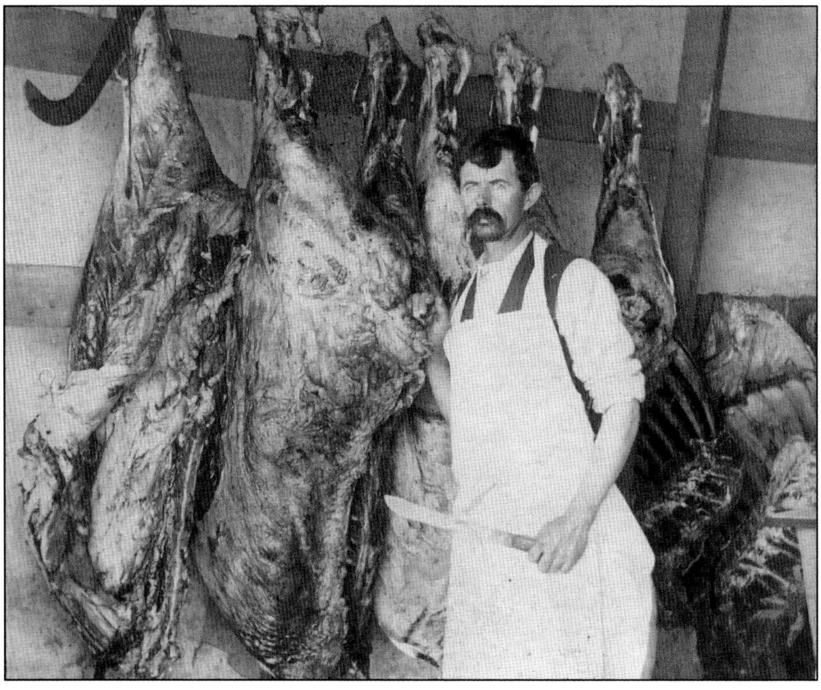

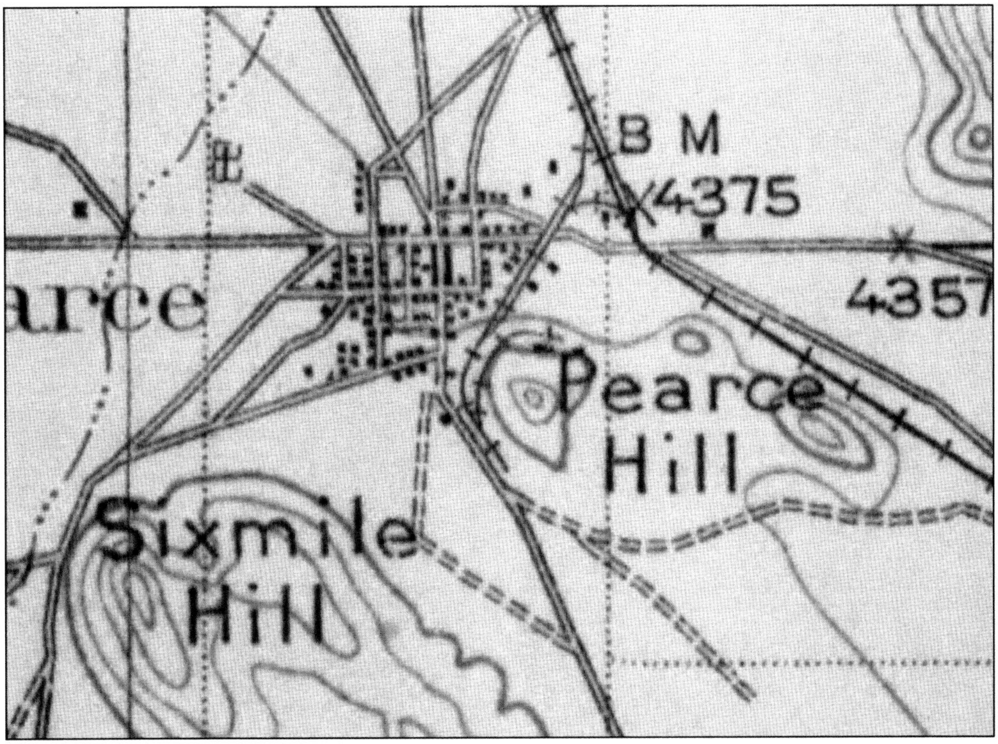

This 1914 map of Pearce clearly shows a growing town. Visible are the many roads leading into town as well as the railroad track. Although Pearce was officially a town in 1896, it was not until 1910 that the county had the town surveyed. That survey was done by John Rockfellow. (Ballard collection.)

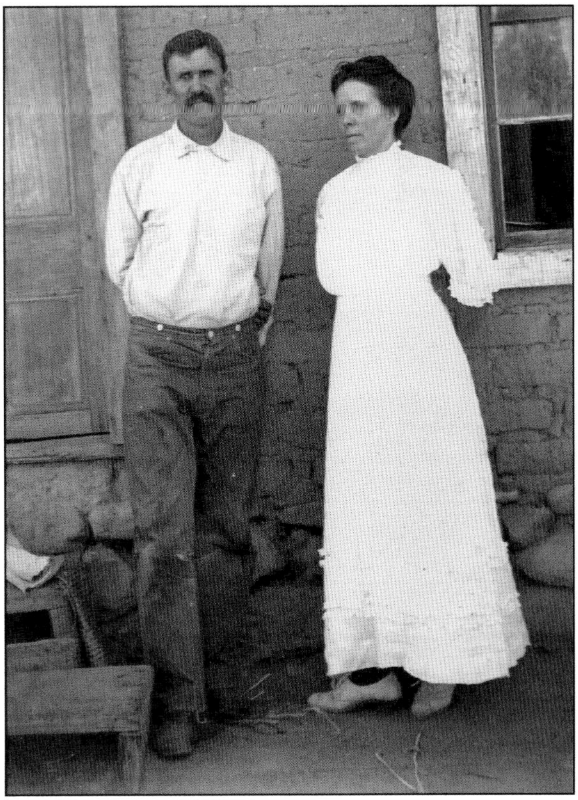

Jackson and Annie Pounds Busenbark were married by Rev. A.J. Benedict in the Cochise Stronghold, on February 17, 1917. In 1921, Jackson Busenbark left the Chiricahua Cattle Company outfit to start his own ranch near Pearce. He bought the *NY* brand from Dave Drew. He and Annie had three children. Joe was born in 1917, Stanley "Bob" in 1918, and Andrew "Jack" in 1920. (Mary Appel.)

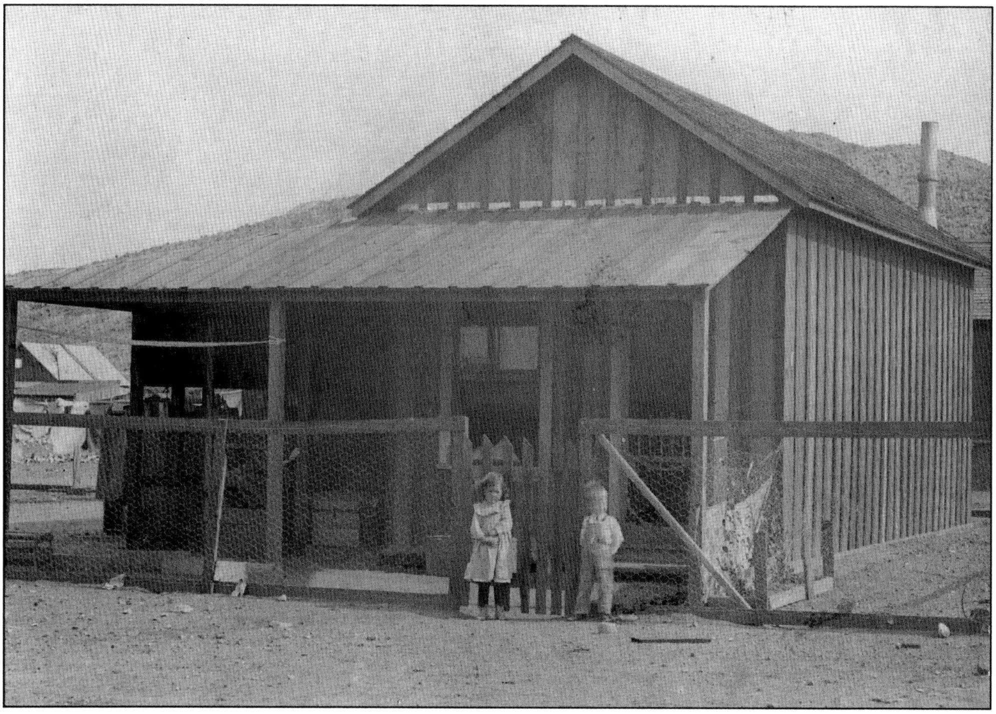

This is the David Stuart Drew house in Pearce; often, the simple clapboard or adobe exterior of a house belied the interior's hominess and beauty. Photographs and framed artwork adorn the walls, and the lace curtains and lovely wallpaper show a woman's gentle touch in a man's harsh world. (Both, Drew family collection, SSVHS.)

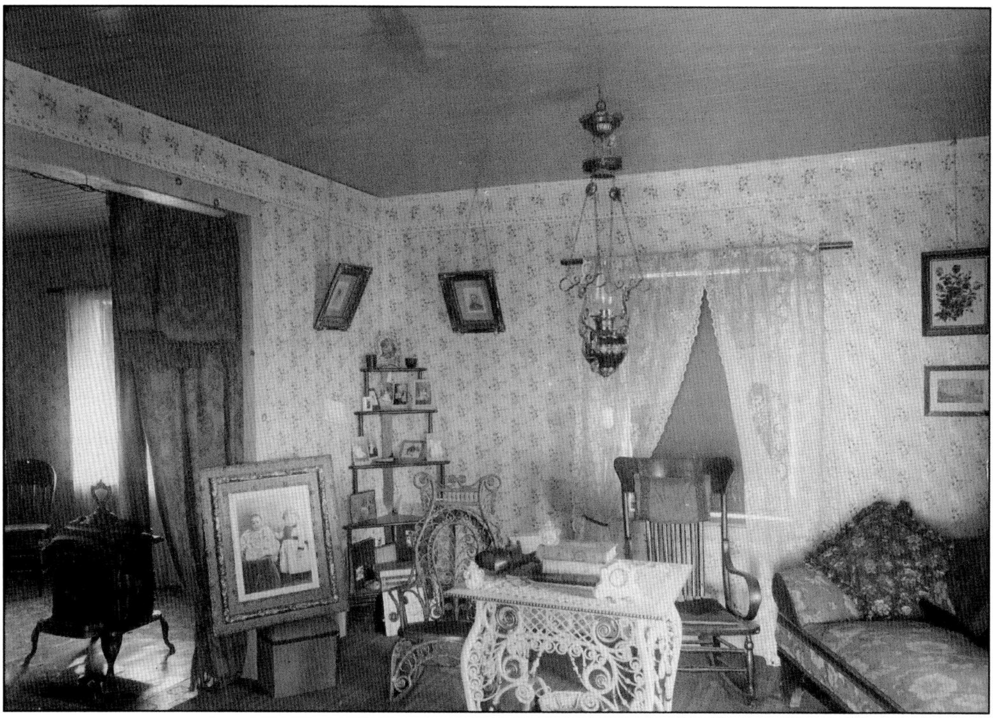

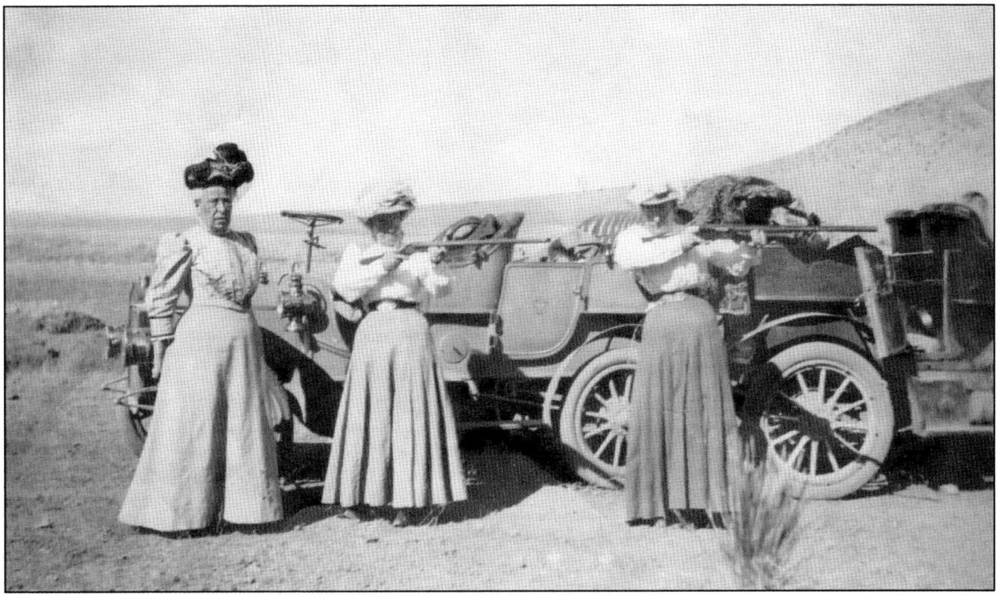

It was not just the men of Pearce who enjoyed shooting. Here, three Pearce women are out for an afternoon of shooting. On some occasions, the Pearce shooting club allowed Mrs. C.K. Barnes to join the contest. (Steven Carlson.)

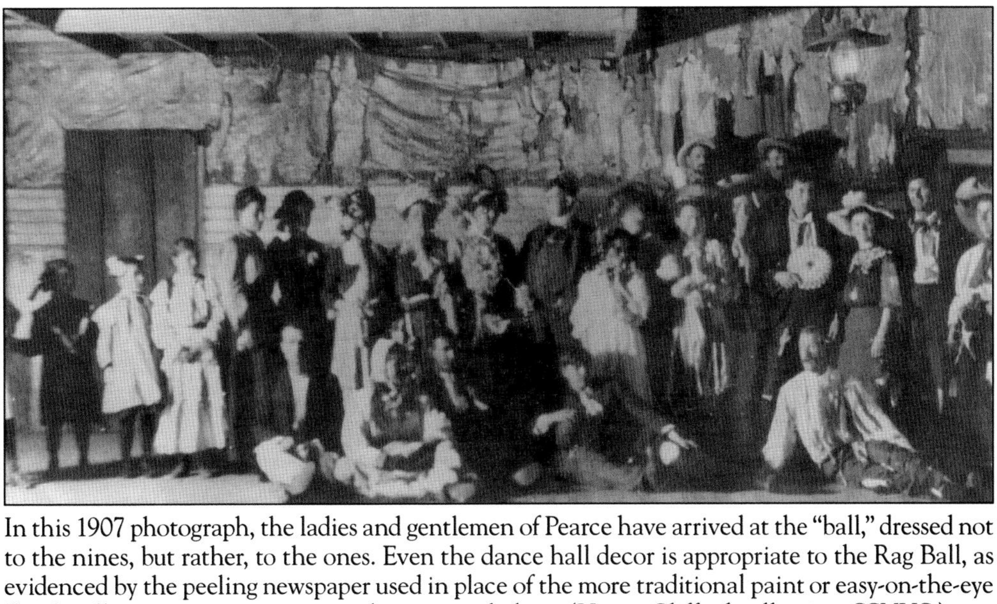

In this 1907 photograph, the ladies and gentlemen of Pearce have arrived at the "ball," dressed not to the nines, but rather, to the ones. Even the dance hall decor is appropriate to the Rag Ball, as evidenced by the peeling newspaper used in place of the more traditional paint or easy-on-the-eye floral wallpapers so appropriate to the time and place. (Henry Clifford collection, SSVHS.)

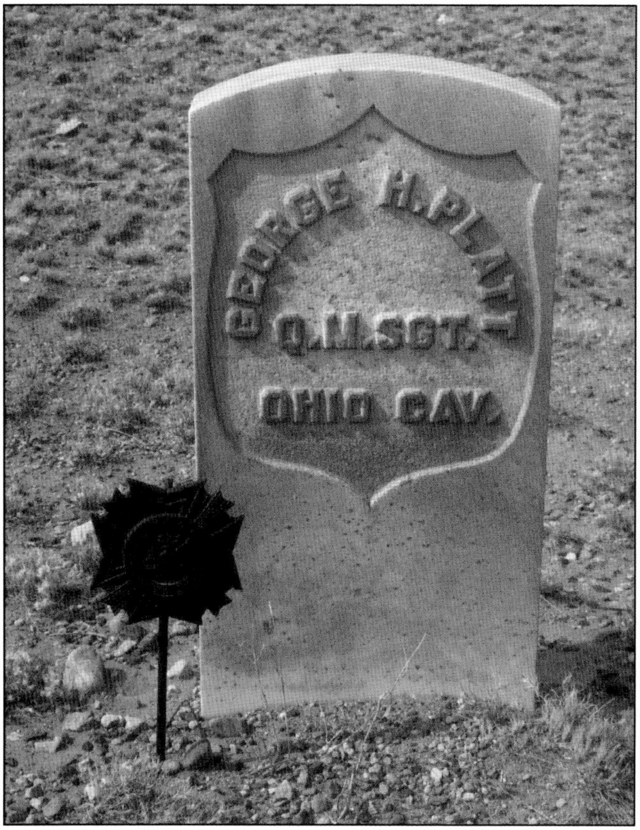

George Platt, bodyguard to Abraham Lincoln? Though a sign states as much as you enter the Pearce Cemetery, little is known of the former quarter master sergeant, who served in the Ohio Cavalry, aside from his storytelling expertise. However, someone must have believed his tales. After his August 1900 death, a letter-writing campaign began asking the government to provide George Platt with a suitable tombstone. The campaign was successful. (Ballard collection.)

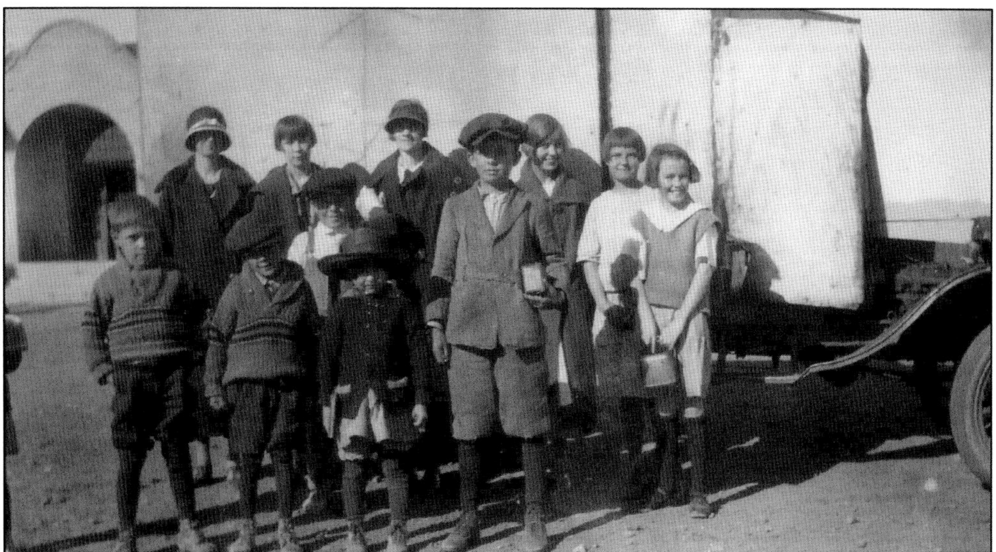

This is one of the Pearce School District's earliest buses, possibly the modified express wagon driven by Mrs. Martin Williams. The vehicle consisted of a solid roof with heavy mesh sides. Automobile seats were fastened down along each interior wall. Once, when the Pick Wick Stage collided with the bus, the back flew open, spilling students, books, and lunches onto the road. No serious injuries occurred. (Mary Appel.)

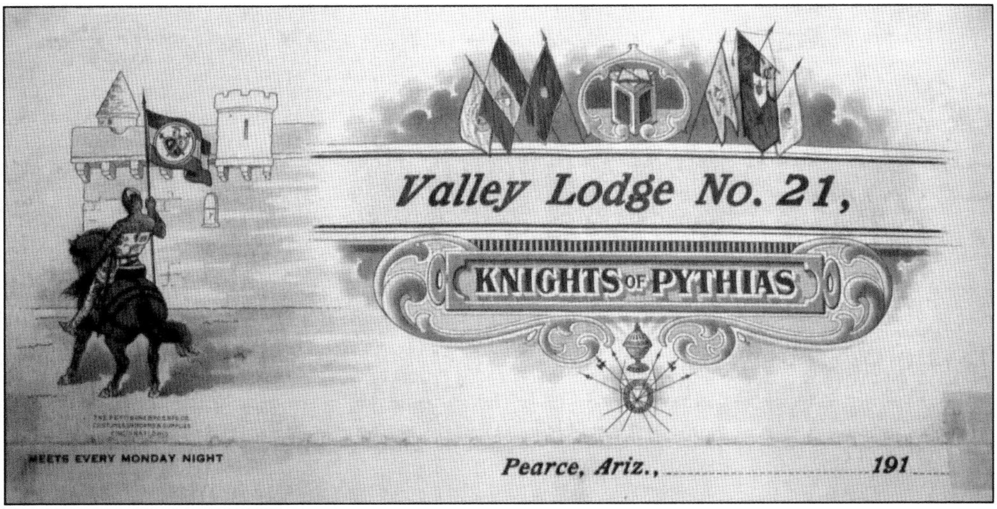

The Knights of Pythias is an international fraternity founded in 1864. Pythians are interested in public affairs, be it local, state, or national, and are eager to enhance their communities. Members of Valley Lodge No. 21 were responsible for establishing the Pearce Cemetery in 1916. Among them were Grand Chancellor William D. Monmonier, George W. Fleetham, Sidney A. Neighbors, and Carson C. Ritter. (University of Arizona Special Collections, Monmonier Papers.)

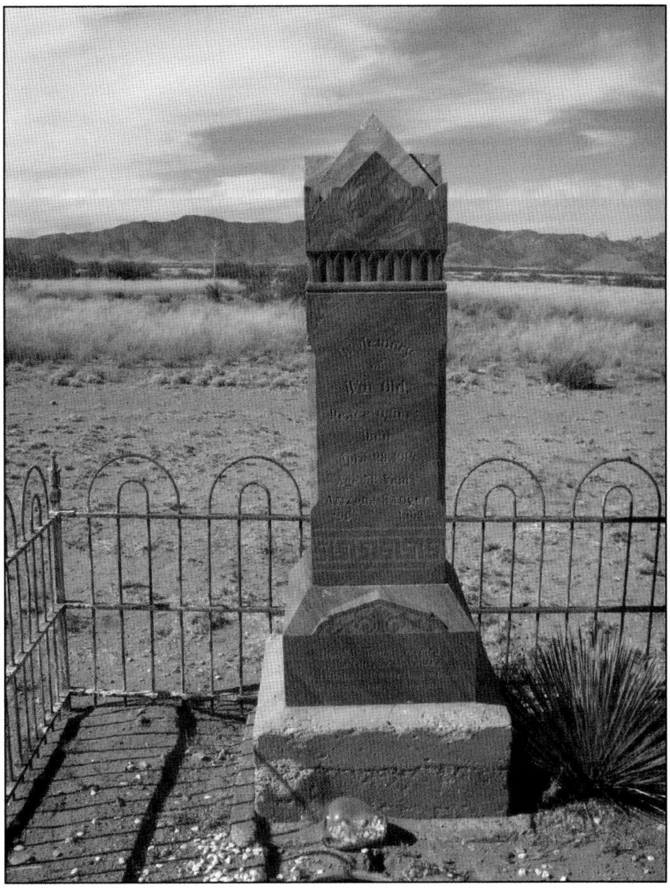

In Pearce Cemetery rests the body of former peace officer William "Billy" Old. William Old died April 28, 1914, the victim of murder, resulting from a single gunshot wound to the chest inflicted by his own wife. He served as an Arizona Ranger from 1904 to 1909, rising to the rank of lieutenant, and continued in law enforcement as a deputy sheriff and constable at Pearce. (Ballard collection.)

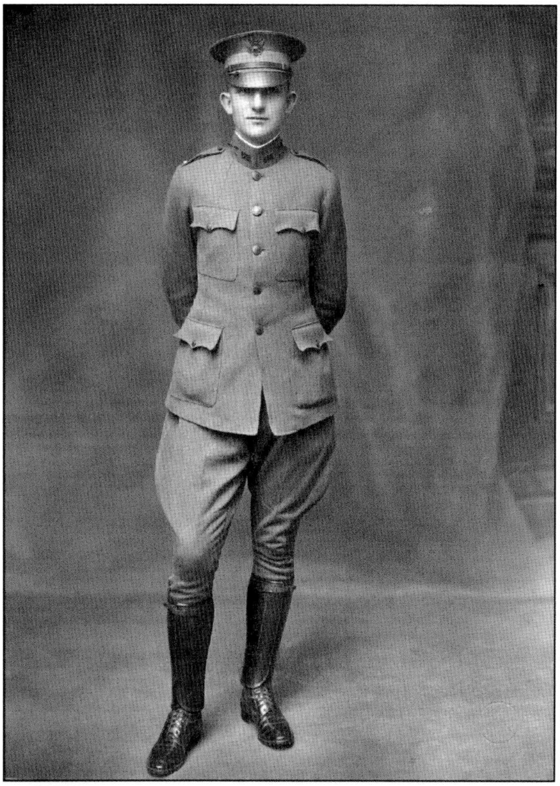

This is the May 1918 graduation photograph of 1st Lt. Lewis Smith, from Presidio, San Francisco. That summer, Lewis was sent to Washington, DC, and from there, was to go to France to join US forces during World War I. Many young men from Pearce also served in World War I, including Ernest and Charlie Renaud, August Junge, and Clay McKnight. (Steven Carlson.)

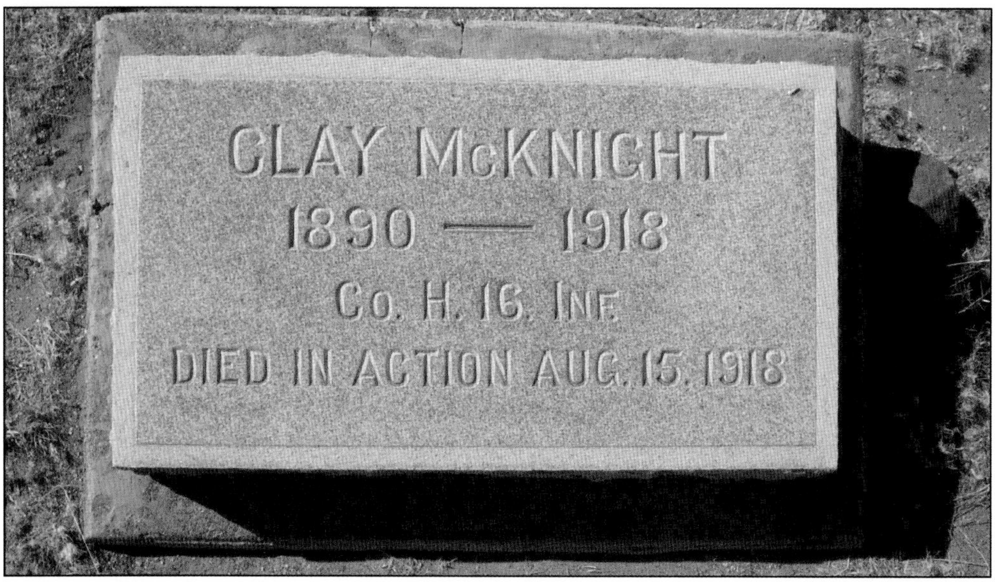

Pearce resident Clay McKnight made the ultimate sacrifice. On August 10, 1918, McKnight's company was caught in a "terrific barrage." Diagnosed with "inhalation of gas and burns of the body," Clay McKnight died on August 15 and was interred the following day in the American Cemetery at Mars. Services in Pearce for the reinterment of McKnight's remains were held January 29, 1921, in the Idle Hour Theater, which "overflowed with friends of the deceased." (Old Pearce Preservation Association.)

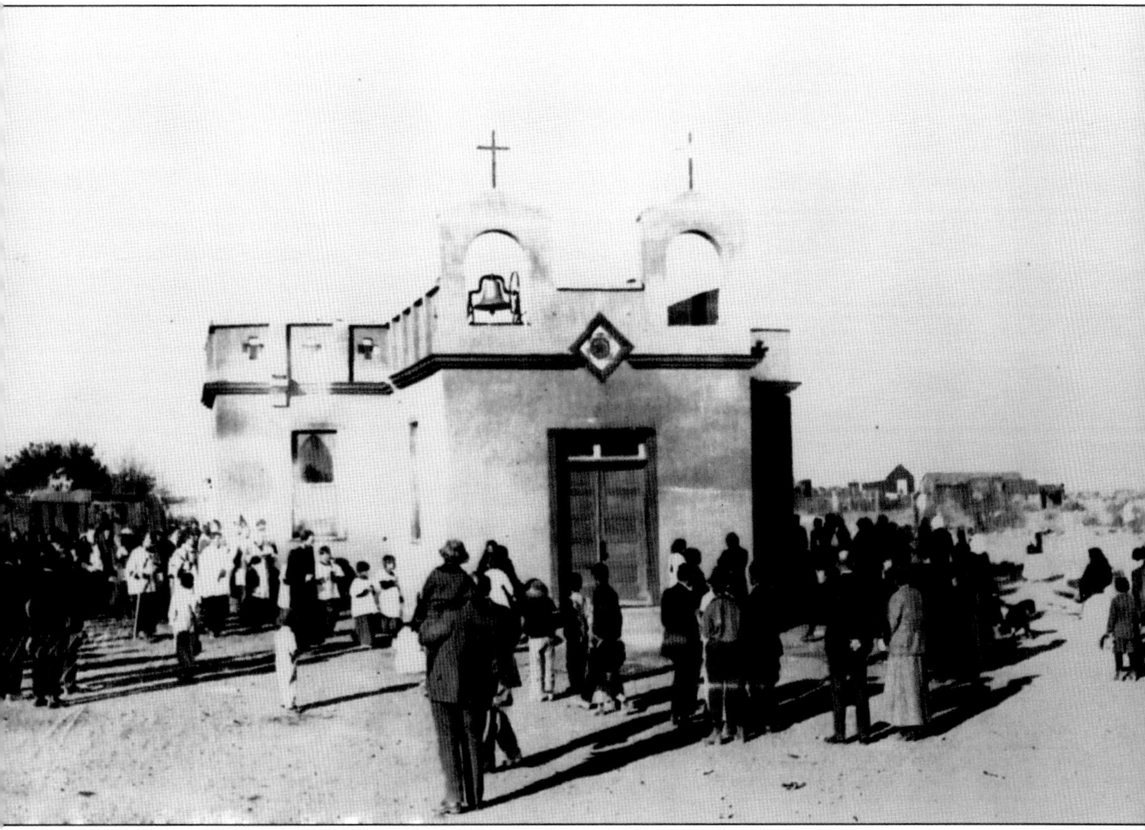

A group of people are attending what is thought to be a wedding at Our Lady of Victory Catholic Church on what is today 4th Street. Note the Sunday-best garb of the ladies and gentlemen. On the left side of the church, the profession of altar boys and officiate can be seen making their way to the front doors of the church. Our Lady of Victory Church was constructed of adobe in the same style as the San Xavier Del Bac Mission, outside of Tucson. The roof was flat with a bell facade on the north front of the building. Stained glass centered the upper-front diamond interface. Shaped in the form of a cross, the sanctuary was in the north wing. Built in 1917, the church served the public until 1969, when the congregation moved to a larger building on South Highway 191. Rev. Thomas Doyle was the last circuit priest to serve the mission. (Old Pearce Mercantile collection.)

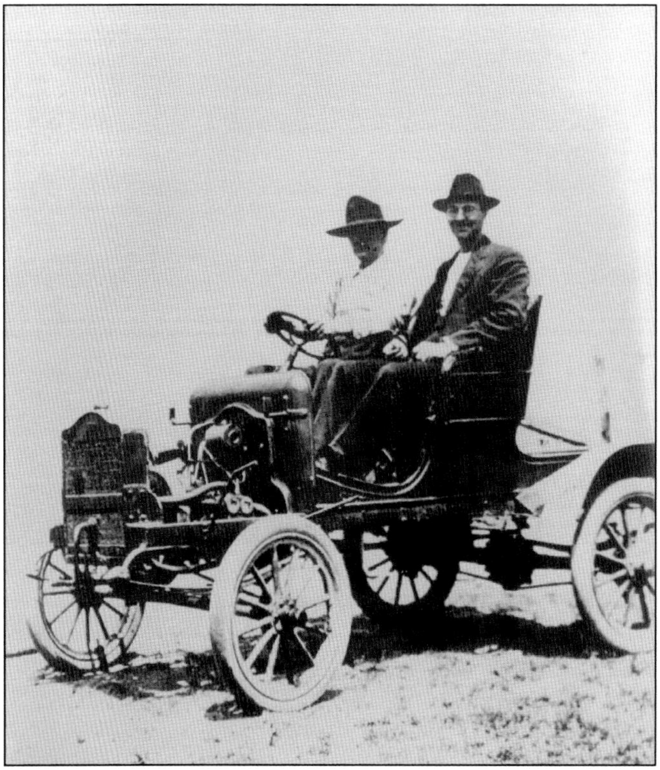

Folks in Pearce really knew how to keep up with modern times. Fulton Gallagher sits behind the wheel of the first automobile in Pearce. What a sweet ride, and by the look on the face of the passenger, he is really enjoying himself. The car in the photograph has been identified by the experts at the Antique Automobile Club of America as a Maxwell. (Henry Clifford collection, SSVHS.)

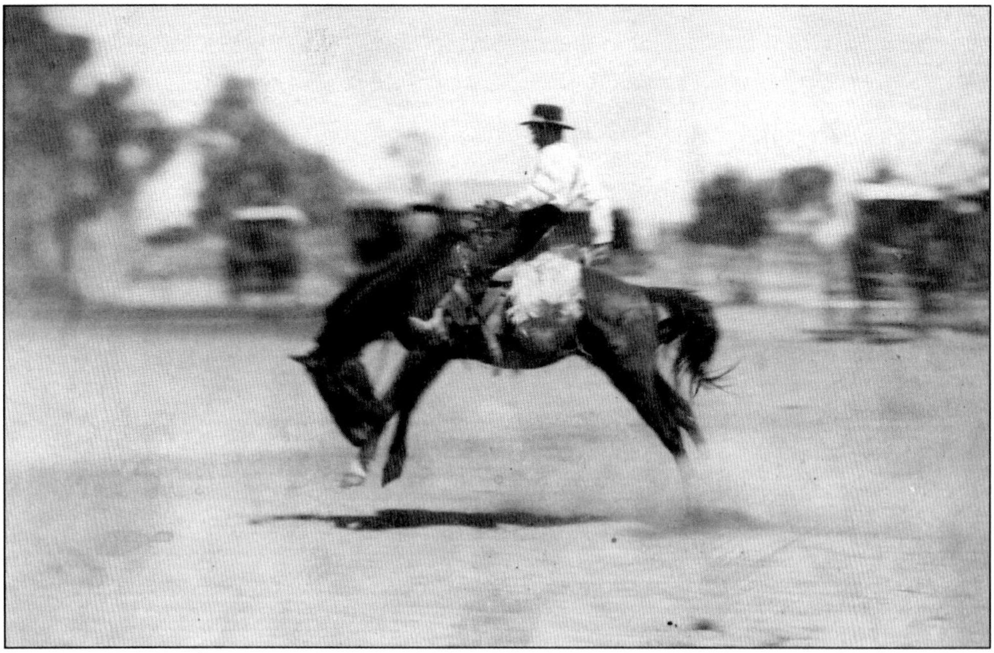

Pearce has a long history of ranching and proving one's skills either on a bucking horse or by roping an unwilling steer, local pastimes that always drew a crowd. To this day, rodeoing goes along with the Western way of life, and the Western way of life was alive and well in early Pearce. (Drew family collection, SSVHS.)

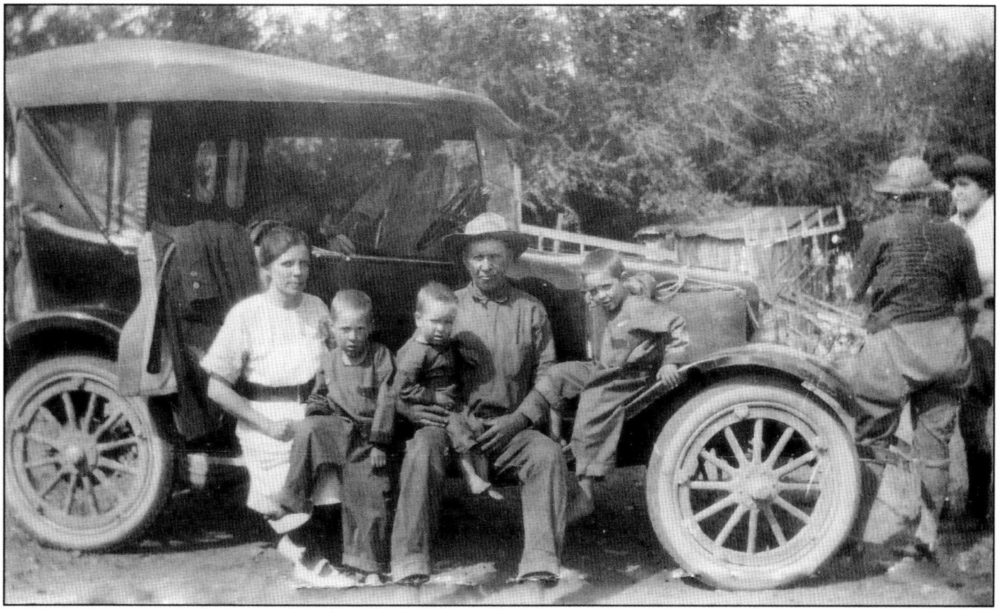

Sitting on the running board is the Busenbark family at the New York Ranch in 1922. The three boys would all take different paths in their lives. Joe Busenbark would become an Air Force pilot in World War II and was shot down over Germany in 1944. Stanley Busenbark worked for a power company in Washington, and Jack Busenbark, also a World War II pilot, would take over the ranch. (Mary Appel.)

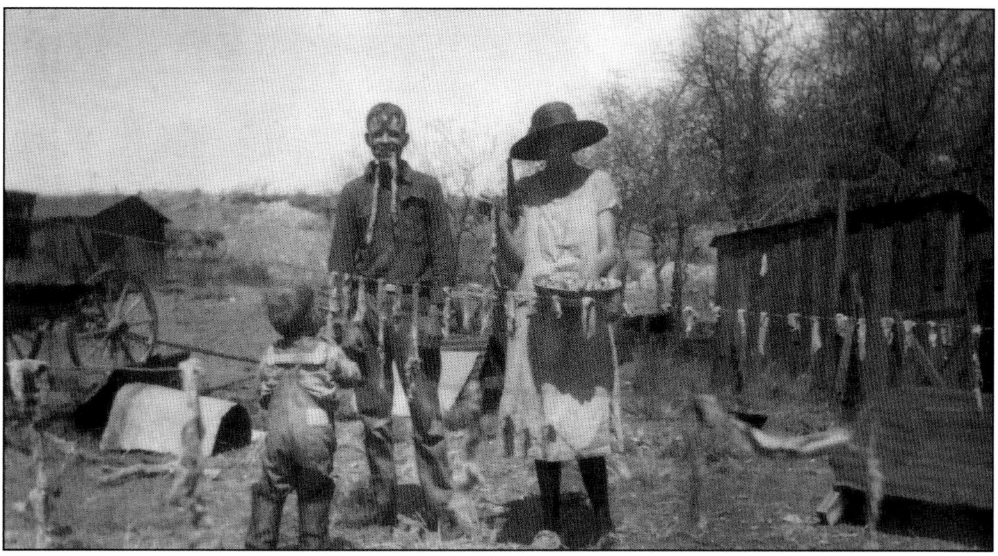

Tex and Bess Mulkey and their little helper, Jack Busenbark, spend a day at the Busenbark ranch making beef jerky. With limited ways of storing food, making jerky was one way to keep meat for a long period. (Mary Appel.)

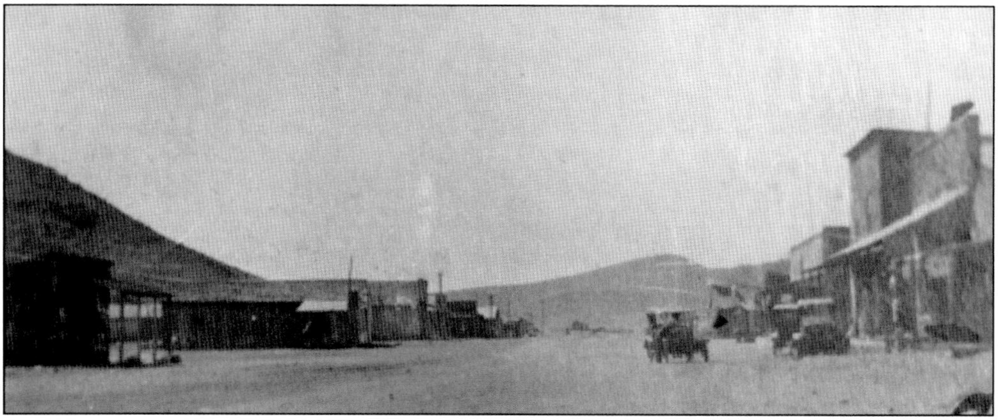

This is downtown Pearce, looking up Main Street. Common-Wealth Hill is visible in the background to the left. The pool hall and saloon, with the wide porch and overhang, where the photograph below was taken, is seen to the middle right. An automobile is parked in front. It is likely the group got together for this photograph, taken in 1907, because of the rare appearance of a traveling photographer in town. (Above, Keith Davis photograph collection; below, Henry Clifford collection, SSVHS.)

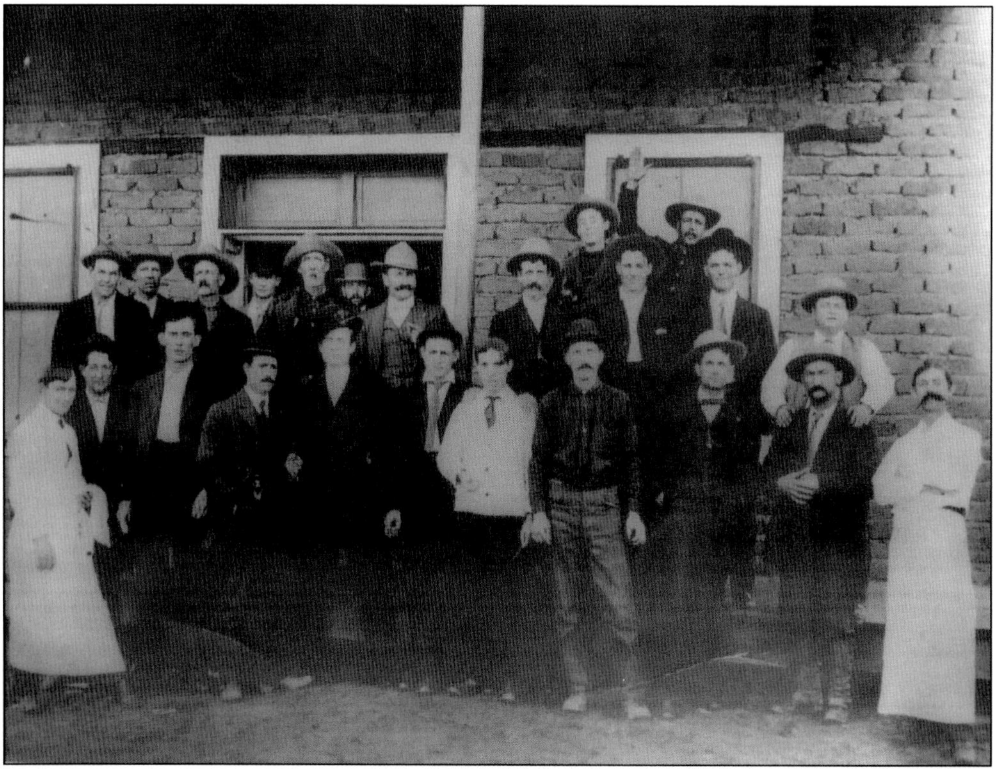

Four

Pearce Struggles to Remain a Town

The Common-Wealth Mine spiraled downward. The cost of retrieving the gold and silver deep within the many shafts was becoming too high. Investors dropped by the wayside. By 1921, the population had declined from a high of 1,500 to 1,000 and by 1928, to 500. Yet the people of Pearce refused to give up on their town. They had invested it with blood, sweat, and tears and meant to make a go of it, no matter the obstacles. Prohibition caused the closing of many a saloon, though entrepreneurs like Joe Bignon wisely turned his bar into the Idle Hour Theater and kept right on working. The price of silver plummeted, and the Great Depression made its way west and into Cochise County. Several men of high standing in the community died, among them William D. Monmonier and A.Y. Smith. The backbone of the community crumbled. Yet others stayed on, working at whatever jobs were available to keep Pearce, their home, a viable community. Good intentions and great heart are not always enough. Pearce lost ground and its people. By 1953, the population had dwindled to 150. What lay ahead?

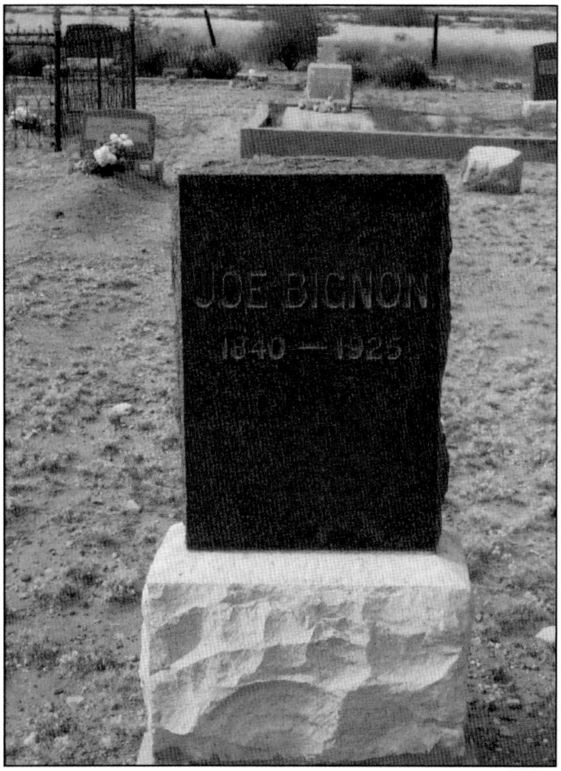

Despite an eventual downward spiral of the Common-Wealth, Joe Bignon remained a staunch Pearce businessman. When Prohibition prevented him from selling spirits in his saloon, an entrepreneur to the end, Bignon changed its name to the Idle Hour and opened a theater. Joe Bignon is buried in the Pearce Cemetery. His wife, Minnie, occupies a grave in the next row over, but still in view of her husband's final resting place. (Old Pearce Preservation Association.)

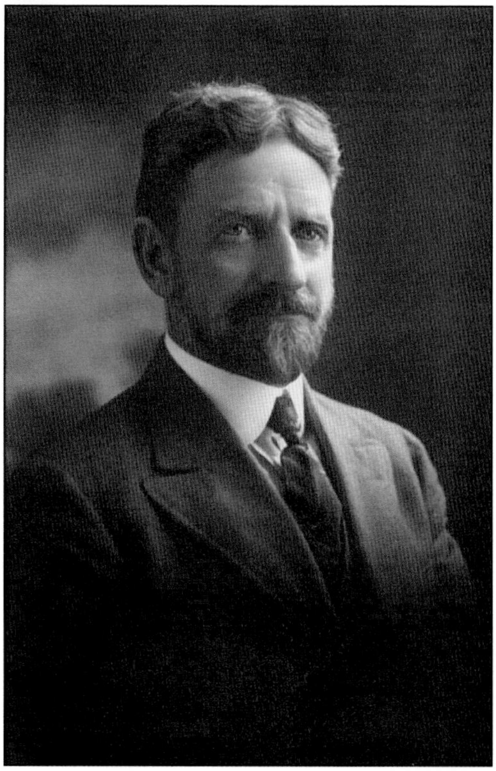

Andrew Young Smith was involved in many civic activities, including serving as an election official, in the Rotary, and on the school board. In the 1920s, seeing the mine slowly losing its shine, he became involved in other enterprises including B-S-B Egg Farm and the Midwest Sugar Company. He did whatever he could to keep Pearce a viable town. On October 13, 1931, he died of a brain tumor. (Steven Carlson.)

In 1930, the Pearce School District purchased its first actual yellow school bus, hiring Dick Olson as driver. He was a strict disciplinarian, a safe driver, and a stickler for punctuality. Previous modes of transportation for Pearce students consisted of parents' automobiles, often driven by the oldest pupil in the family. The most impressive of these vehicles was a Pierce-Arrow luxury car, owned by John Gradall, of the Kansas Settlement. (John Magoffin.)

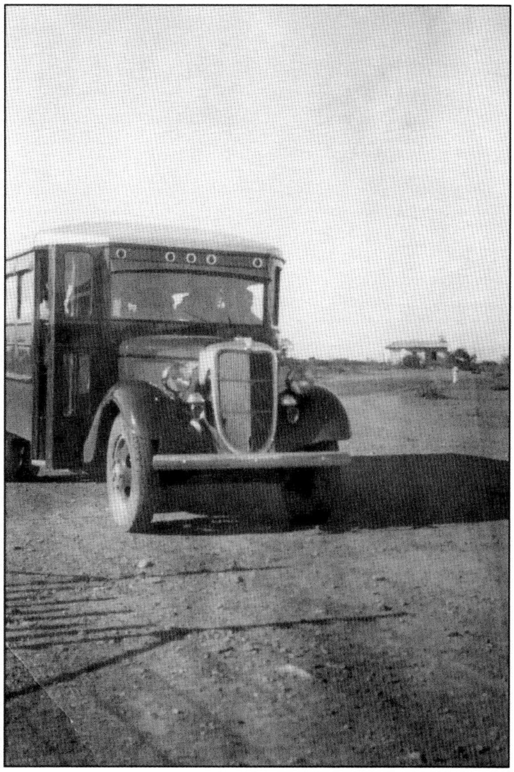

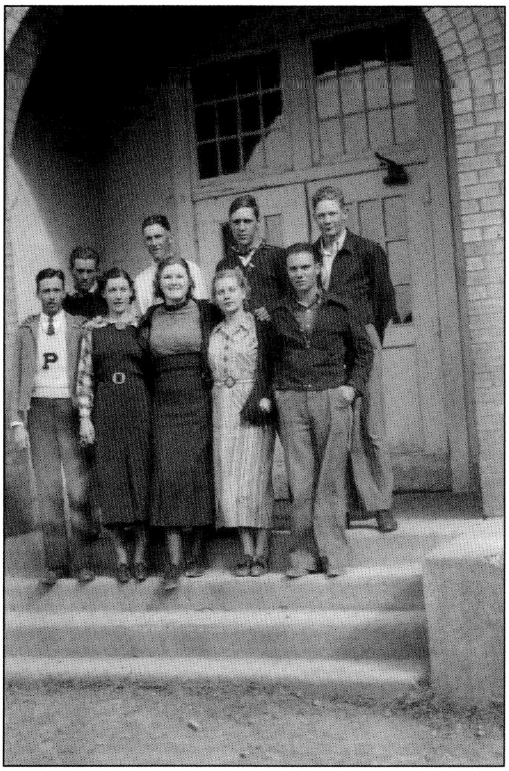

In September 1920, Pearce Union High School was founded with approximately 50 students; a principal, Mr. Carouthers; and a staff of three teachers. To graduate, students had to complete four years of English, two years of math, two years of science, two years Spanish or Latin, and four electives. Pictured here is the senior class of 1936. (Mary Appel.)

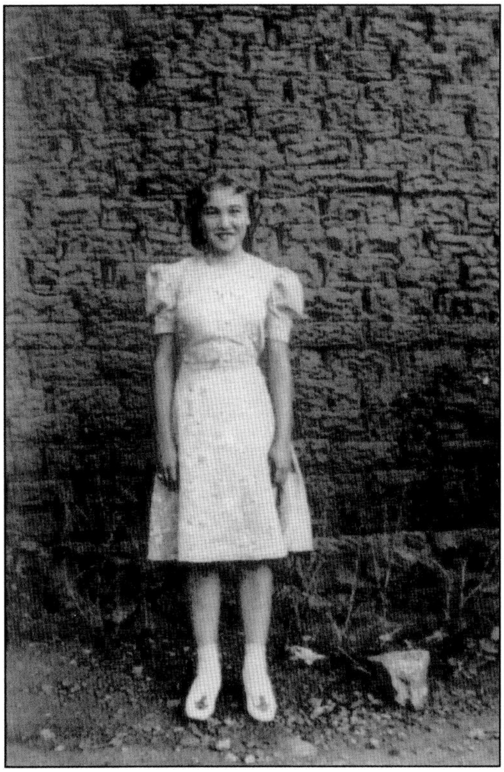

Jean Newman stands outside the Pearce mercantile in 1936. She worked as a clerk when the store was owned by Albert Rothe. Her family came to Pearce from Kansas. Her father worked briefly for the mine, but after an injury fighting a fire in the Chiricahuas, his employment opportunities were limited. With the town population and jobs decreasing, the family moved to Tucson. (Old Pearce Preservation Association.)

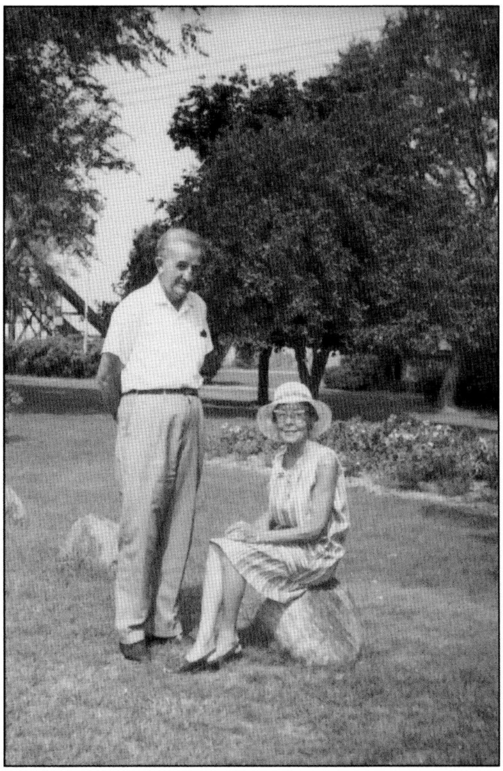

After his military service, Lewis Smith worked in Washington, DC, for the Department of Mines. He returned to Pearce briefly in the late 1930s and worked as a surveyor. He left Pearce for Morenci, where he worked for Phelps Dodge. Lewis is pictured in 1966 with his wife, Claire. (Steven Carlson.)

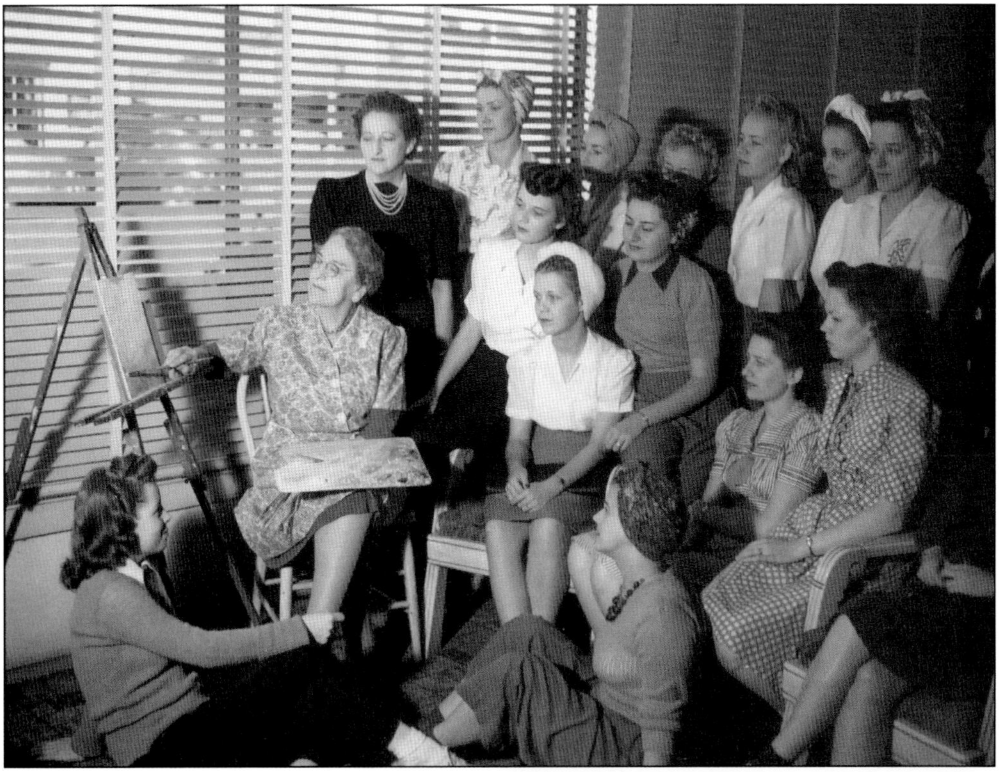

Effie Anderson Smith studied painting at the National Academy in New York, with May Bradford Shockley at the Stickney School of Fine Arts, and with Anna Althea Hills. Known for her use of color, her Arizona landscapes became nationally known. In 1931, an exhibition of her paintings was held in Corcoran Hall in Washington, DC. She soon became known as Arizona's dean of women artists. (Steven Carlson.)

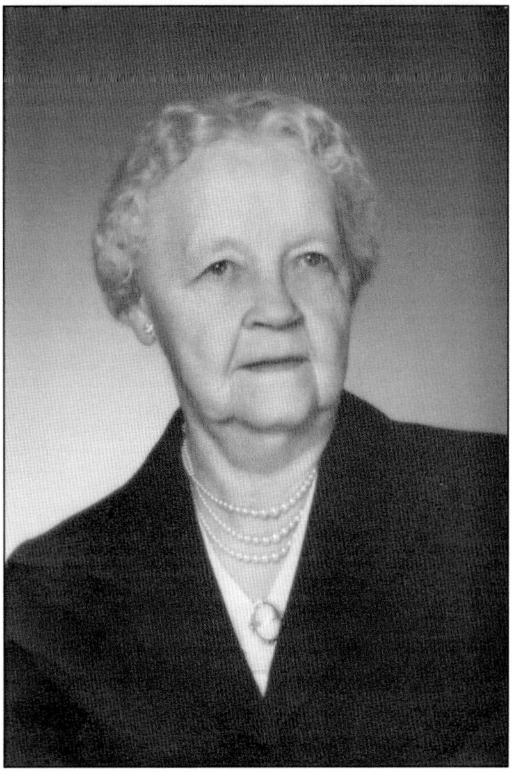

Sometime in the 1940s, Effie Anderson Smith moved out of Pearce. In November 1951, she moved to the Arizona Pioneers Home in Prescott. After four years there, she passed away on April 21, 1955. Of the 60-plus years she had lived in Arizona, over 40 were spent in Pearce. (Steven Carlson.)

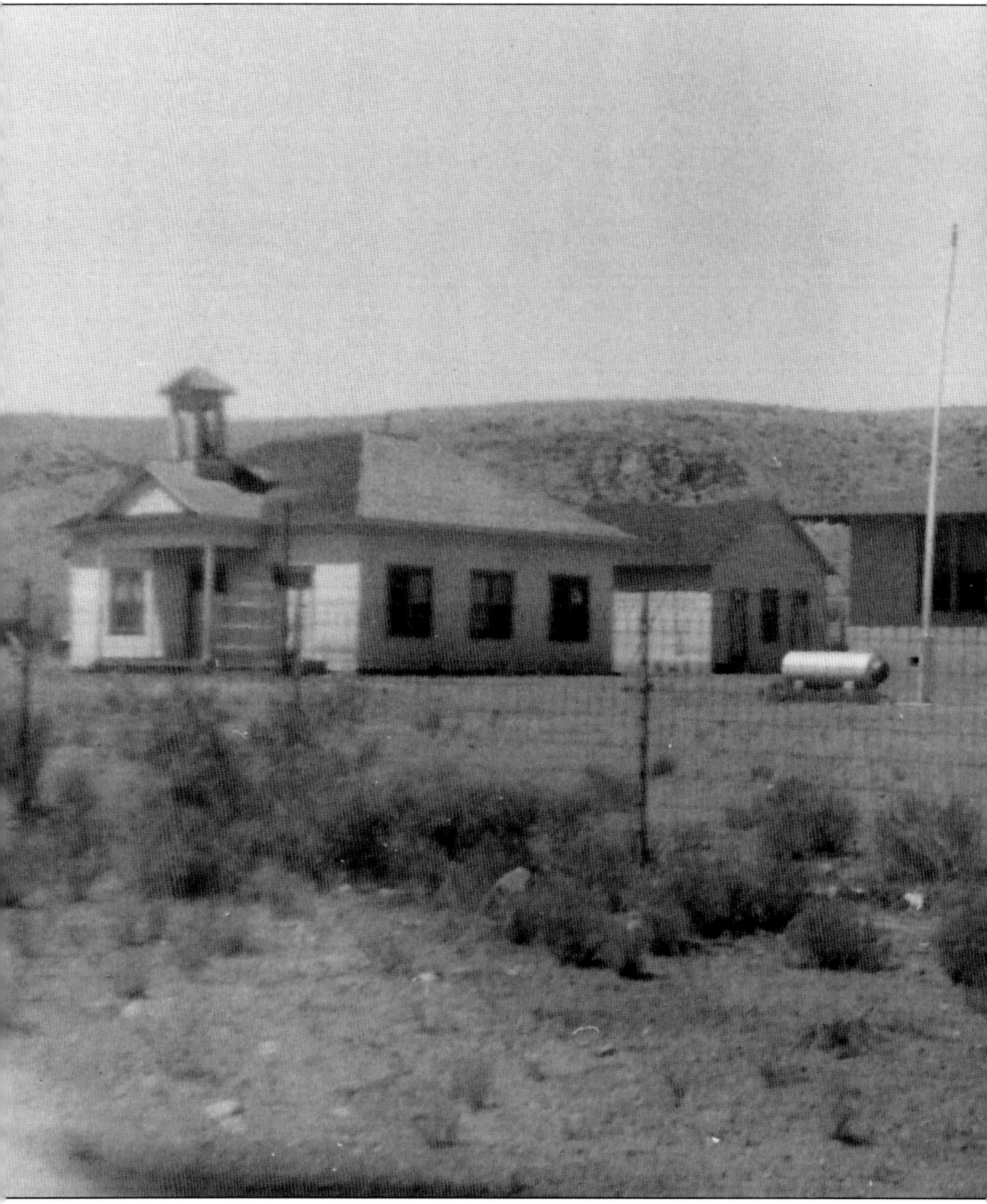

The outstanding building behind the elegant arch is the brick incarnation of the Pearce School. This imposing edifice was built in the Arts and Crafts style in 1912. Land was donated by the Common-Wealth Mine Company. Originally, it was a four-room school. Each room included a cloak room. The school included first through twelfth grades, until the high school was moved to the town of Elfrida in 1948. The church-like frame structure to the left of the 1912 building is

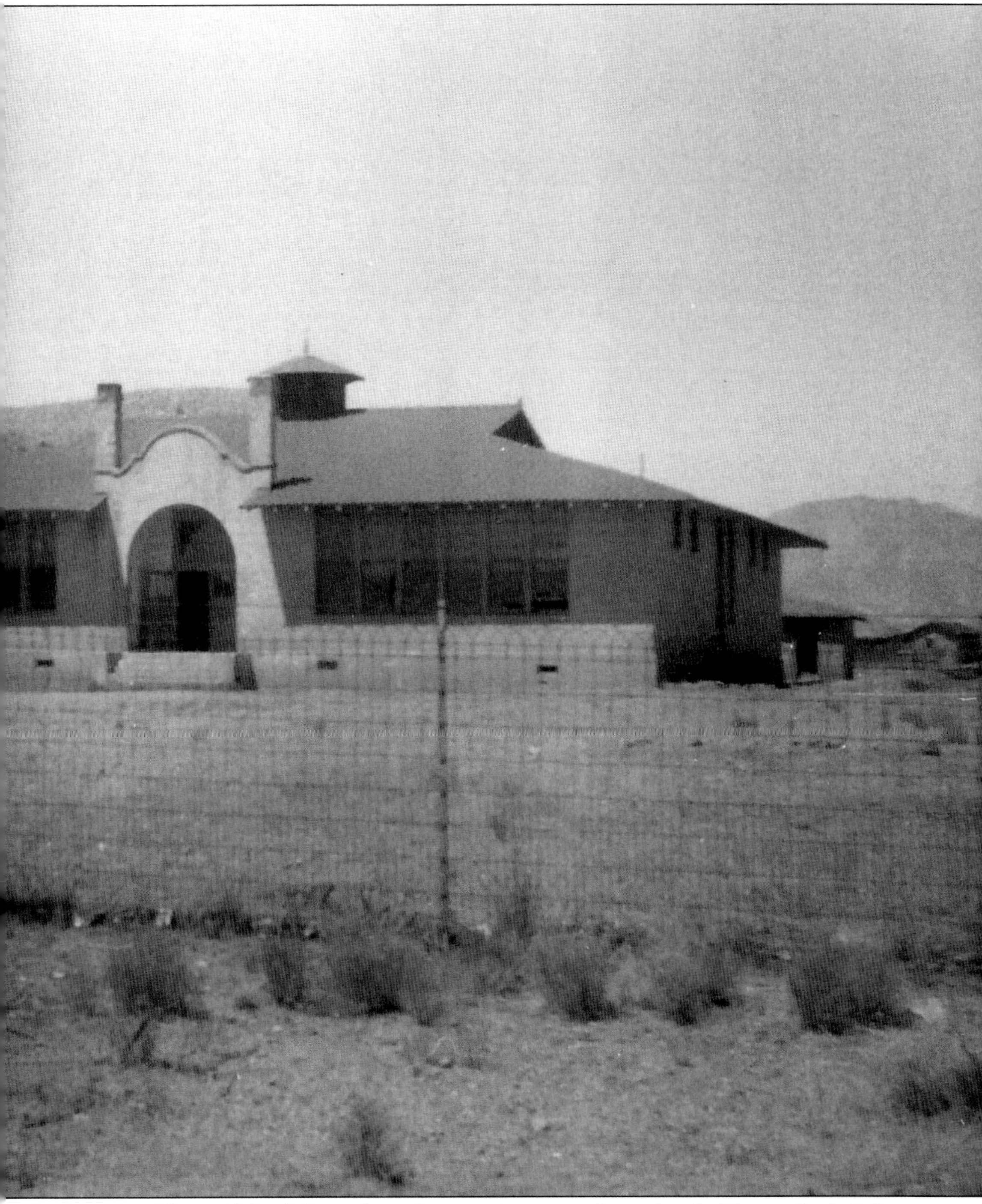

the original Pearce School. Fittingly, it also sometimes served as a church. The smaller building behind this one, also frame, was brought over from the town of Servoss to expand the town's school capacity as the Pearce population grew and before the construction of the new school in 1912. (Mary Appel.)

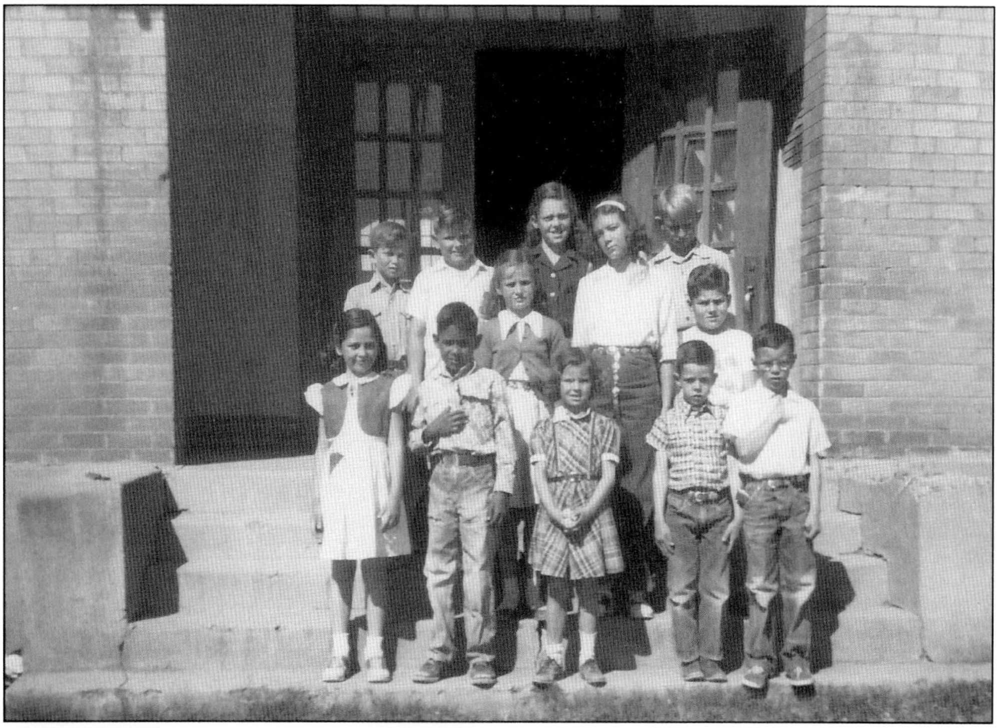

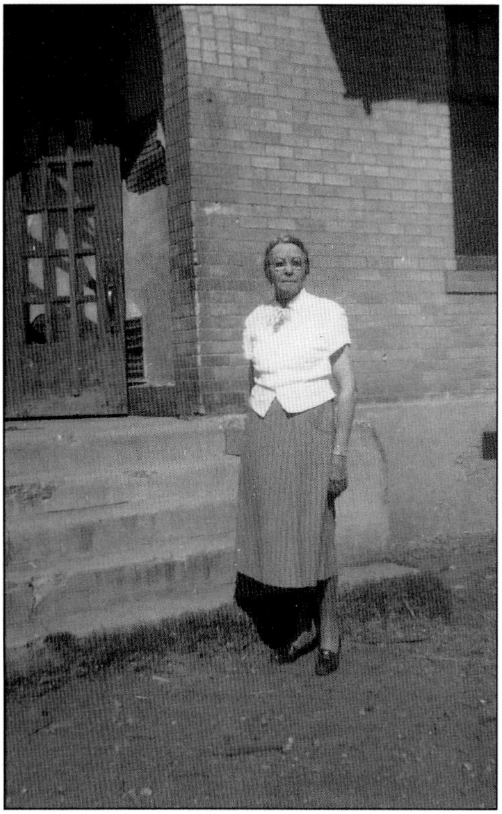

In August 1948, the high school moved its students to Elfrida, to the school that later became Valley Union High. With the high school grades gone and a dwindling population, the entire student body of 1955 stands in stark contrast to the senior class of 1936 (shown on page 49). (Mary Appel.)

Mrs. McSparron, a teacher, was living near Sierra Vista with a year left until retirement but no class to teach. Pearce was in need of a teacher, so Jack Busenbark brought her over to Pearce. She was considered a fine employee and was asked to stay for another year, but declined. (Mary Appel.)

Bobbie King was a teacher at Pearce School for several years in the 1950s. Fluent in Spanish, she taught English to the children who only spoke Spanish. By the time they were in third grade, they could speak English well and were up to grade level in their schoolwork. She is remembered by students as being a wonderful teacher. (Mary Appel.)

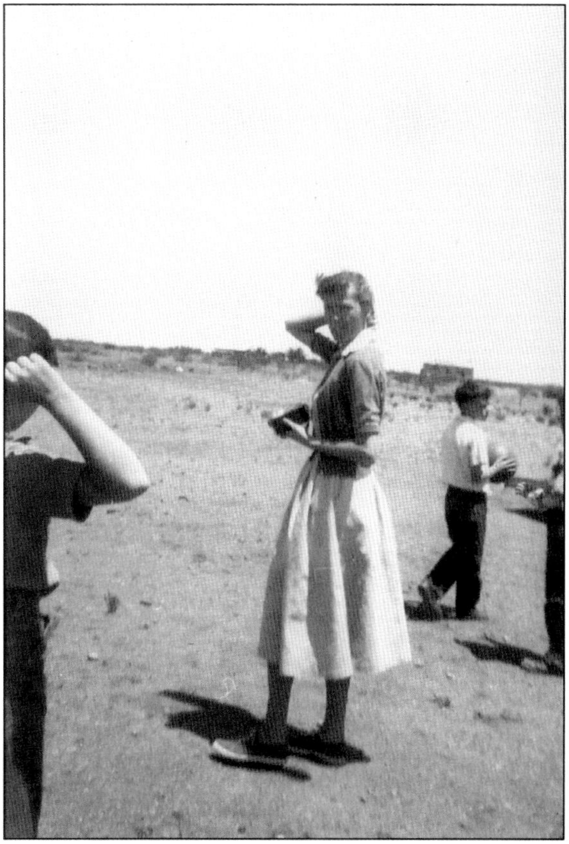

Teacher Grace Solms stands with the students of Pearce Elementary from 1956. From left to right are (first row) six unidentified students, Rusty Hatley, Jo-Ann Busenbark, Brian Hatley (head turned), and Judy Meek (behind Jo-Ann with her head turned); (second row) Grace Solms, Doris Meek (peering over display), Sharon Stevenson, Margaret Gallager, Bobbie Meek, Mary Busenbark, and an unidentified boy. Grace Solms later became county school superintendent. (Mary Appel.)

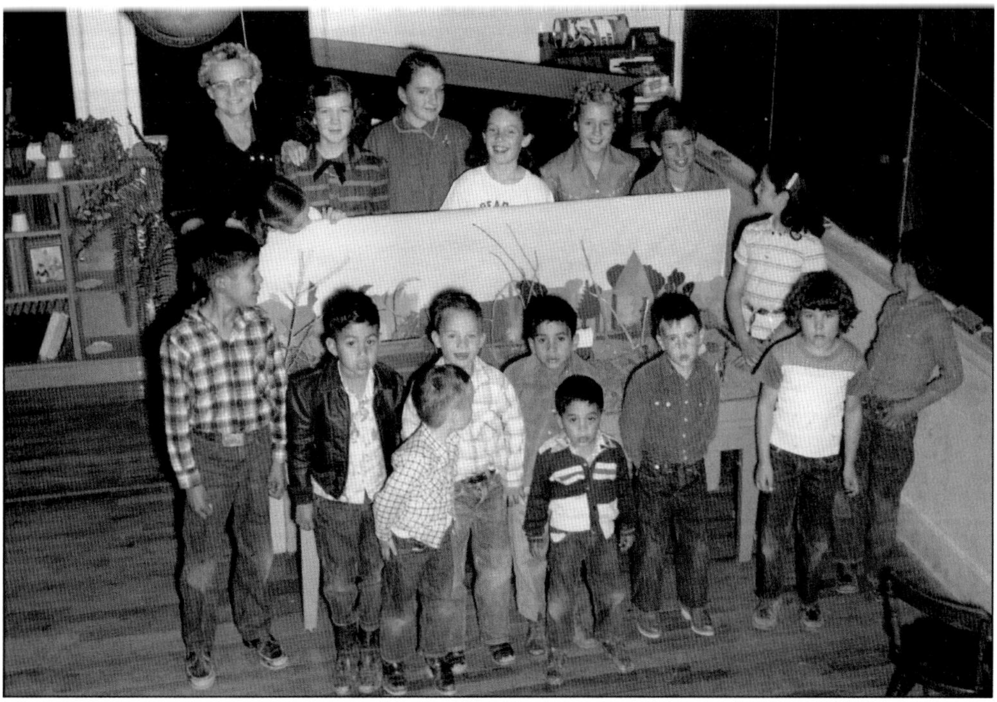

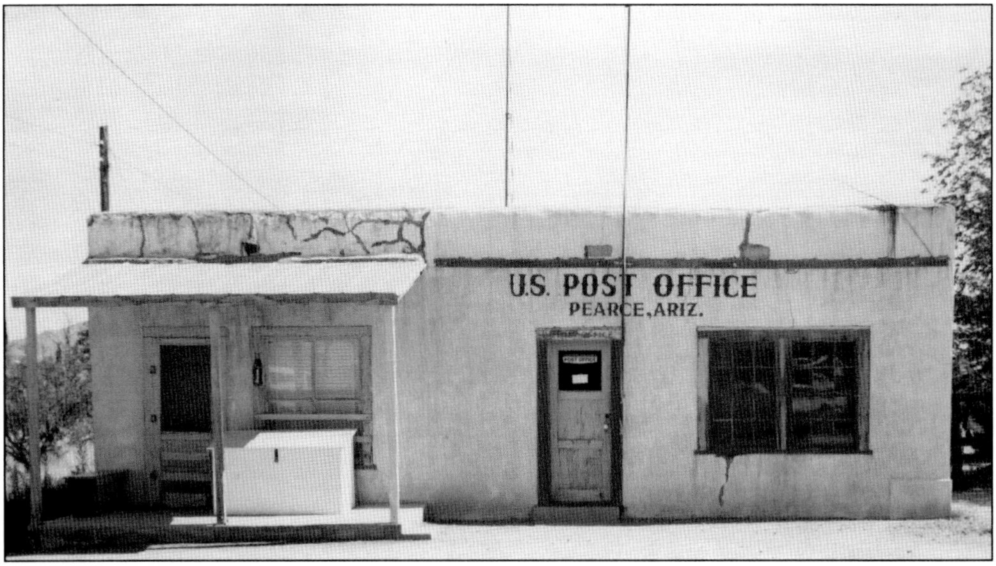

Situated across the road, east of the Pearce Mercantile, the post office was built from adobe, had plank flooring, and oak post office boxes. The north part of the building housed the Pearce Cafe. In 1967, with the population shifting to the Sunsites community, it was decided to move the post office there. This was another blow to the town of Pearce. (Postal History Foundation.)

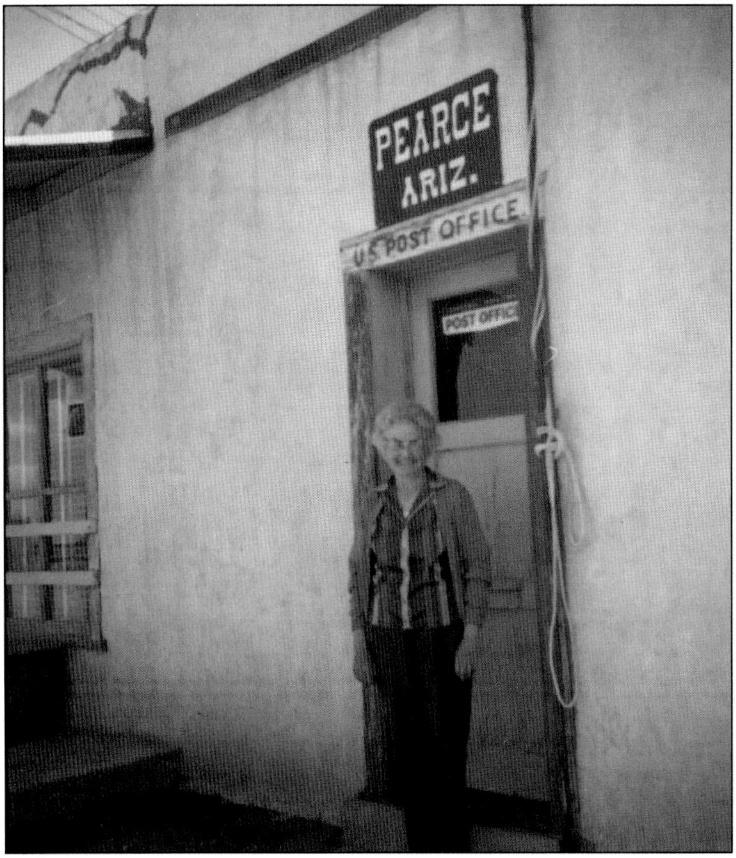

Gladys McCleod, seen here, was the last postmaster at the Pearce location, serving for over 35 years. Gladys's mother, Mary Huddy, had also been postmistress of Pearce. (Postal History Foundation.)

Modern ladies, stepping out in Old West style, gather in front of the Old Store. Even in the late 1950s and early 1960s, the female population of Pearce knew how to keep the spirit of this once-booming mining town alive. (Old Pearce Mercantile collection.)

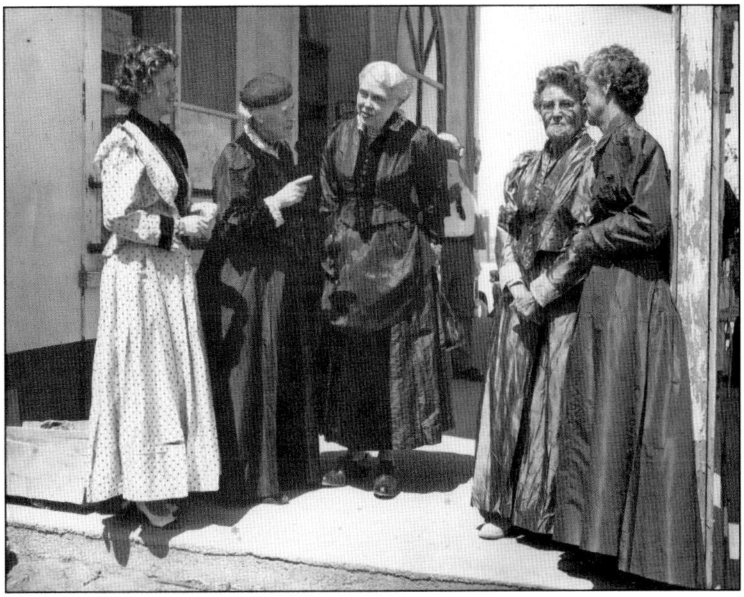

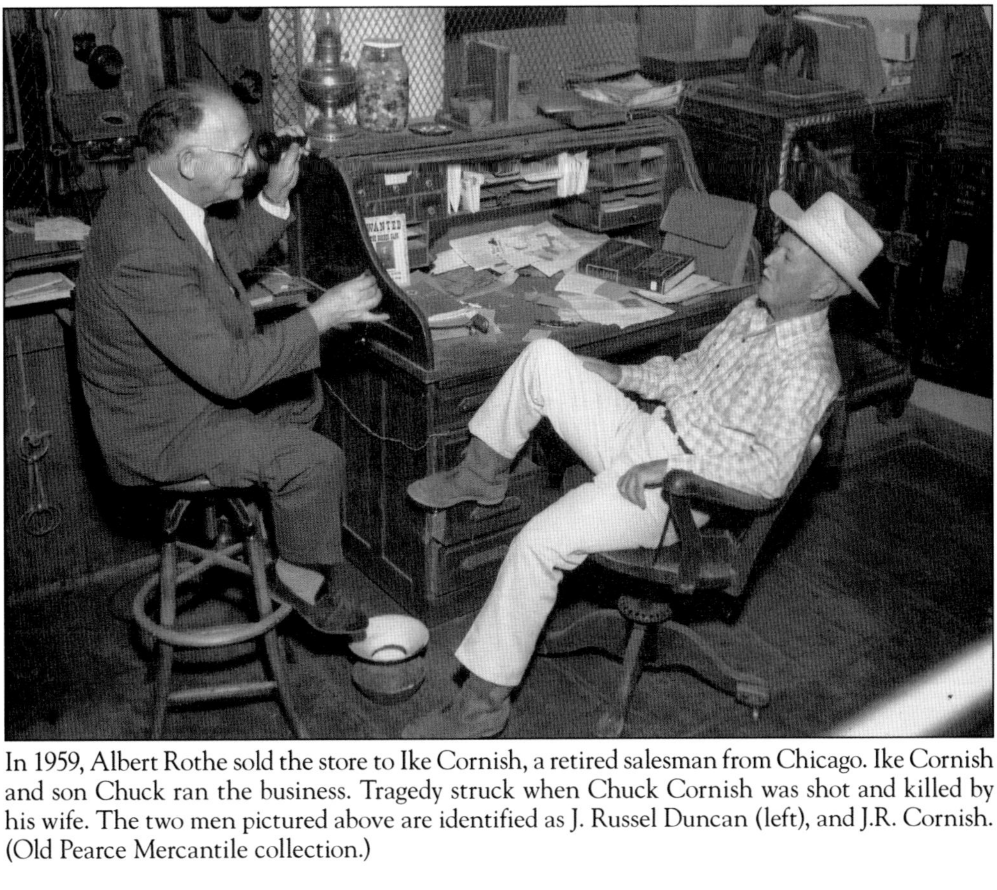

In 1959, Albert Rothe sold the store to Ike Cornish, a retired salesman from Chicago. Ike Cornish and son Chuck ran the business. Tragedy struck when Chuck Cornish was shot and killed by his wife. The two men pictured above are identified as J. Russel Duncan (left), and J.R. Cornish. (Old Pearce Mercantile collection.)

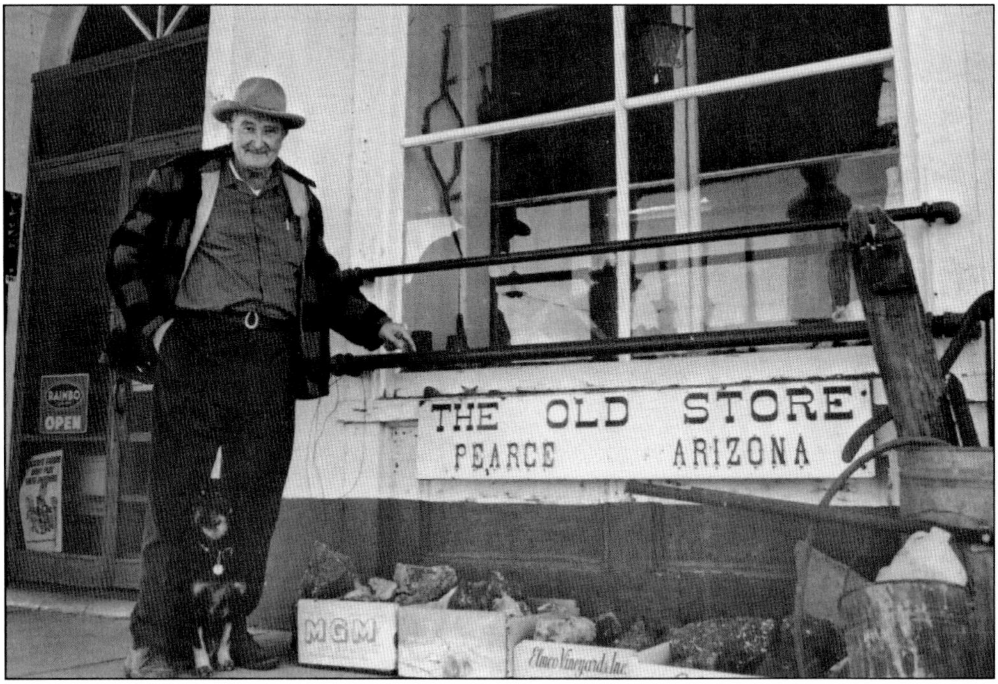

Ben Seaton managed the Old Pearce Mercantile, known simply as the Old Store, in the 1960s. He and his dog Buddy were local fixtures. A "Greetings from Pearce, Arizona" postcard describes the store: "The Old Store has seen it all . . . the noisy excitement of a few years and the long silence of many. Here, on display, are hundreds of items ranging from the antiques of those old days to period and contemporary pieces of the Great Southwest. . . . You'll find Buddy and me waiting to greet you at the Old Store, Pearce, Arizona, on Route 666 [renamed Route 191 in 1992] between Willcox and Douglas in fabulous Cochise County." (Above, Old Pearce Mercantile collection; below, Cochise County Historical Society.)

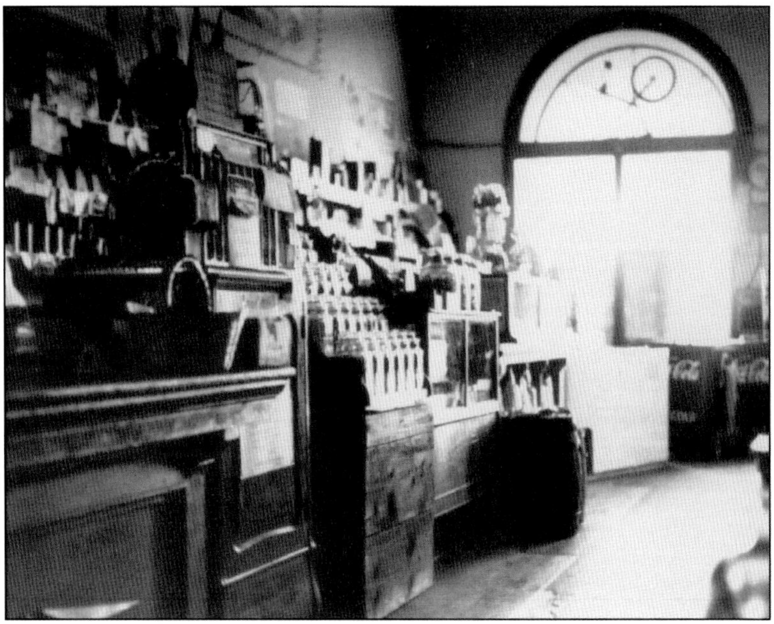

In February 1973, a film crew arrived in town to shoot an advertisement for Olympia Beer. Since then, other filming has been done, including a Taco Bell advertisement and the television show *Little House on the Prairie*. (Old Pearce Mercantile collection.)

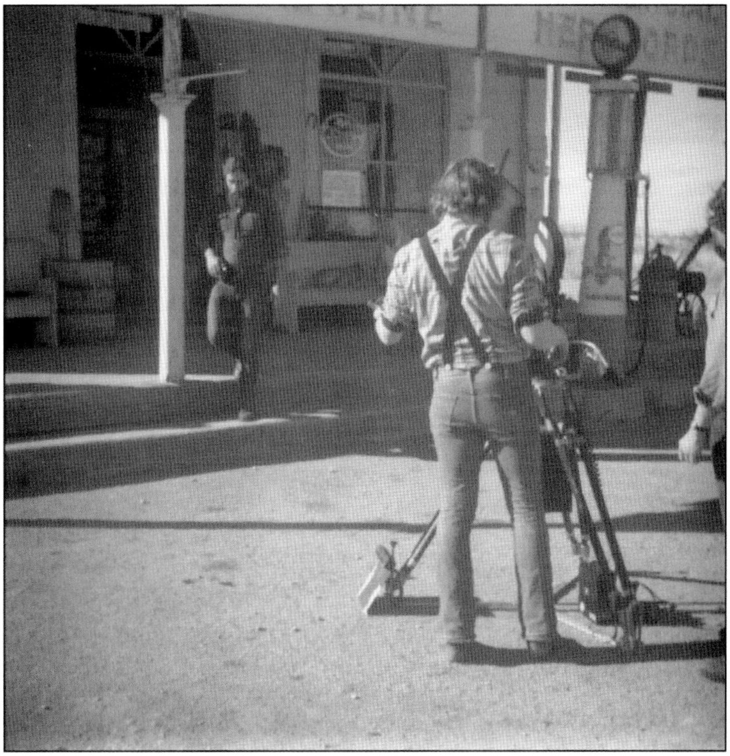

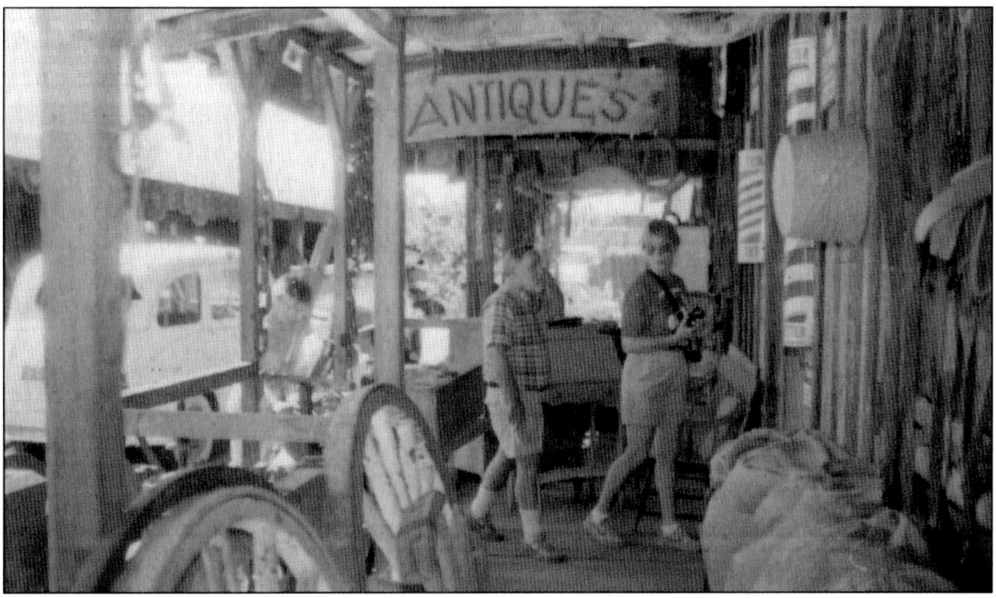

John and Ginger Thurman bought the store at the end of 1969. Through the early 1970s, their hard work made the mercantile a success. But in 1975, John died unexpectedly. Ginger, with the help of family, kept the store running. Pictured here, a couple passes through the south entrance of the store. (Old Pearce Mercantile collection.)

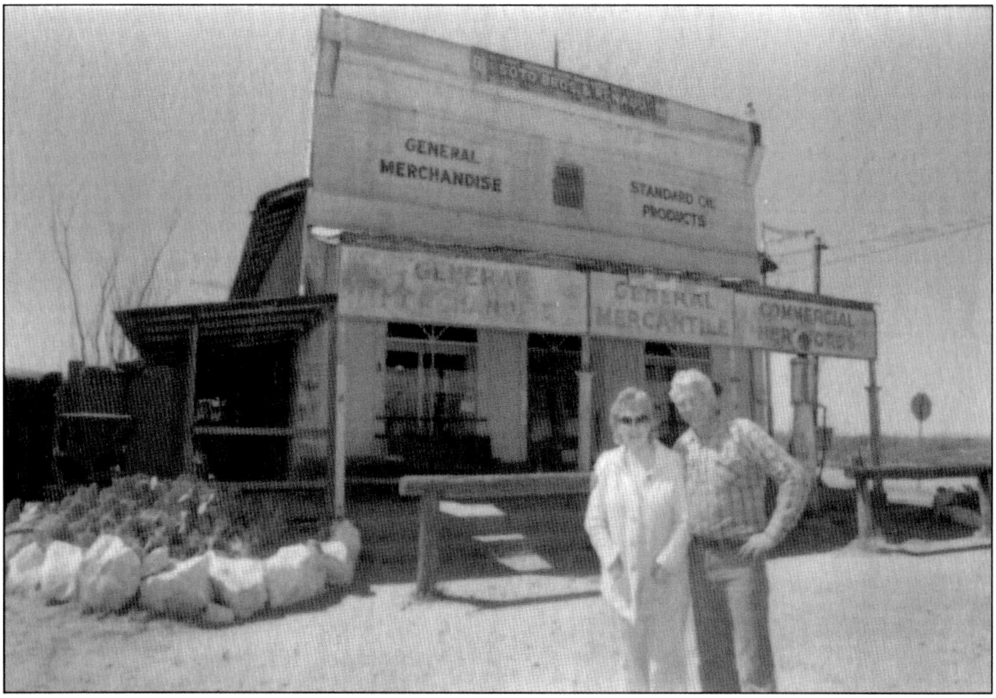

In 1978, Ginger married Dave Davison, a retired Marine who had recently moved to the area. Dave's many skills, including blacksmithing, helped him with renovations, improvements, and maintenance of the store. Also in 1978, the building was added to the National Register of Historic Places. Dave passed away in 1993. Eventually, Ginger decided to sell the store and moved to Tucson. Ginger passed away in 2010. (Both, Old Pearce Mercantile collection.)

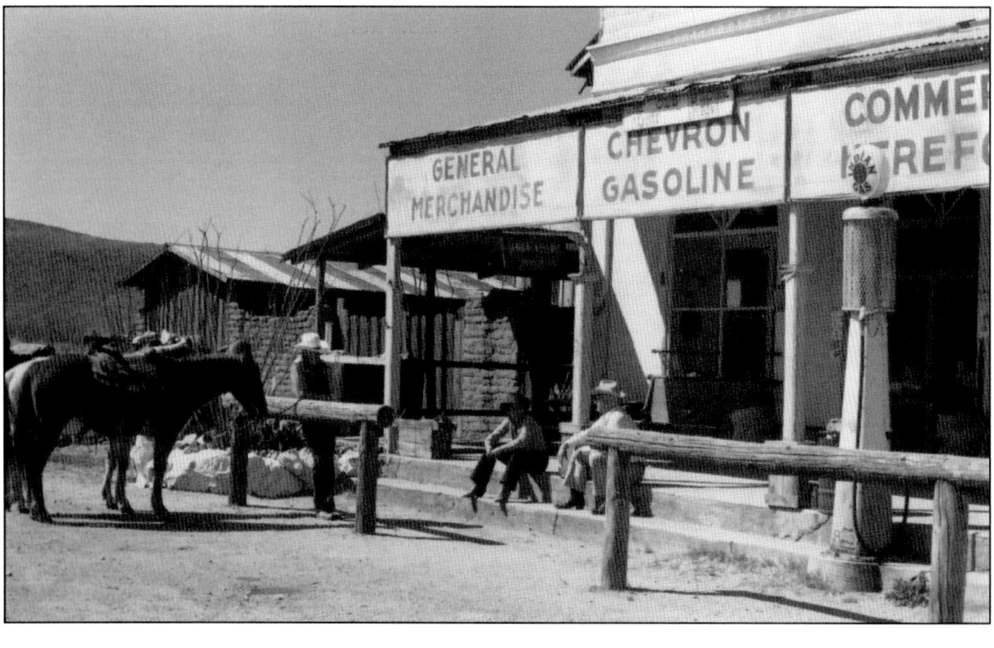

Five

Horizon and Sunsites in the 1960s

The 1960s impacted the lives of two distinctly different generations. Baby boomers struggled through a decade that included Martin Luther King's dream and assassination, Vietnam's violence, Pres. John F. Kennedy's assassination, and Elvis Presley's new competition, the Beatles. The other generation, characterized by journalist Tom Brokaw's moniker the "Greatest Generation," looked forward to retirement. They survived the Great Depression and World War II, and they wanted an active, carefree lifestyle. Almost simultaneously, two Arizona companies enticed them to the sunny Southwest. On January 1, 1960, Del Webb kicked off the 1960s with Sun City, the nation's first planned active-adult retirement community, on the site of ghost town Marinette, near Peoria, Arizona. In Cochise County, landowners in the area of Pearce, another ghost town, sold vast stretches of acreage to Horizon Land Corporation, founded by Joseph Timan and Irving Geist. Timan, a former New York lawyer and real estate investor, had grand plans that included selling land and building communities in Arizona, New Mexico, and Texas. Horizon promised ideal weather, beautiful surroundings, and inexpensive land to future retirees from chilly Midwest, Northern, and Northeastern states. Oversized newspaper advertisements offered "Full Acre Homesites in Beautiful Arizona Sunsites, Total price $495, No Interest Charges! No Carrying Charges!, and $10 Down/Month." Horizon introduced a policy that credited trip expenses to those who purchased more than $2,000 in land. Investors used their trip allowances to visit Arizona and to view their lots. On March 26, 1965, Willcox's *Arizona Range News* published a supplement celebrating the third anniversary of Sunsites. In 1967, Horizon marketing literature announced that Sunsites had 92 resident families, including 65 children. Many of Horizon's promotions featured children, a concept that set it apart from Sun City and its age restrictions. The decade ended on a somber note. On May 11, 1969, residents dedicated Vonderheide Memorial Falls, honoring popular young Horizon Project Manager Marvin O. Vonderheide, who died in 1968. Volunteers built the waterfall on the lush executive golf course from the finest and most colorful rock specimens they could find.

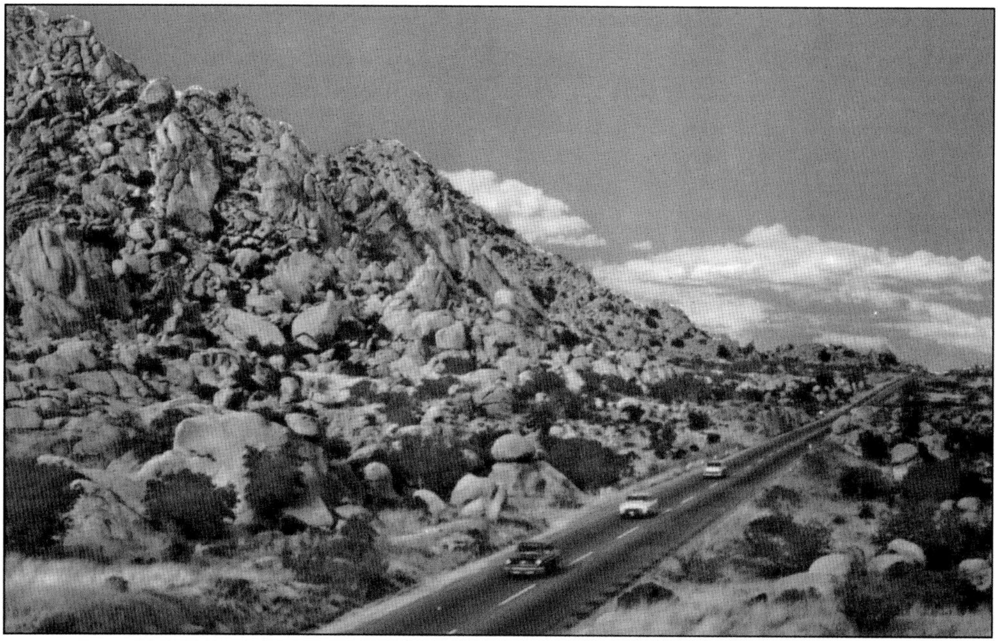

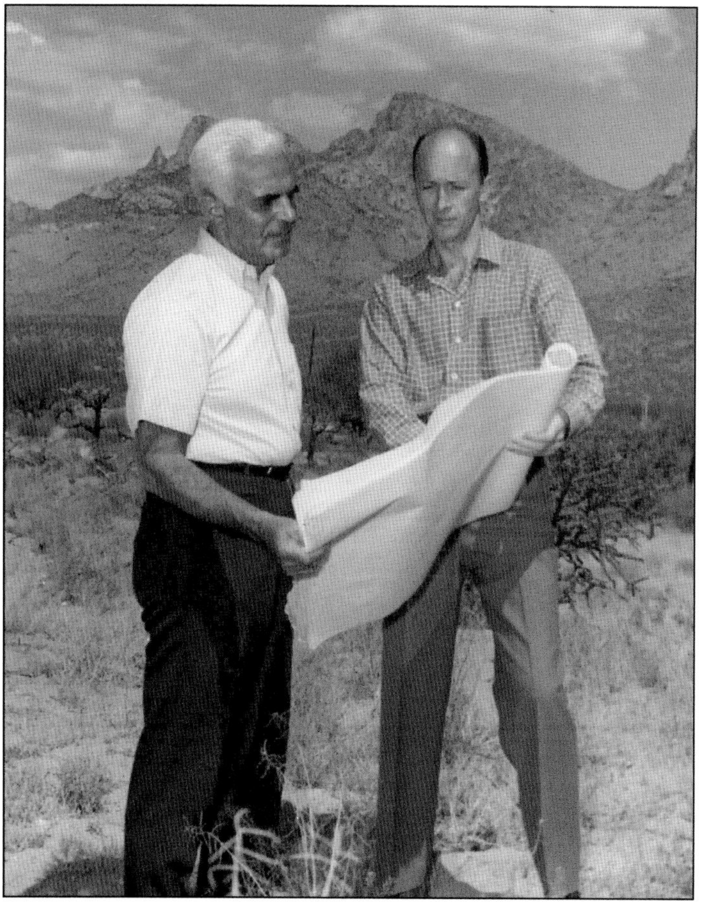

Long before it became Interstate 10 in the 1960s, US Highway 86 cut through the Dragoon Mountains and Texas Canyon. Travelers exited at US Highway 666 and drove south to reach Sunsites. In 1992, US Highway 666 was renamed US Highway 191. (Library Archives.)

Against the backdrop of the Dragoon Mountains, Joseph Timan (left), founder and president of Horizon Land Corporation, and Sidney Nelson, executive vice president, review land engineering maps for Horizon property in the Sulphur Springs Valley. Horizon claimed, "every site is perfect for building." (SSVHS.)

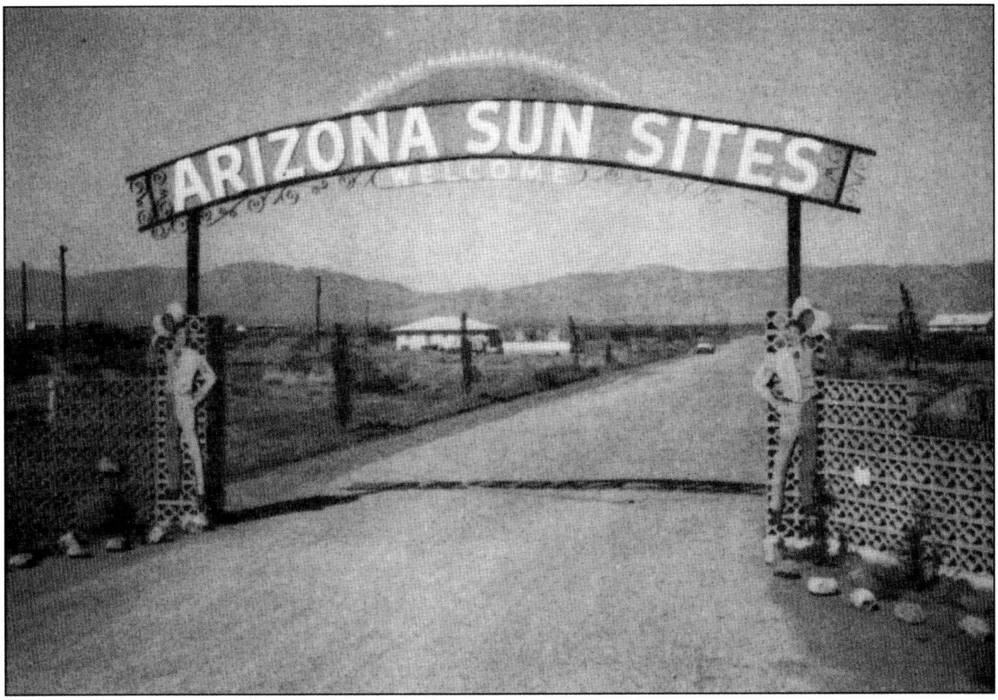

The entry arch, flanked by cowboys and located at the High Street and US Highway 666 intersection, welcomed visitors to "Arizona Sun Sites." Horizon Land Corporation featured this photograph in marketing materials for several years. In the 1960s, Horizon used several variations of the town's name; frequently, more than one style was used within one document or publication. John Pearce photographed the restaurant adjacent to the entry arch when he visited Sunsites in the early 1960s. The arch and the restaurant sign show just two of the variations for spelling Sunsites. The restaurant changed owners numerous times; today, the building houses a real estate office. (Both, Library Archives.)

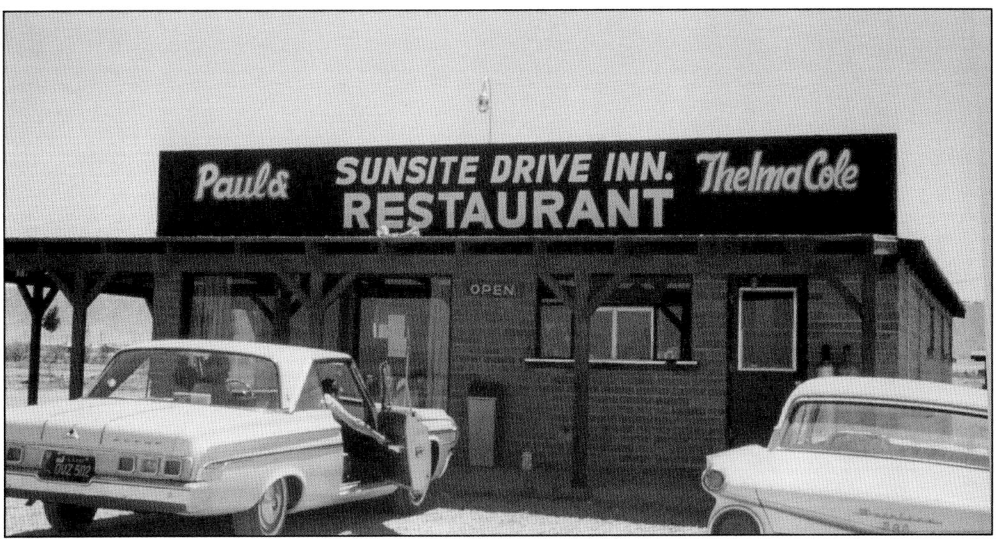

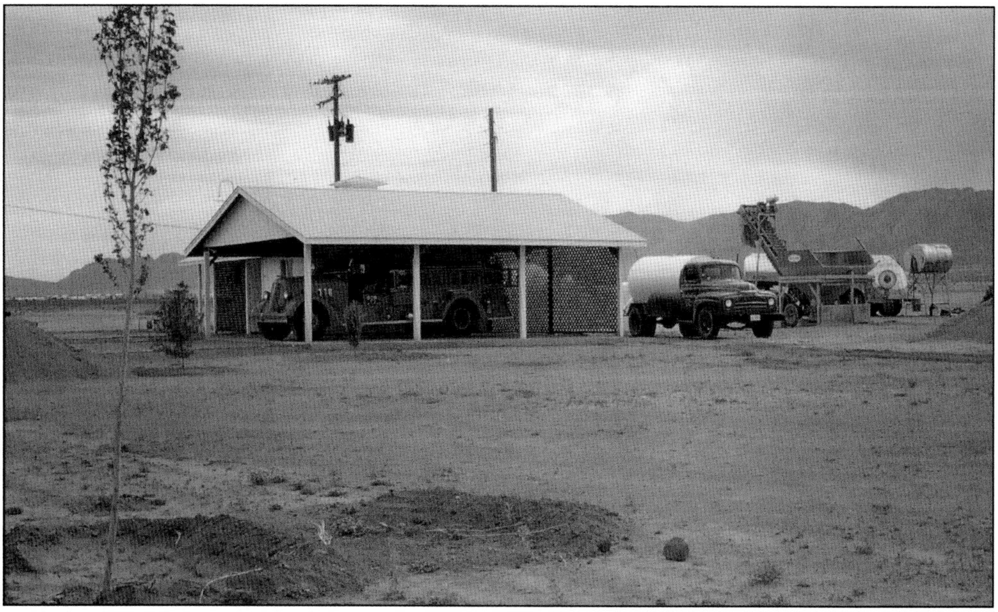

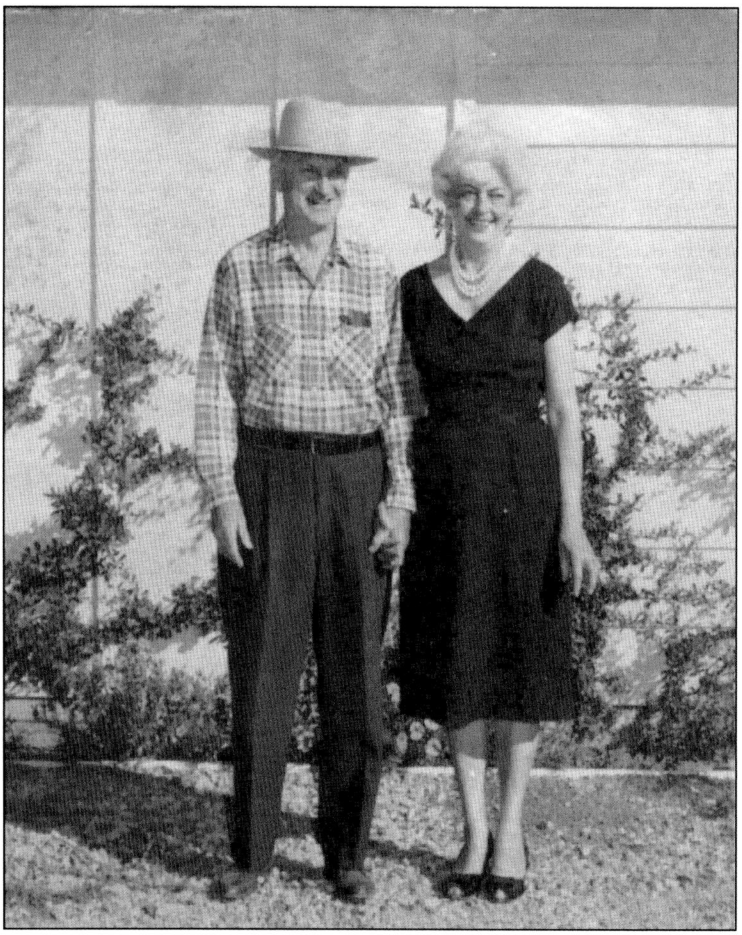

The fire station was one of the first structures built in Sunsites. The fire truck shown in this photograph, taken by John Pearce in the early 1960s, was later purchased by Sunsites residents Rose and Russ Vandeyacht. (Library Archives.)

According to Horizon Land Corporation marketing literature, Mr. and Mrs. H.P. Barnard, of Rolla, Missouri, purchased the first house built in Sunsites. Bea and Clem Clemmons purchased the first contracted home. (Library Archives.)

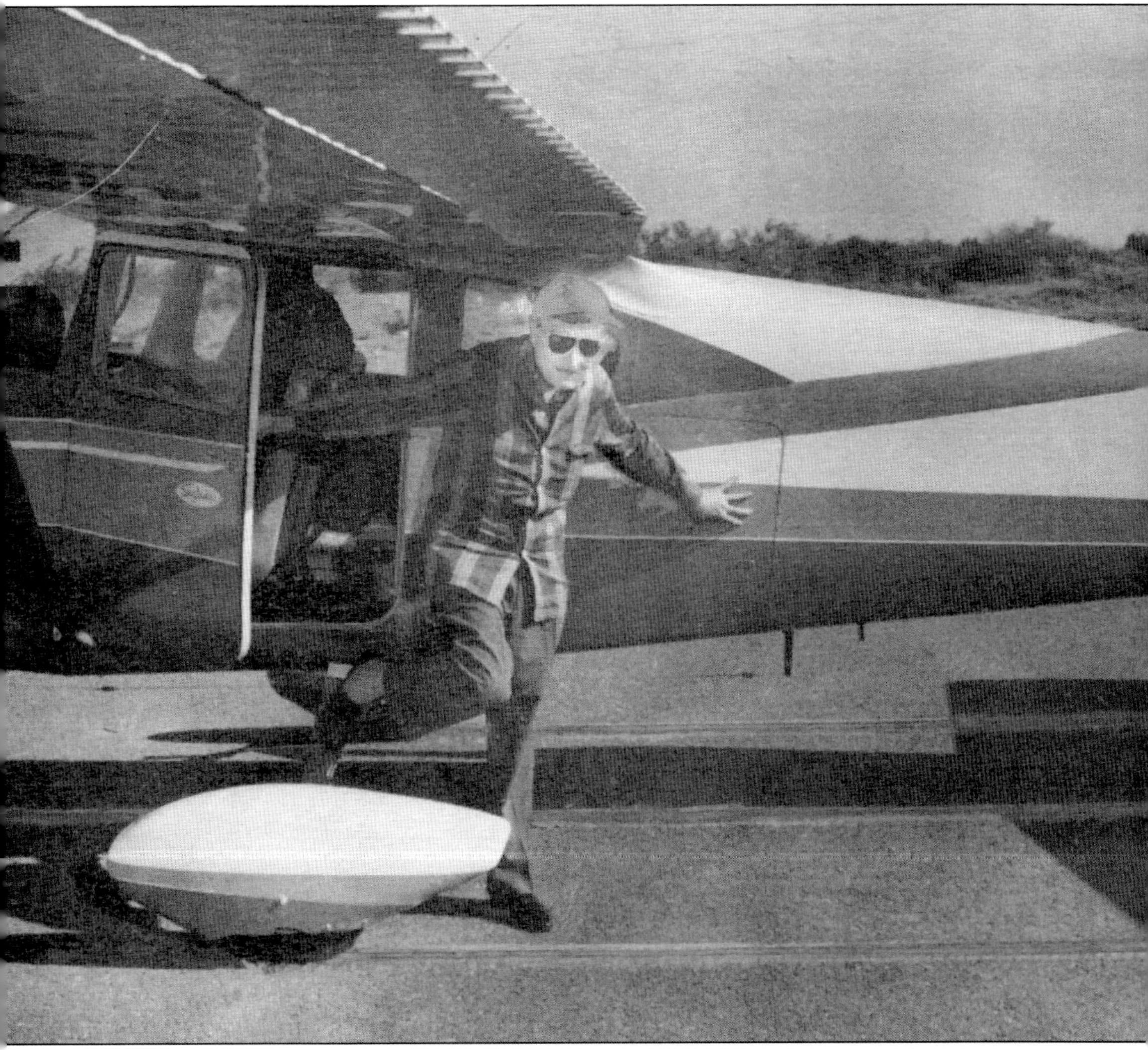

Ranch roads in the area of Sunsites made a handy landing strip in 1962 for directors of the newly formed Valley Telephone Cooperative. This photograph of an unidentified man exiting a plane that had just landed appeared in the October 1962 *New Horizons* newsletter. The photograph accompanied a story about a directors' meeting at the home of Dr. D.W. "Doc" Ingram, located south of Sunsites Heights. The *Arizona Range News* explained in a special edition devoted to Sunsites's third anniversary that light planes used Sunsites streets as landing strips. (Teri and Frank Bessler.)

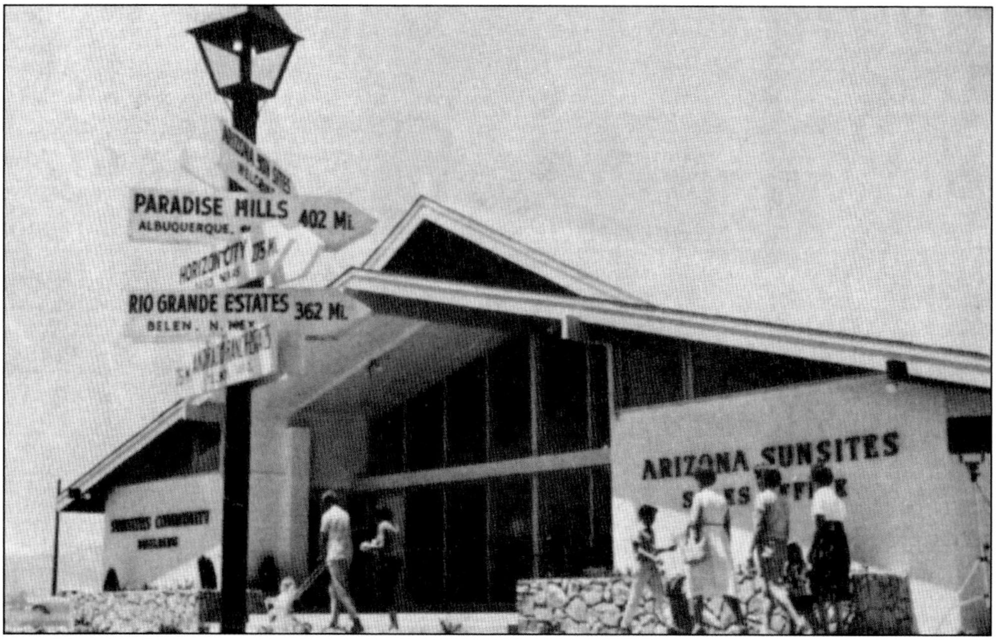

Horizon dedicated the Sunsites Community Center in May 1963. Horizon president Joe Timan officiated. More than 1,000 people attended the dedication. One side of the building housed Horizon's sales office. The signs on the lamppost name other Horizon developments. (Library Archives.)

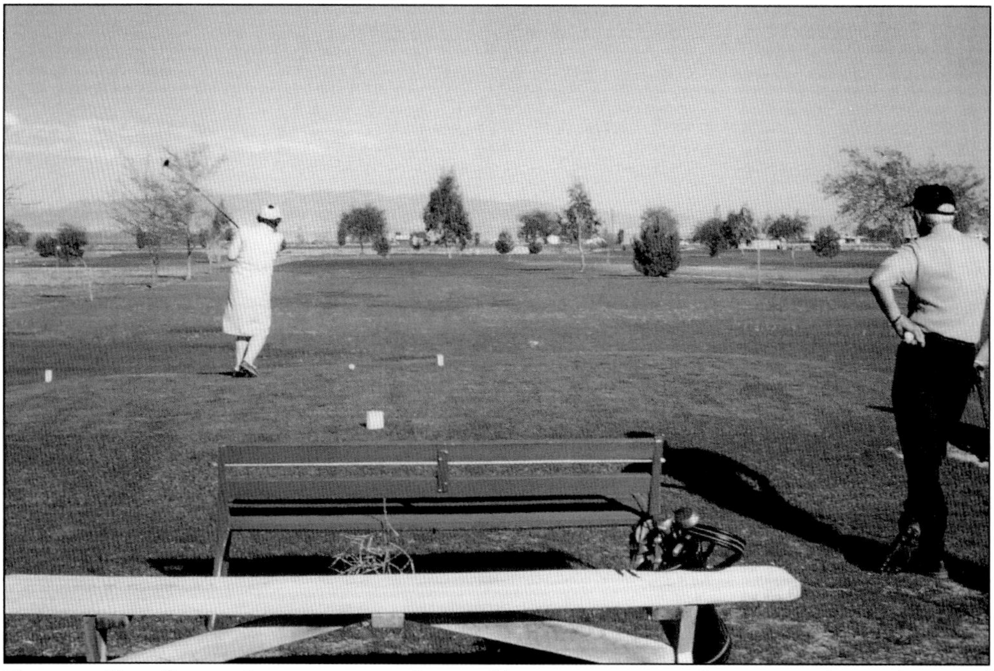

Playing golf on Sunsites's executive par-three golf course was a popular pastime for residents and visitors. John Pearce captured this iconic moment during his trip to Sunsites and Arizona in the early 1960s. (Library Archives.)

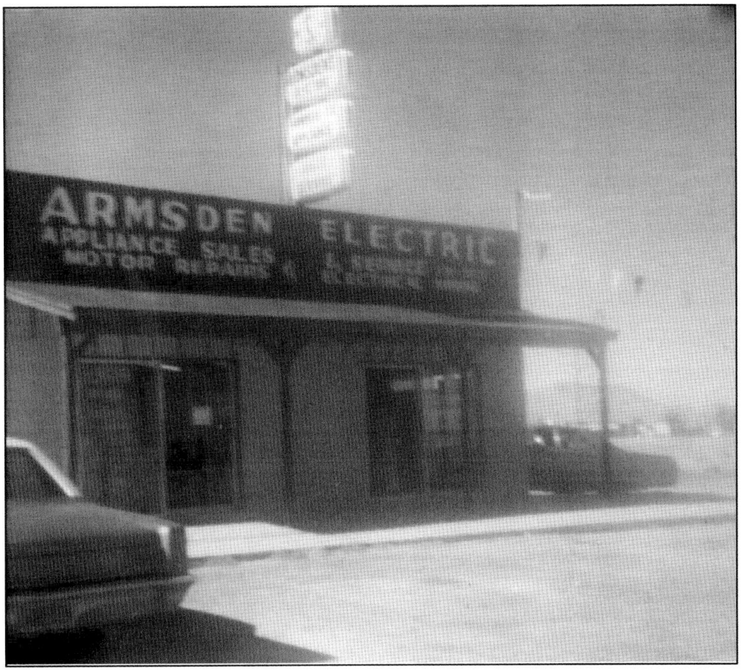

Armsden Electric was a welcome addition to the fledgling Sunsites community when it opened in 1964. Ed Armsden moved from Kendall, New York, to open an appliance sales and service business, settling with his family in a home on Christmas Tree Lane. (Diana Armsden.)

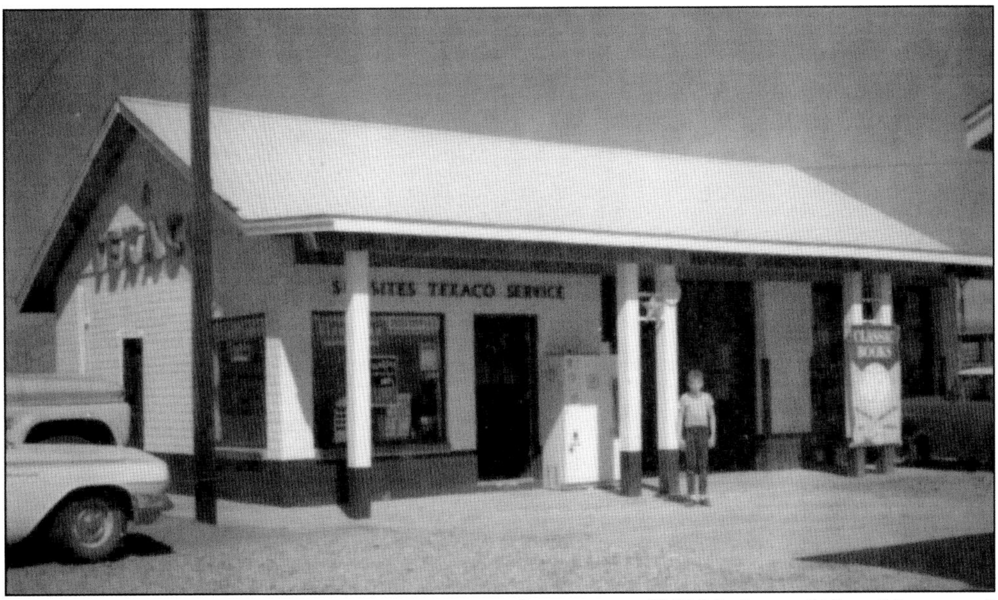

Joe Iazzetta built this Texaco service station at the corner of US Highway 666 and Ironwood Road in 1964. Joe, his wife, and four children moved to Sunsites from New Jersey. The boy in the photograph is Joe's son Mike. (Mike Iazzetta.)

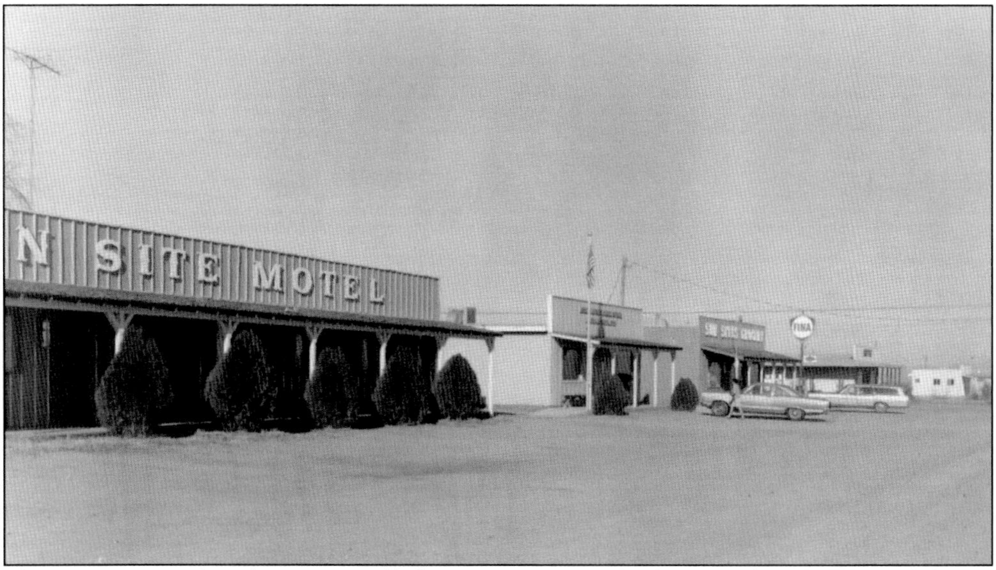

The Sunsites Motel, with its sign spelled as "Sun Site Motel," dominated Frontage Road during the 1960s. The US Post Office relocated from Pearce to the building next to the Sunsites Motel in January 1967. (SSVHS.)

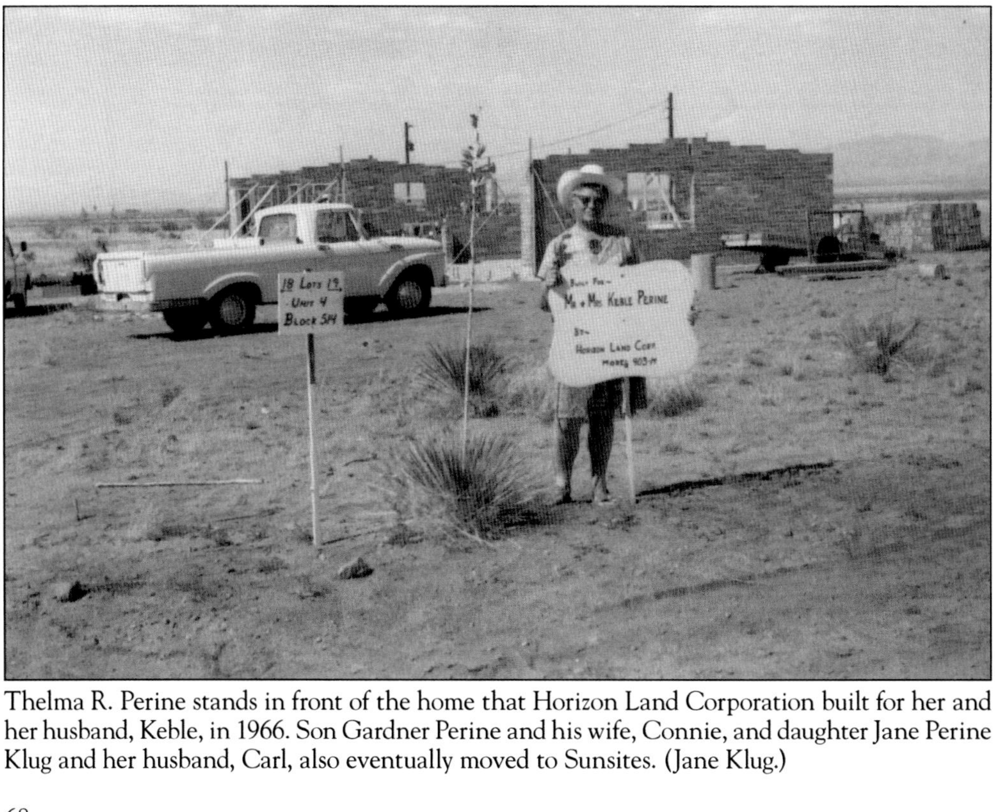

Thelma R. Perine stands in front of the home that Horizon Land Corporation built for her and her husband, Keble, in 1966. Son Gardner Perine and his wife, Connie, and daughter Jane Perine Klug and her husband, Carl, also eventually moved to Sunsites. (Jane Klug.)

Walter Hieber meticulously used photographs to document each step of the construction of his home on Christmas Tree Lane in October 1962. It was among the first homes built in Sunsites. (Walter Hieber.)

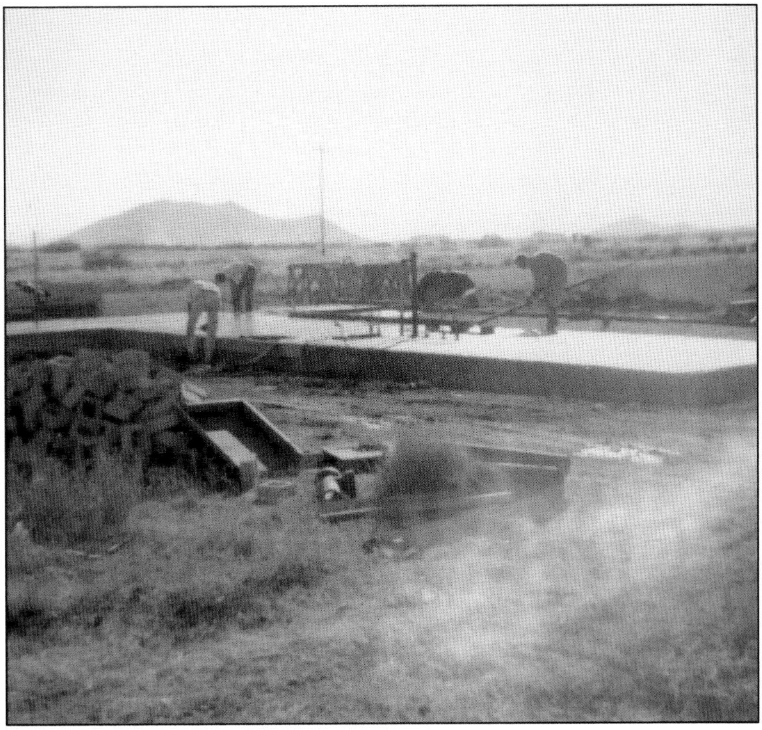

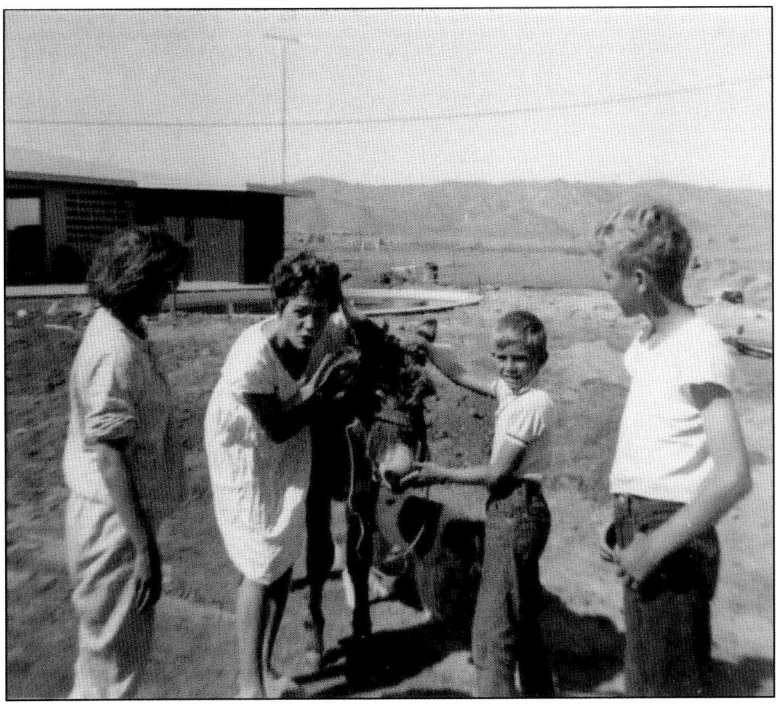

Chapo the donkey was a source of great fun for Claire Iazzetta (center) and her children Sue (left), Tom, and Joe. Son Mike is not pictured. Their swimming pool, built in 1964, was a popular gathering spot. The Iazzetta family got the donkey from Mary and John Magoffin. (Mike Iazzetta.)

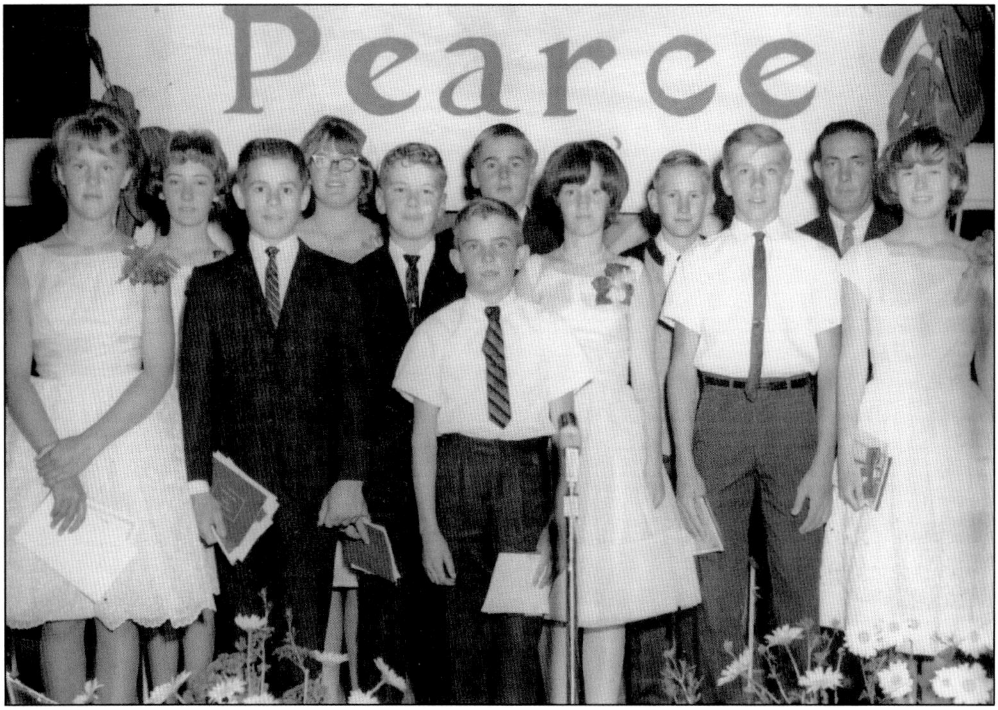

In 1965, the Pearce Elementary eighth graders had graduation ceremonies on the stage of the Sunsites Community Center. Mike Iazzetta stands center-front. Standing behind him are, from left to right, Mary Frei, Meg Magoffin, Mark Hapton, Martha Cunningham, Mark Brown, Talbott Starling, Gail D'Elia, Glenn Williams, Keith Karnok, principal Roy Watson, and Patty Lewis. (Mike Iazzetta.)

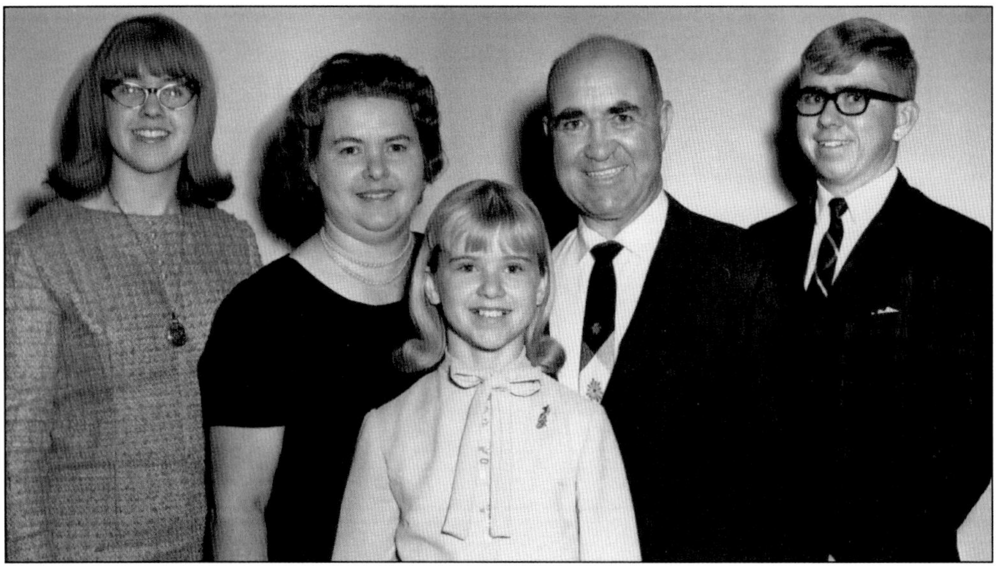

Eschol Cosby founded and built the first church in Sunsites. Cosby's obituary stated that he also served as pastor of the Branded for Christ Baptist Church for about 40 years. This picture of the Cosby family was printed in the *Arizona Range News* on February 2, 1967. Shown are, from left to right, Becky, Joan, Cathy, Rev. Eschol Cosby, and Bobby. (SSVHS.)

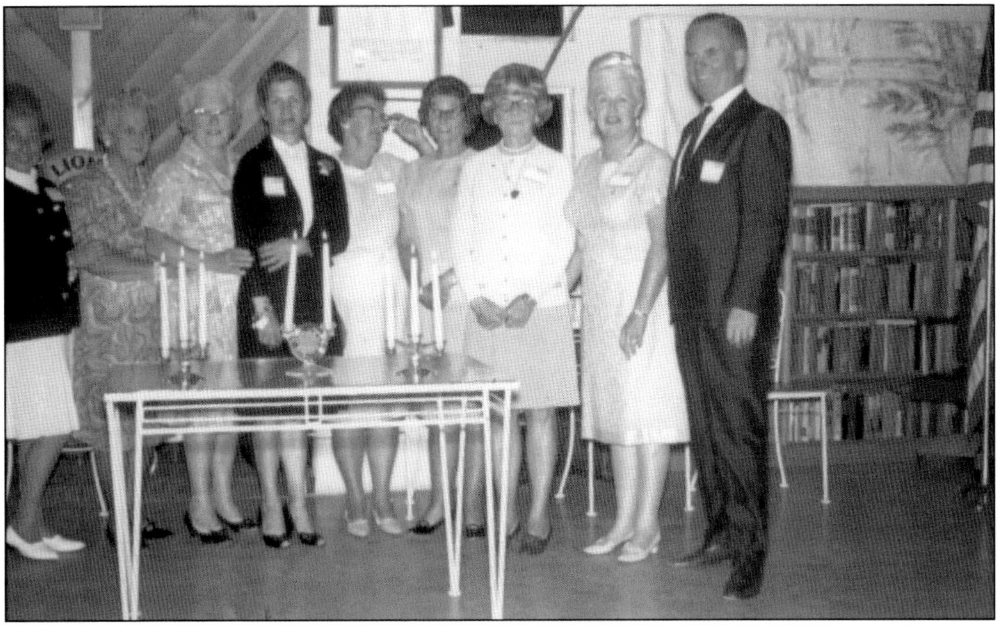

Lions Club district governor Tom Clewes (far right) installed officers of the Lionesses on October 6, 1969, at the Sunsites Community Center. The officers are, from left to right, Mrs. Jerry Benes, Mrs. John Stahl, Mrs. George Muller, Mrs. Ted Sharp, Mrs. Harold Bushman, Mrs. Joe Sitarz, Mrs. Edwin White, and Mrs. Alan Witherspoon. The bookcase on the right side of the stage served as the first library. (SSVHS.)

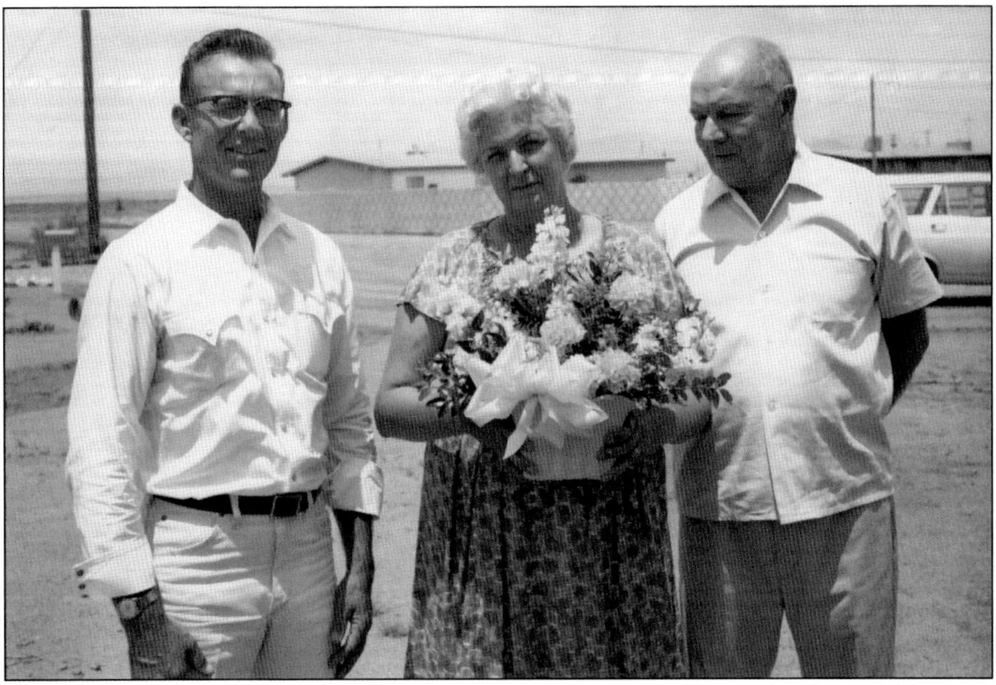

New Sunsites residents Mr. and Mrs. Arthur Bennett got a welcome with a beautiful bouquet from Marvin Vonderheide, Sunsites project manager. The Bennetts, both teachers, arrived in 1967. (SSVHS.)

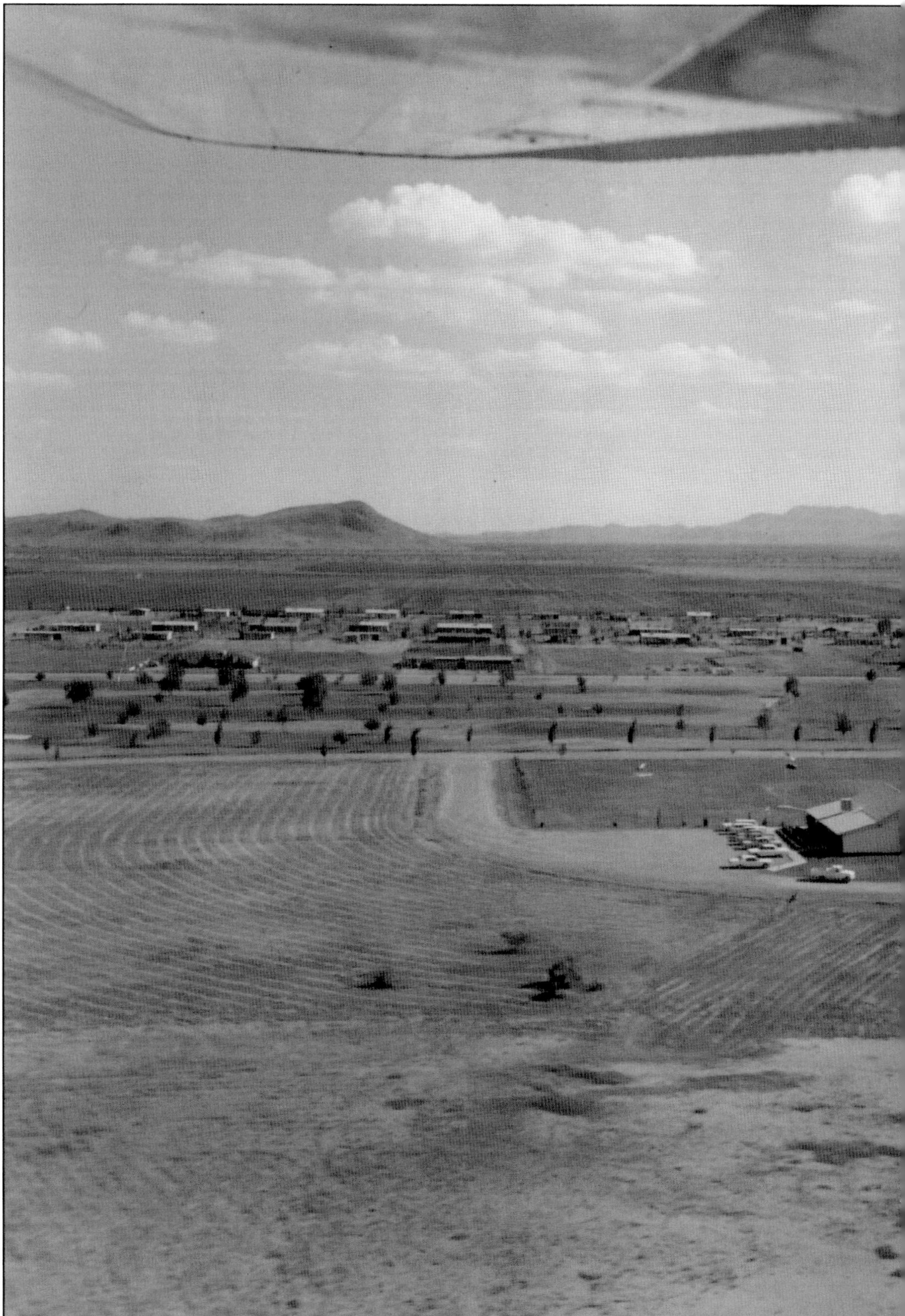

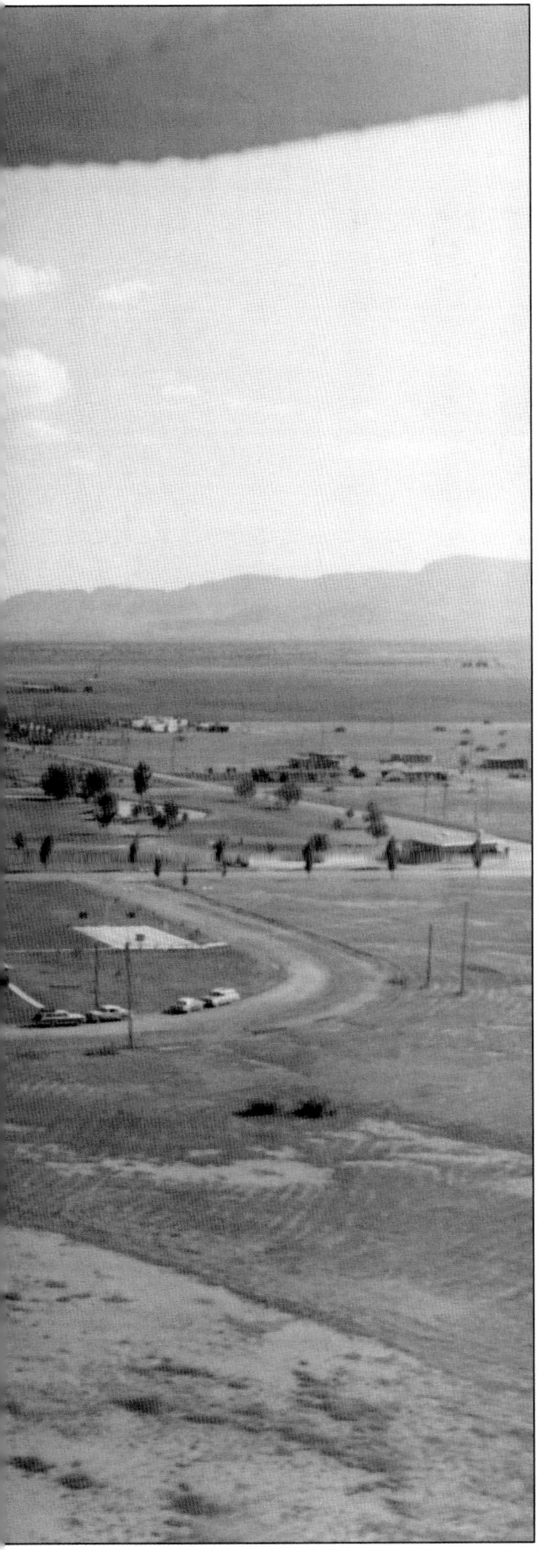

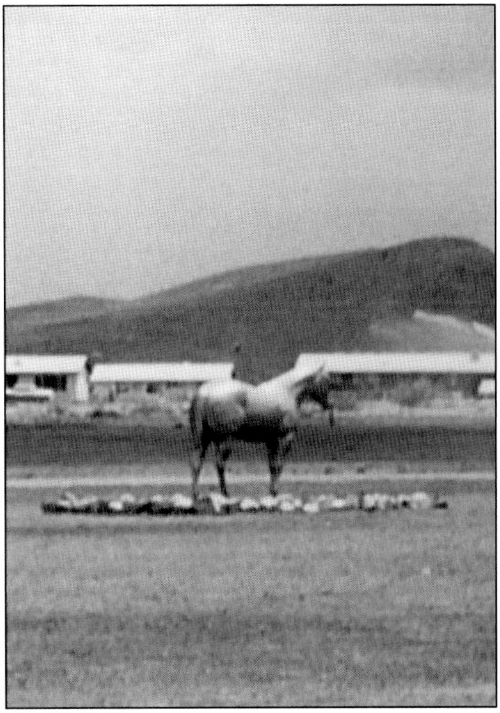

This aerial view of Sunsites was part of a Horizon film that premiered at the Willcox Rotary Club on February 15, 1968. The film *The Southwest Story* was one of many movies and television shows utilized by Horizon to promote their developments in the Southwest. The photograph shows much of Sunsites, looking southward. A horse statue is barely visible on the front lawn of the building used as a community center and a sales office. John Pearce took the only known close-up view of the statue during his visit to Sunsites in the early 1960s. Horizon painted the statue gold, but referred to it as "a graceful bronze horse statue." They considered it a symbol of the "free and unspoiled" West. The statue disappeared mysteriously, and there are several differing stories about who removed the statue, why it was removed, and its final whereabouts. (Left, SSVHS; above, Library Archives.)

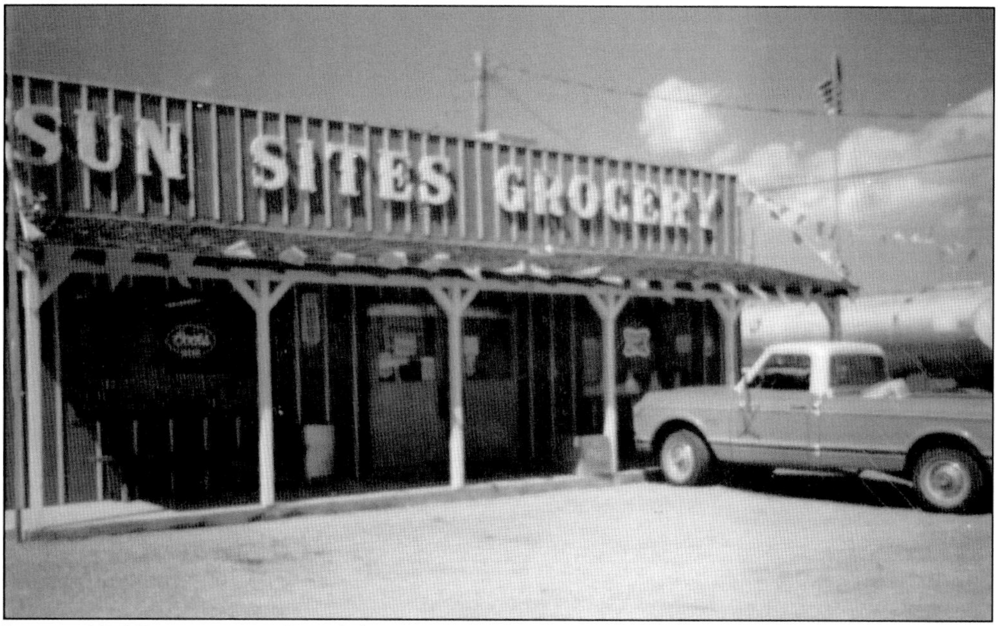

Jean and Ed Borgnaes purchased the Sunsites grocery store in 1969. The grocery store and the motel, two of the earliest businesses in Sunsites, and located just steps away from each other on Frontage Road, had different versions of the *Sunsites* name. Today, Valley Appliance, owned by Susan and John Hellsten, occupies the building. (Jean and Ed Borgnaes.)

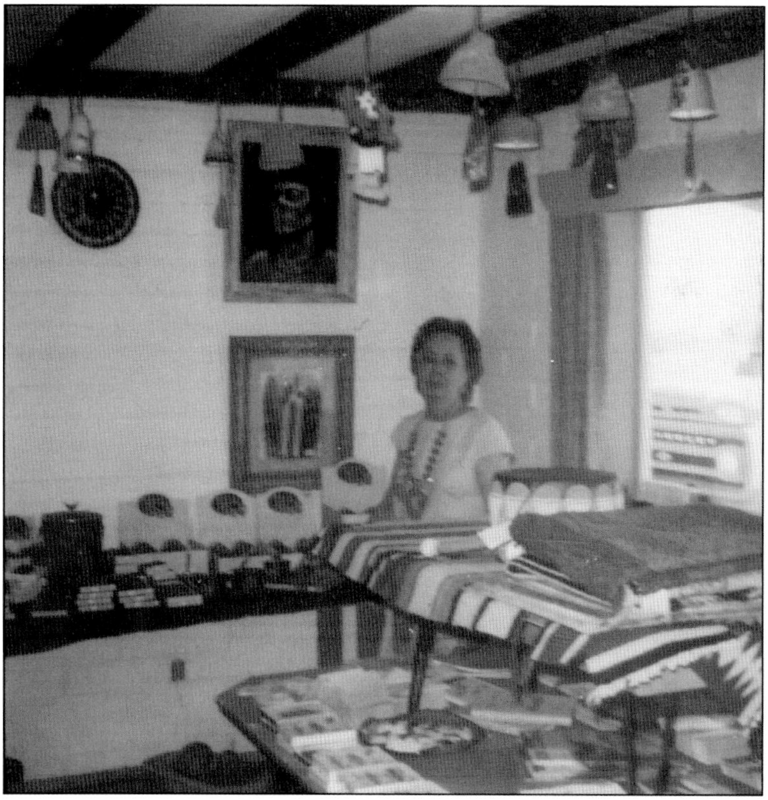

Bea Hessler proudly displayed the variety of items for sale at Cochise Indian Trading Post in this 1969 photograph. She and her husband, Bill Hessler, specialized in authentic Indian jewelry. Bill Hessler wrote the popular cookbook *Good Grazing Along the Southwestern Border*. On October 2, 1985, Bea disappeared mysteriously on Soren's Pass Road. (Sue Smith.)

Six

Music and Magic in the 1970s

Sunsites residents enthusiastically enjoyed homegrown entertainment during the 1970s. They performed for every audience they could find, much like the "backyard musicals" popularized in movies starring Judy Garland and Mickey Rooney. J.T. Holt's series about Sunsites, published in 1999 in the *Arizona Range News*, reported that at one time, there were between 35 and 40 clubs for fewer than 1,000 residents. Musician Julia Witherspoon founded many of those clubs, including Desert Community Arts, Sunsites Squares, and Valley Chorus. In 1976, Sunsites residents produced an ambitious three-day extravaganza. Chaired by Betty Mayo, the Last Frontier bicentennial event included a museum, music, and skits. In the mid-1970s, a magician arrived on the scene. Retired Air Force colonel Howard Shonting and his wife, Rene, moved from New York to Sunsites. He founded the popular Way Off Broadway Little Theater. Described as 2,456 miles from Broadway, members of the theater put on productions that included musical revues, comedy skits, marionettes, dancing, and magic. Nationwide, the economy turned sour. The OPEC oil embargo put the brakes on travel. The Watergate scandal shook confidence in government. In Tucson, Horizon contended with the impact of the economic downturns and with its own missteps. Now known as Horizon Corporation, after changing its name from Horizon Land Corporation in 1968, the company went from heralding success stories to settling suits. In 1971, the Horizon directors elected Joseph Timan as chairman of the board and chief executive officer. At the same time, they named Sidney Nelson as president. The Federal Trade Commission filed a complaint against Horizon for its advertising and sales practices in 1975. The *Sunsiter* printed Sidney Nelson's rebuttal on the front page of the April 1975 edition. The State of Arizona filed a civil suit on similar grounds, which it settled through a consent agreement in 1978. For Sunsites, the 1970s brought a new bank, new churches, the first nine holes of an eighteen-hole golf course, renovation of the commercial area, and a new fire station. In 1977, the Apache Generating Station began a $22 million expansion, designed to meet future needs.

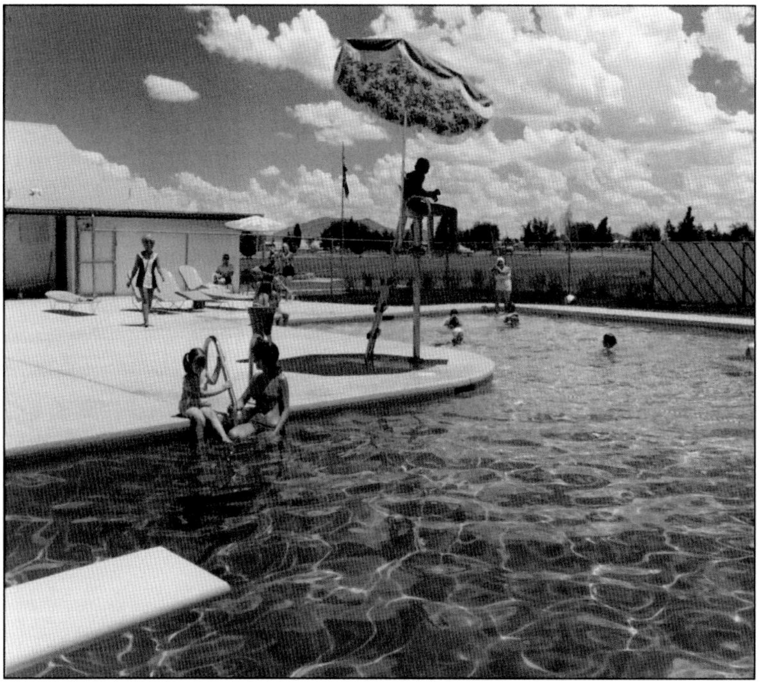

The swimming pool at the Sunsites Community Center opened June 1, 1971. The *Arizona Range News* reported on July 22, 1971, that the new swimming pool attracted people from the entire Sulphur Springs Valley. (SSVHS.)

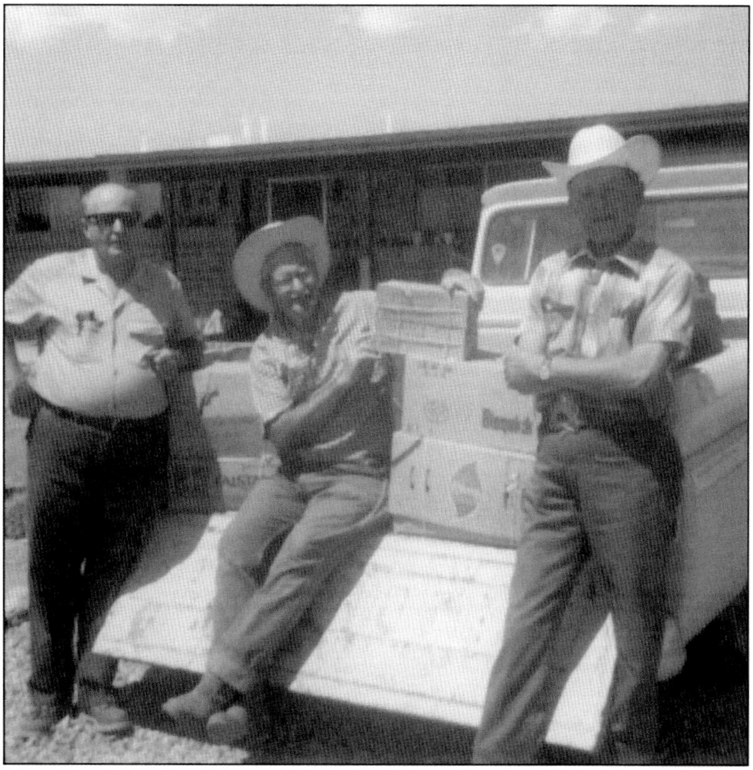

Cochise Stronghold Lions Club members show off a truck filled with books, magazines, and postage stamps, bound for the Veteran's Hospital in Tucson. The *Arizona Range News* published this photograph on July 29, 1971, and identified the members as, from left to right, Austin Neff, William Silva, and Joseph Sitarz. (SSVHS.)

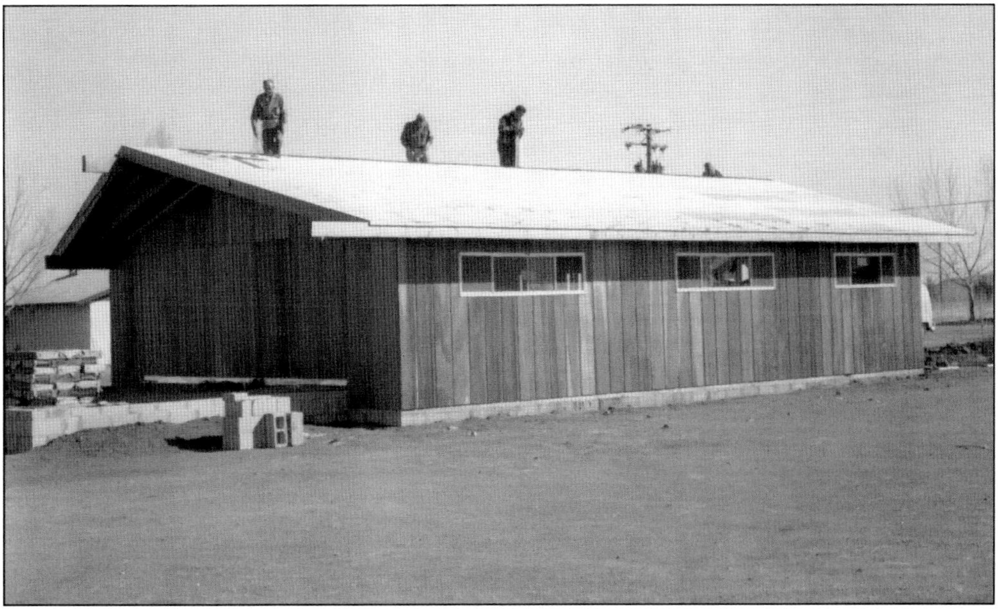

This photograph, published in the *Arizona Range News* on March 11, 1971, shows Sunsites residents putting the finishing touches on the Arts and Crafts Building adjacent to the fire department. The library that began as a collection of books on the stage of the Sunsites Community Center moved into a portion of the new building. Horizon Corporation furnished the land and the materials for the building. Today, the building serves as a dormitory for the fire department EMTs. (SSVHS.)

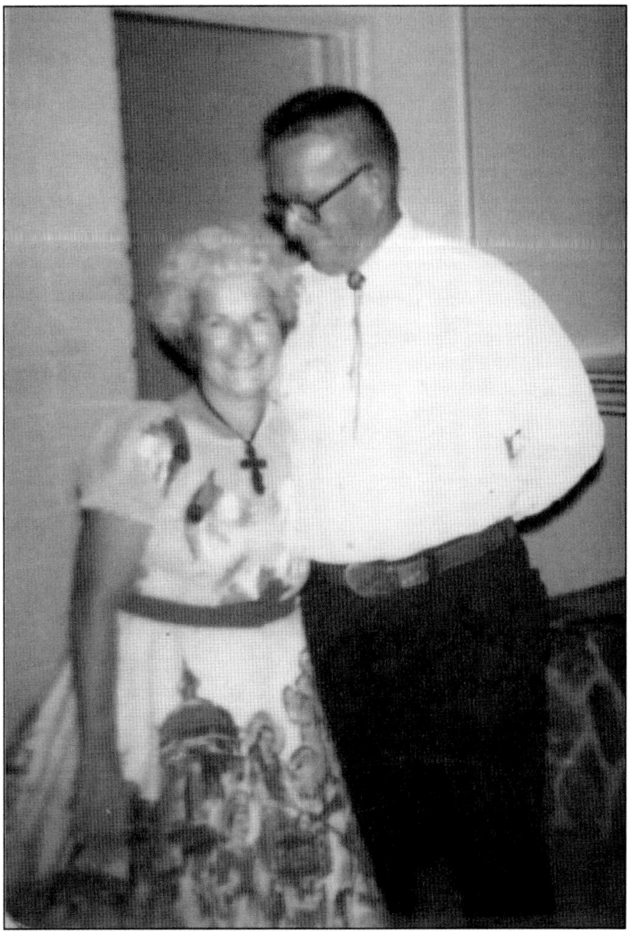

Yvonne and Bruno Lauraitis helped to found the Sunsites Squares in 1973. The couple guided the group through its first year and then continued to serve as its advisors. After Sam Green, from Benson, called dances at a Mid-West "7" Club party, the guests at that party formed the square dance club. The Mid-West "7" Club was a social club for residents who moved to Sunsites from Midwestern states. (Yvonne Lauraitis.)

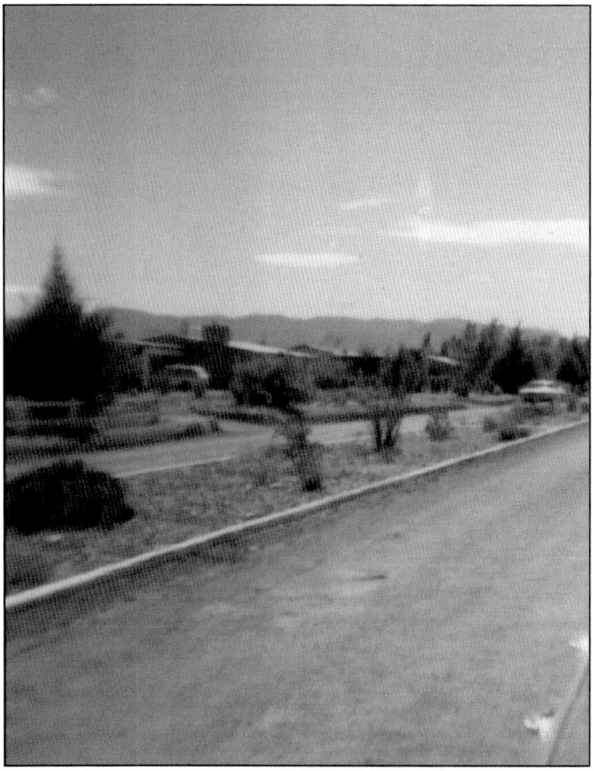

In 1974, Walter Hieber took this rare photograph of the median that once divided Christmas Tree Lane. Most of the earliest homes in Sunsites were built on Treasure Road or on Christmas Tree Lane, reportedly named for the green landscaping and evergreen trees that lined the street. (Walter Hieber)

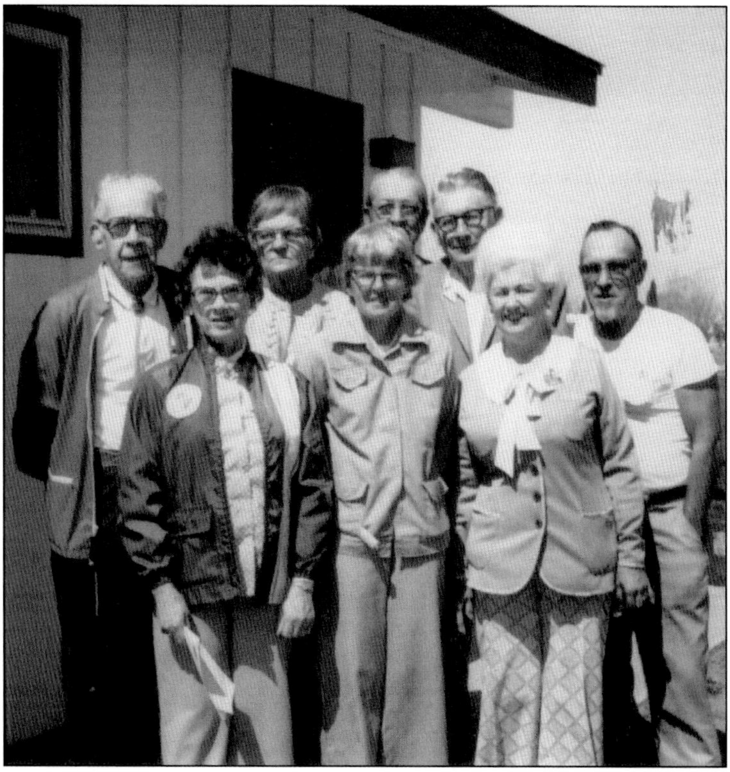

The 1976–1977 Sunsites Homeowner's Association officers and board of directors include, from left to right, (first row) director Evangeline Seger, treasurer Alice "Tommie" Sawyer, and first vice president Julia Witherspoon; (second row) president Ralph Marmor, director Virginia Seffen, director Ray Kirsten, director Ed Wood, and secretary Eugene Whitney. Second vice president Herbert Kinney is not pictured. (SSVHS.)

Millie Giles, of Sunsites, and Gerald Duke, of Willcox, show off their winning trophies at the second annual Sunsites Invitational Golf Tournament. The *Arizona Range News* reported on July 11, 1974, that there were 91 entries in the two-day event. (SSVHS.)

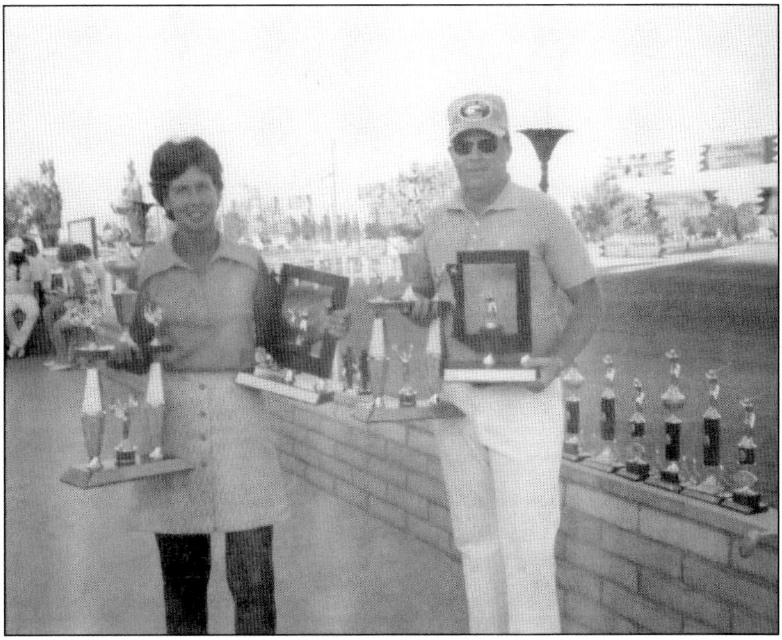

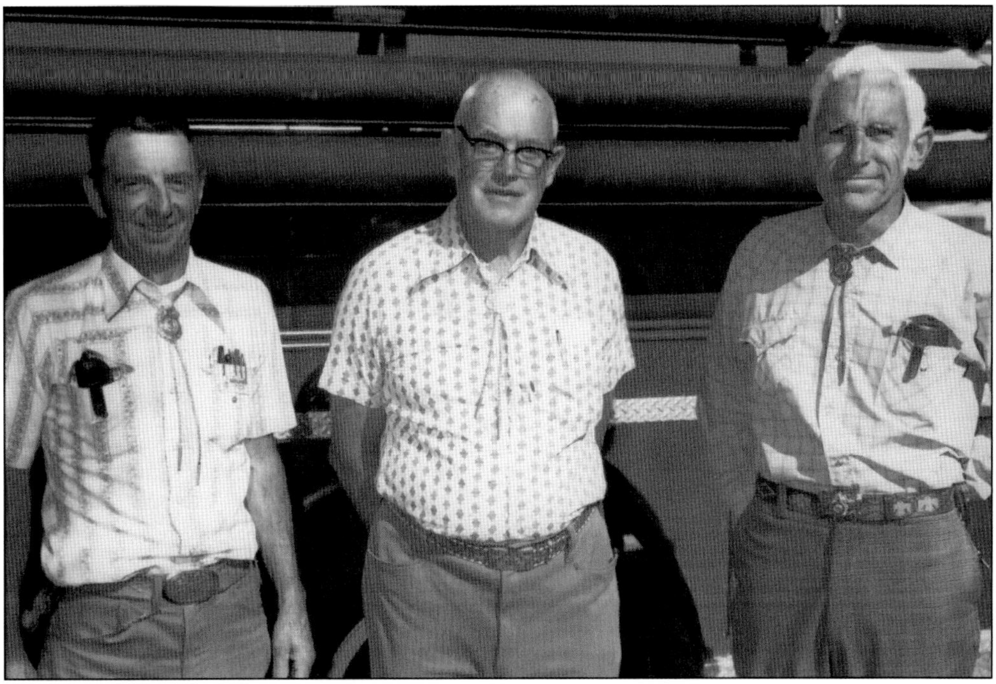

Sunsites fire chiefs pose for this photograph, which ran in the *Arizona Range News* on May 2, 1974. They are former fire chief Andy Szcepanik (left), Chief Bob Davenport (center), and former fire chief Bill Davidson. (SSVHS.)

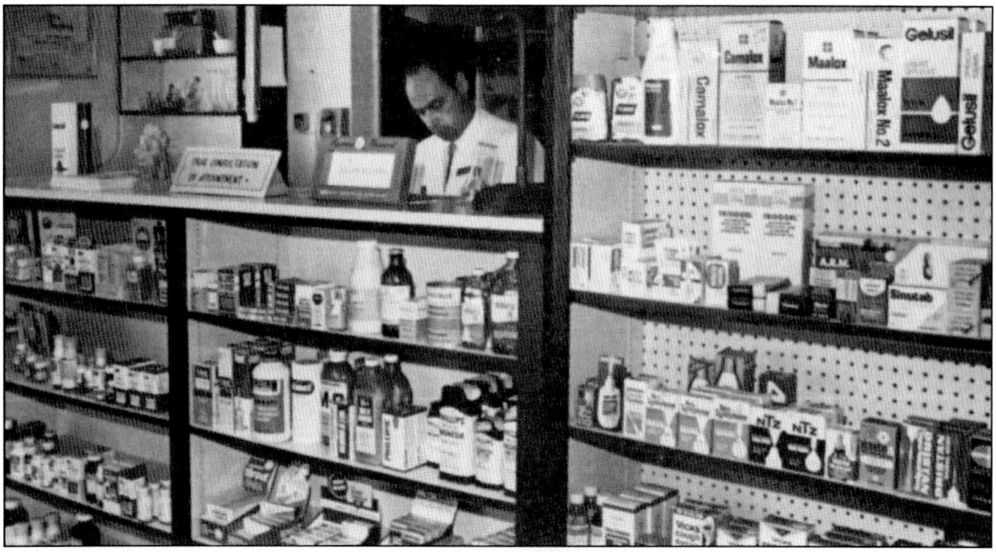

William Kuchynka, shown in this 1975 photograph from Horizon literature, ran the Sunsites Pharmacy. The pharmacy shared space with the Family Health Center, both located in the Medical Building on Irene Street. (Library Archives.)

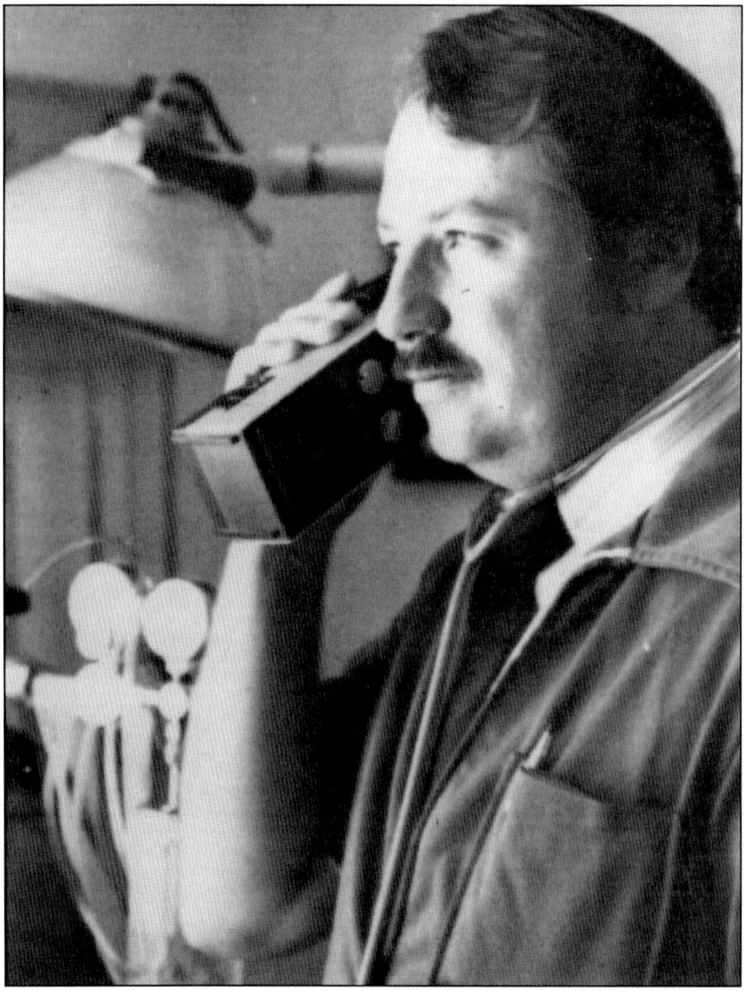

Physician's Assistant Eric Anderson, in a 1979 photograph, uses a walkie-talkie to speed up local communications at the Family Health Center. Horizon Corporation published literature that included photographs and stories about residents of their communities to illustrate the amenities available. (Library Archives.)

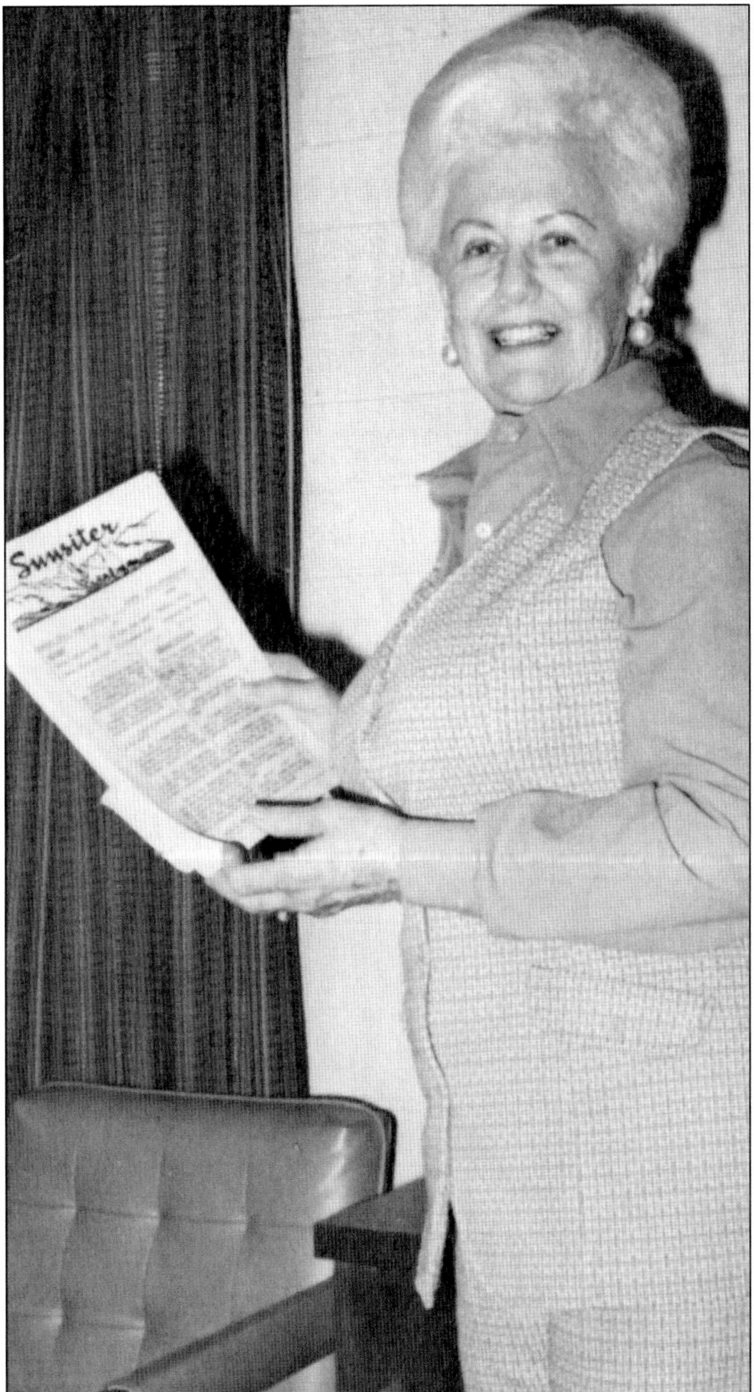

Julia Witherspoon shows off the *Sunsiter* monthly bulletin that she founded and edited. The first issue of the *Sunsiter* was distributed in 1973 and was sponsored by the homeowner's association. Julia and her husband, retired Army major Alan Witherspoon, moved to Sunsites in 1968. (Library Archives.)

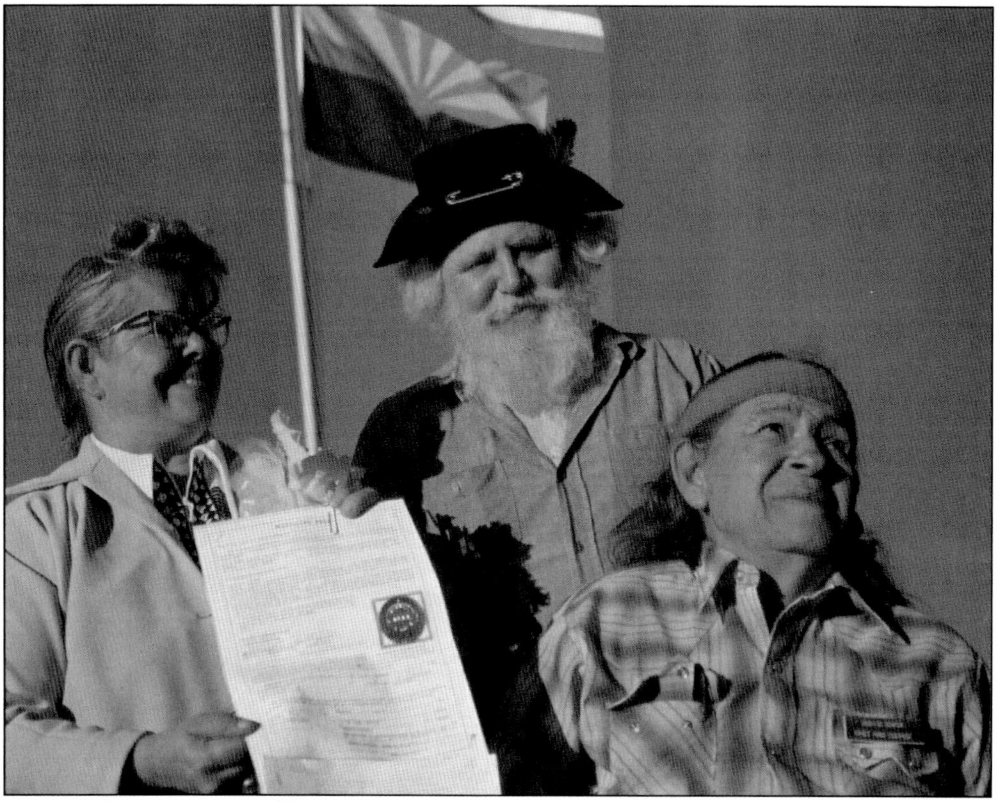

Nino Cochise, a 99-year-old Apache who claimed to be the grandson of Cochise, was honored at Arizona Sunsites during Thanksgiving week in 1973. Sidney Nelson, Horizon's president, presented a five-acre parcel to him, located 10 miles west of Arizona Sunsites, near the Cochise Stronghold. From left to right are Nino's wife, Minnie, displaying the deed, an unidentified man, and Nino Cochise. His claims of relationship to the leader Cochise have not been verified. (Library Archives.)

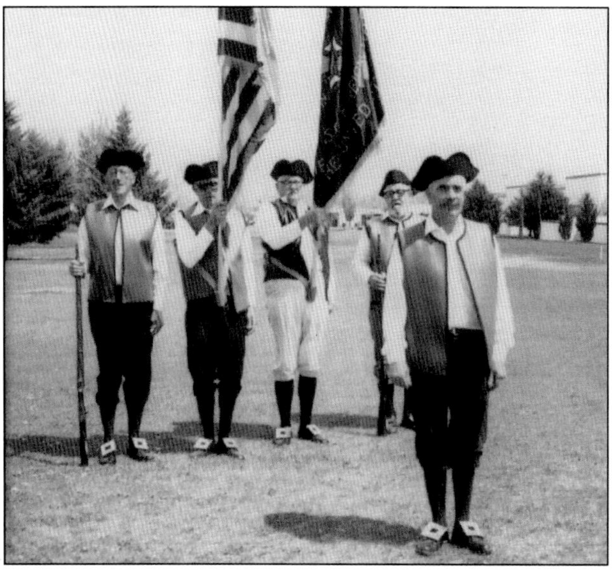

Members of the Veterans of Foreign Wars (VFW) are dressed in Revolutionary War uniforms to perform the daily parade of flags ceremony at the three-day Last Frontier bicentennial celebration at the Sunsites Community Center April 30–May 2, 1976. (Library Archives.)

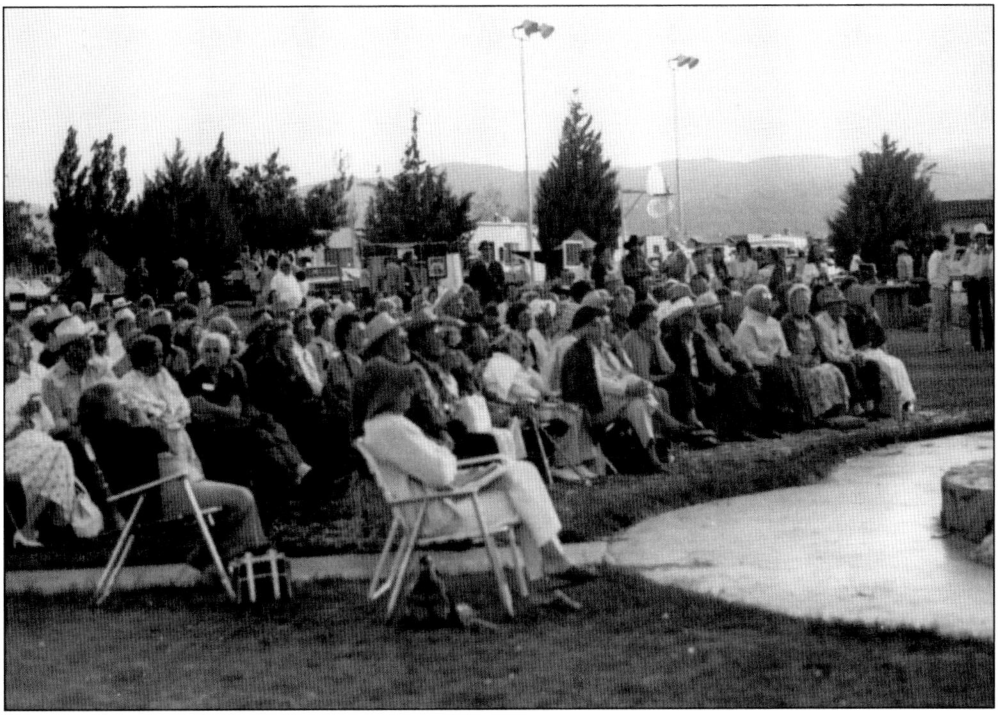

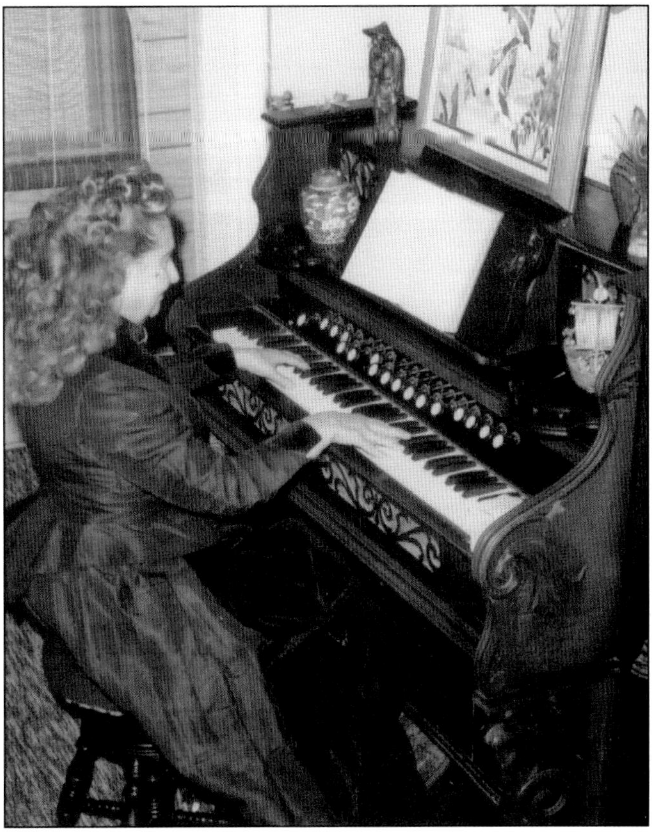

There were large audiences for the programs at the Last Frontier bicentennial celebration. In addition to the entertainment, there were a variety of exhibits. Mrs. Lyle Davis shows off the pump organ owned by Mr. and Mrs. Robert Spinney in the Frontier Home, furnished by the Cactus Wren Homemaker Club. Other exhibits included the Valley Pioneer Museum, a children's exhibit, a gem and mineral exposition, an art show, an Arizona State Mineral Resources Department film (shown daily), History on Wheels, Blacksmith at Work, and animal exhibits. Mary Bolles wrote and directed *The Last Frontier*, described as a "Historic Pageant of the Sulphur Springs Valley." Julia Witherspoon was musical director for the pageant. (Above, SSVHS; right, Library Archives.)

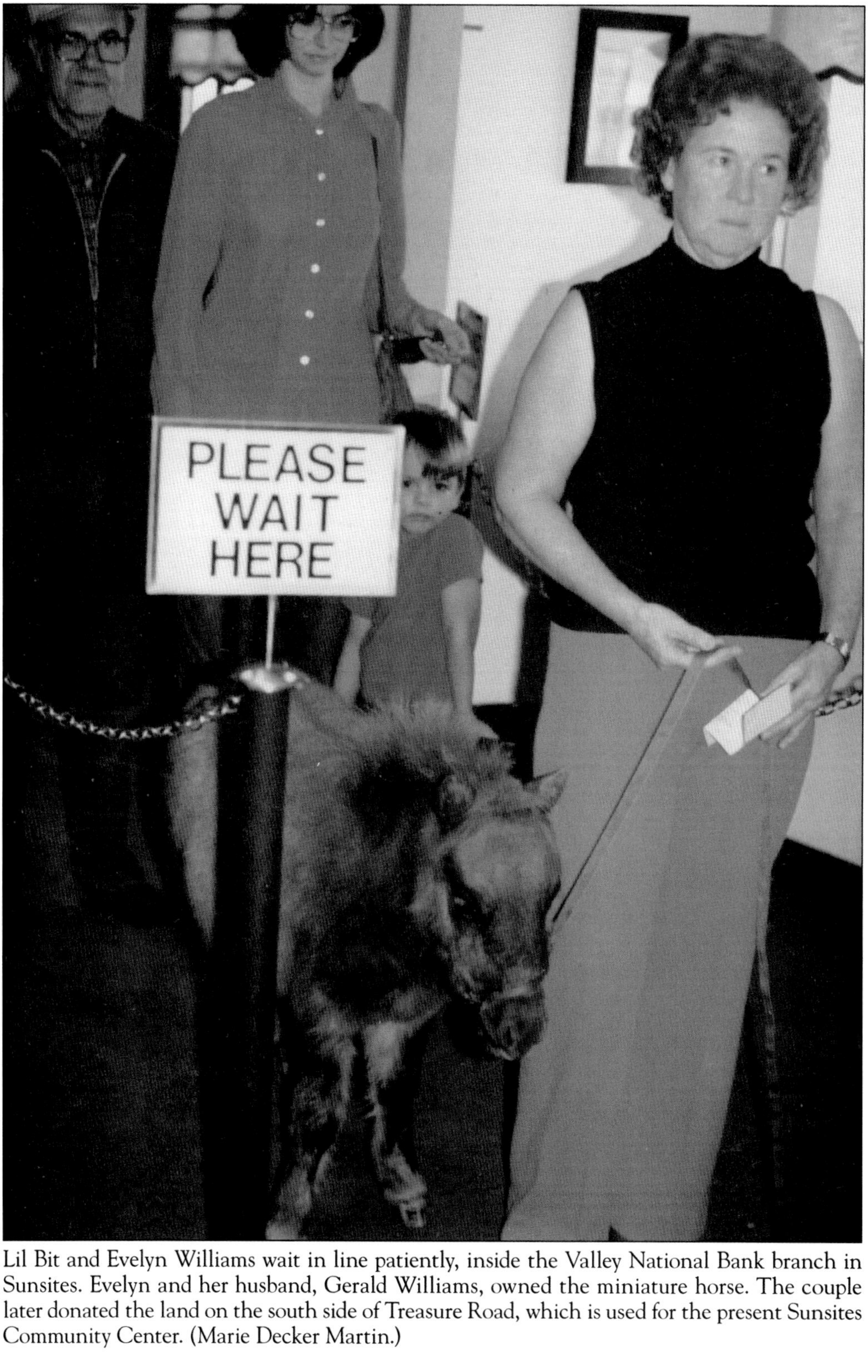

Lil Bit and Evelyn Williams wait in line patiently, inside the Valley National Bank branch in Sunsites. Evelyn and her husband, Gerald Williams, owned the miniature horse. The couple later donated the land on the south side of Treasure Road, which is used for the present Sunsites Community Center. (Marie Decker Martin.)

In this photograph taken in 1978, Ed Borgnaes shows off the coveted Shillelagh award that he won at the annual Saint Patrick's Day Tournament in Sunsites. Every year that the tournaments were held, one Shillelagh was ordered from Ireland, and no two were alike. (Ed Borgnaes.)

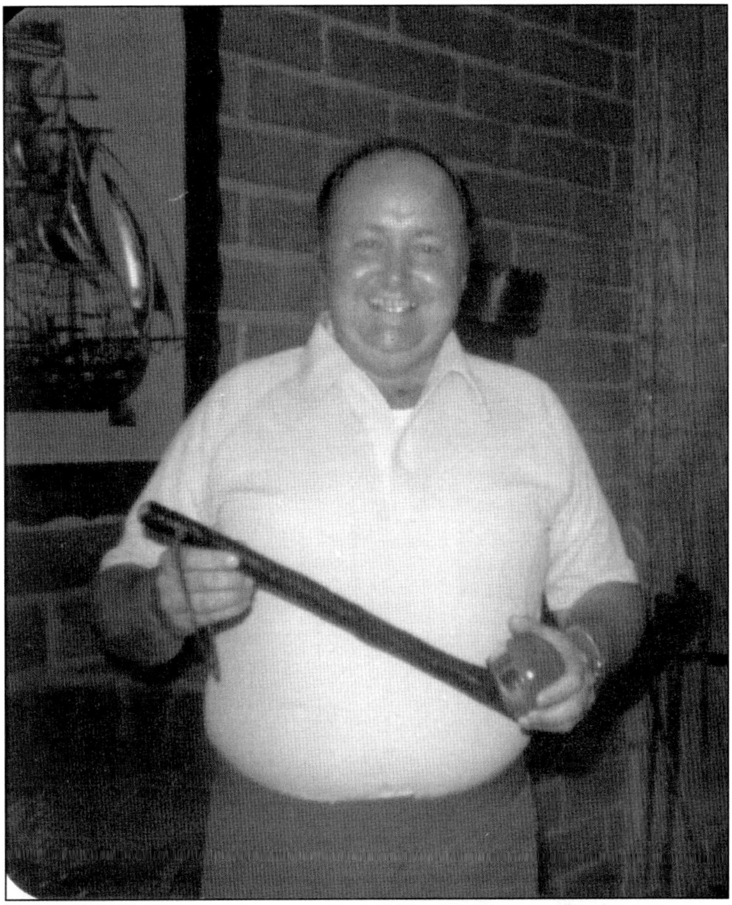

The Sunsites Gem and Mineral Club is one of the oldest groups in Sunsites. They organized in April 1965 and in 2010, had 84 members. Members are shown at the club's second annual Tailgate Rock Show in May 1977. (Sunsites Gem and Mineral Club.)

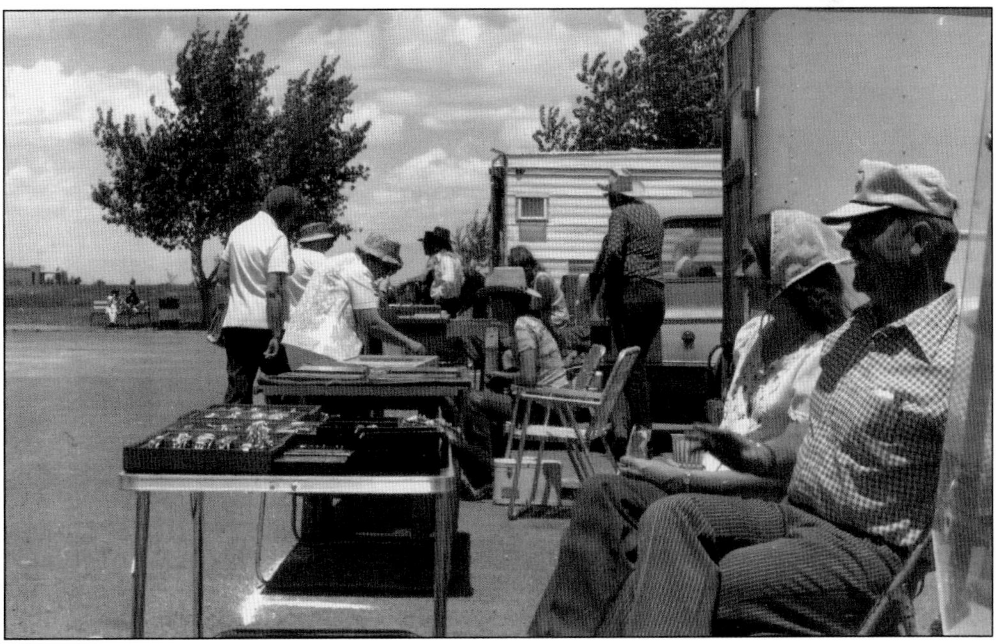

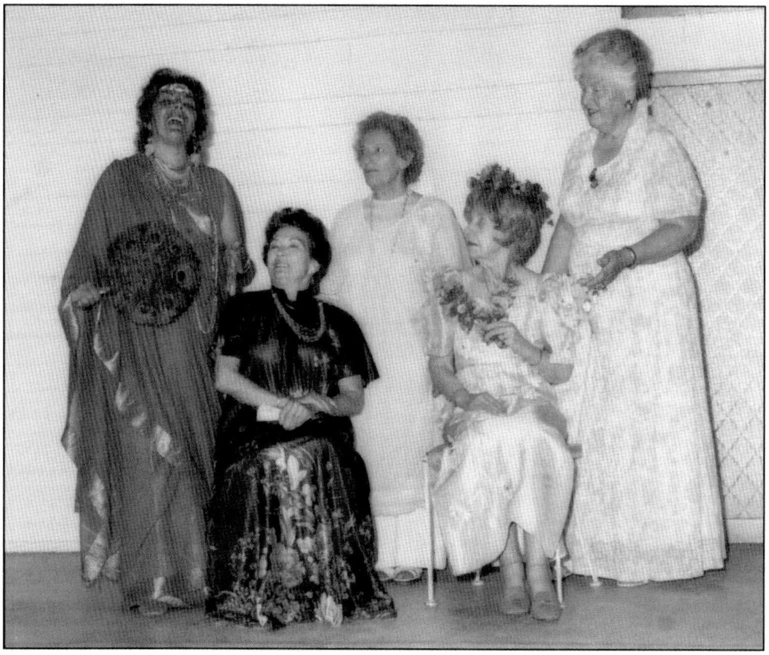

This cast of Sunsites residents performed the one-act play *When Shakespeare's Ladies Meet* for the Desert Community Arts annual dinner and business meeting on April 1, 1979. The performers are, from left to right, Murial Woods, Gertrude Settles, Terry Zollars, Myrtle Johnson, and Mary Bolles. (SSVHS.)

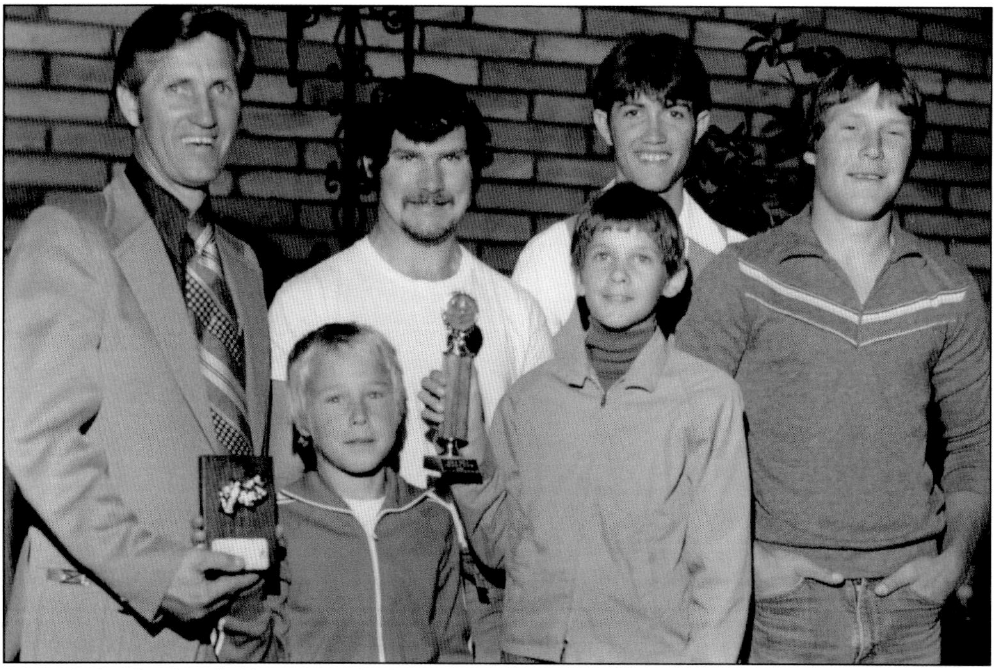

Rev. Clyde Thacker (left) poses with the Broken Arrow Boxing Club of Sunsites in a photograph from April 1979. Boxing club members are, from left to right, (first row) Cori Bradshaw and Jeff Mack; (second row) Gene Lauve, Ed Thacker, and Kenny Bradshaw. Reverend Thacker's life was cut short in 1994 when two teenaged boys shot and killed him. (SSVHS.)

Seven

Mystery and Uncertainty in the 1980s

The story of Sunsites in the 1980s reflects a deflated economy and changes within Horizon Corporation. Horizon's new pattern of giving with one hand and taking away with the other tested residents' resilience. In 1981, the FTC and Horizon reached an agreement, which weakened the company's financial position. In 1985, the mysterious disappearance of popular businesswoman Bea Hessler baffled not only law enforcement, but also those who knew her. Travelers discovered her car on Soren's Pass Road, but Bea had vanished. The case remains unsolved. Horizon's relationship with Sunsites during this decade was equally bewildering. They allotted $10,000 for trees for the golf courses and for the sewage treatment plant, and announced completion of the final nine holes for the regulation golf course and a $5 million project that included a shopping center. Simultaneously, however, the corporation pulled Horizon employees out of Sunsites, and it shocked residents in 1984 when it announced plans to convert the community center into a country club, closing the swimming pool, tennis, and shuffleboard area. Sunsites residents rallied, and a committee reached an agreement with Horizon that would permit the committee to operate the community center and related facilities as a non-profit organization. Horizon continued its pattern of giving while it systematically reduced its presence in the community. It donated parcels of land to the library and the VFW for new buildings, and it turned the architectural review board over to the Sunsites Community Association. While community leaders navigated the changes in Horizon's relationship with Sunsites, organizations thrived. The Gem and Mineral Club, the VFW, and the Lions Club celebrated 20th anniversaries. The *Sunsiter*, Way Off Broadway Little Theater, and Sunsites Squares celebrated 10th anniversaries. Other milestones included establishing the Buzz Stop and purchasing transportation buses, averting closure of the medical clinic, creating a chamber of commerce, and doggedly working to improve the appearance of the village during Action Arizona competitions. In 1988, Valley Chorus gave its last Living Christmas Tree performance.

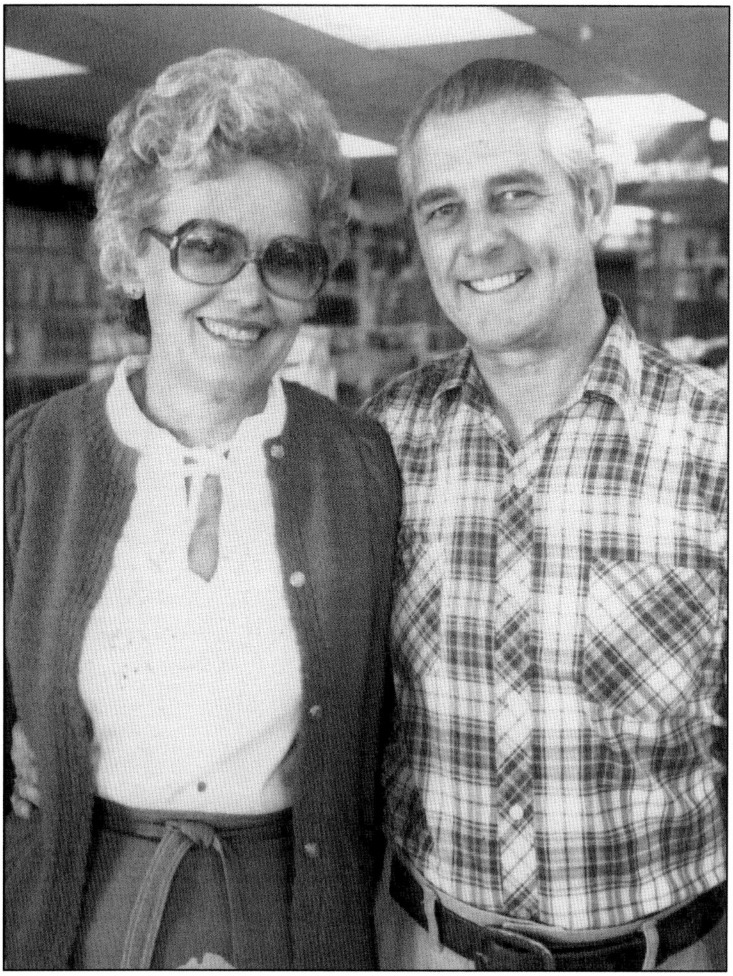

Bob and Nina Peterson purchased the Ace Hardware Store in April 1980, renaming it Peterson's Ace Hardware. This photograph appeared in the *Arizona Range News*, when the Petersons announced the store's grand opening in October 1980. (SSVHS.)

Sunsites residents stayed busy with groundbreakings and construction in the 1980s. Red Fox took this photograph in 1981 during the groundbreaking for the VFW building on Ford Road. Pictured from left to right are Jim Healy, Al Morvay, Francis Jones, Harry Withrow, Vern Merritt, and Art Hardesty. (Cochise VFW Post 9977.)

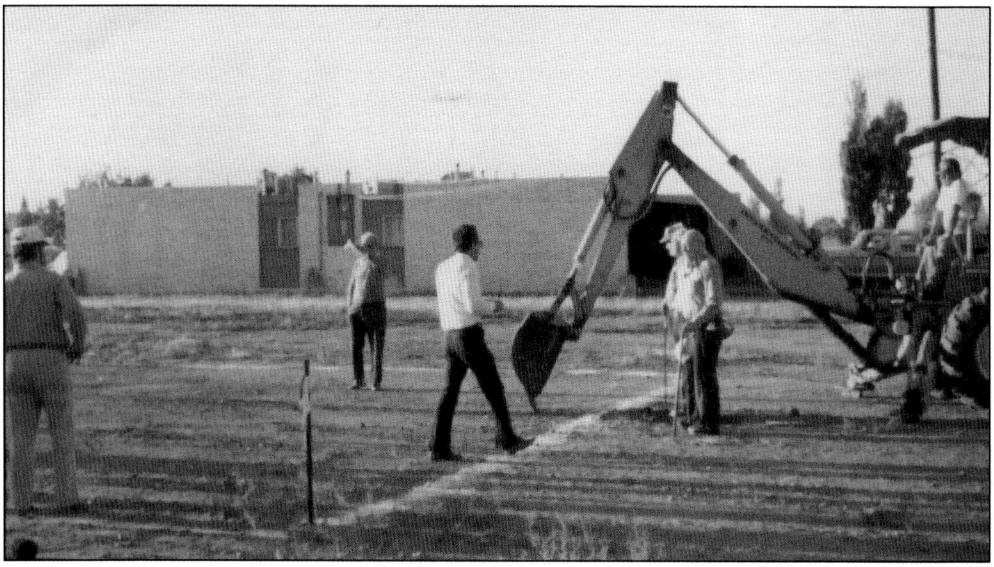

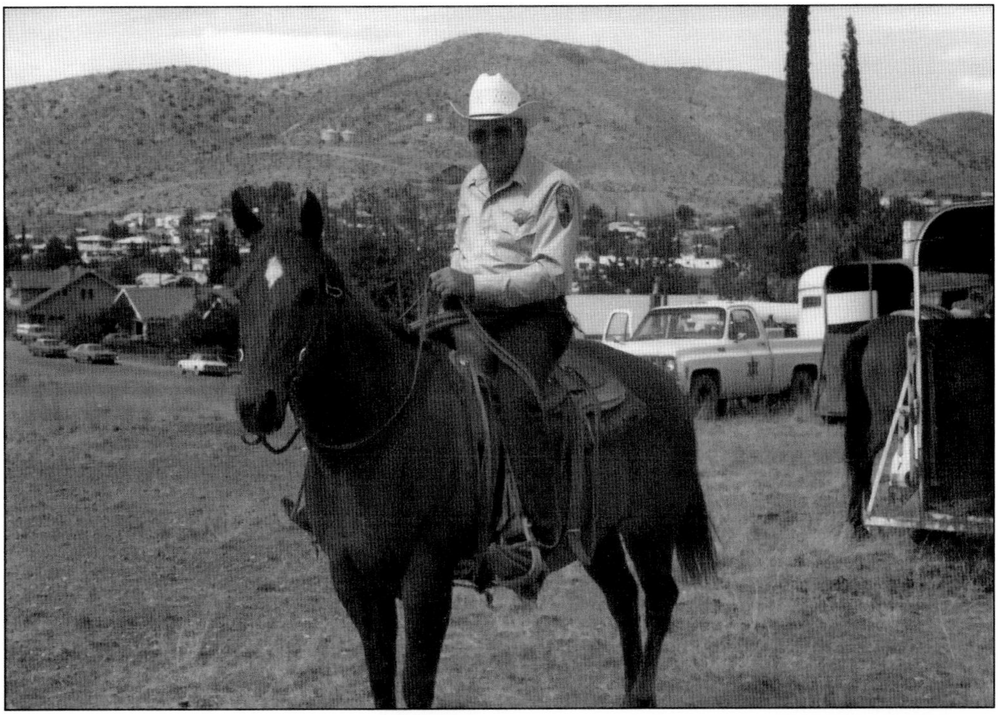

Jack Busenbark, shown in this 1982 photograph, was a deputy sheriff in Cochise County for 15 years, but he was also a pilot and a rancher. He bought the Joe Bignon homestead north of Pearce and the Fred and George Fleetham homesteads south of Pearce. (Mary Appel.)

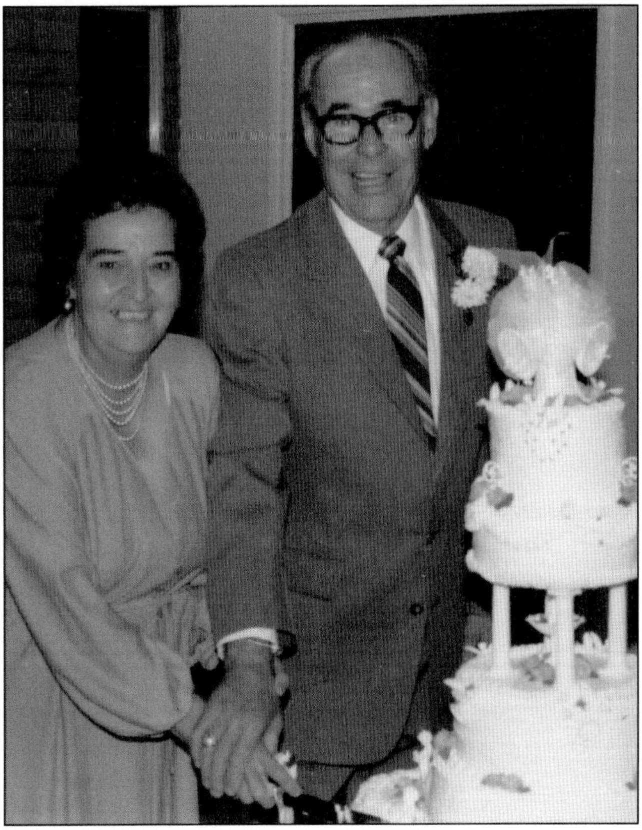

Billie McDonnell's and John Lally's wedding in 1981 typified remarriages for Sunsites residents. The Social pages of the *Sunsiter* regularly ran stories about couples who had second marriages after the death of a spouse. The Lallys volunteered in many organizations. They were honored for their work with the Lions Club in the areas of vision and hearing. (Billie Lally.)

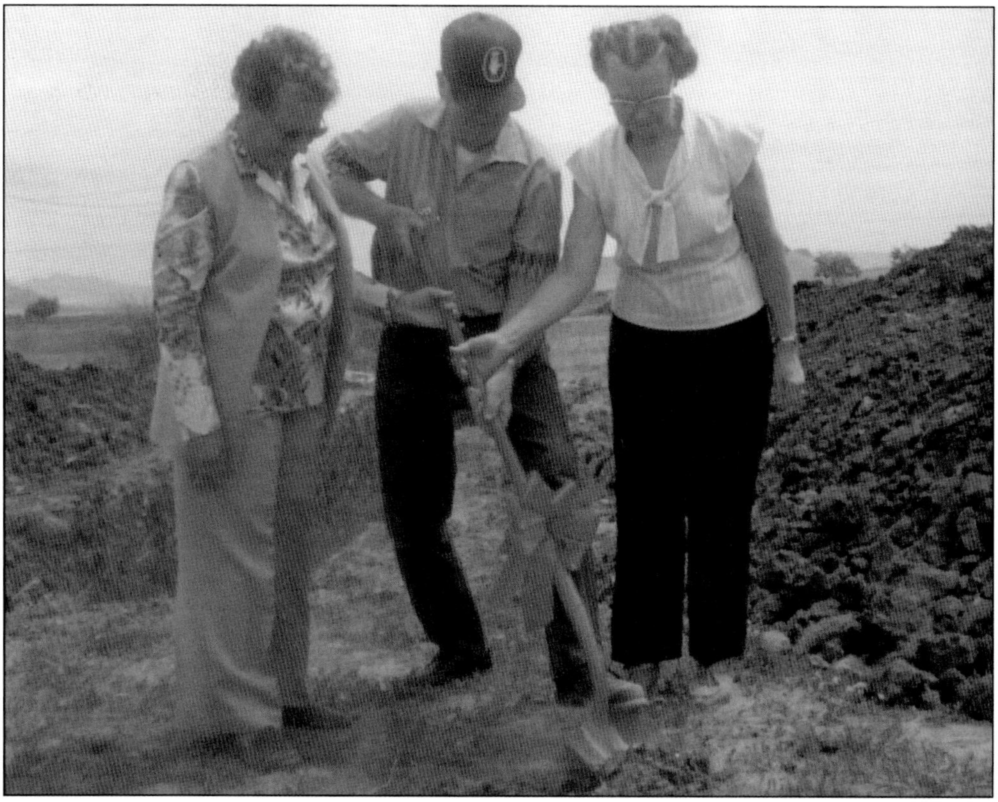

Shown above on April 30, 1983, construction manager Ivan Hawkinson turns the first spade of dirt at the groundbreaking for the rammed-earth community library. Assisting Hawkinson are Kelsey Mansir (left) and Barbara Rogers. Residents of Sunsites put in more than 4,000 hours of volunteer labor and support to the crew during construction of the library. (Both, Library Archives.)

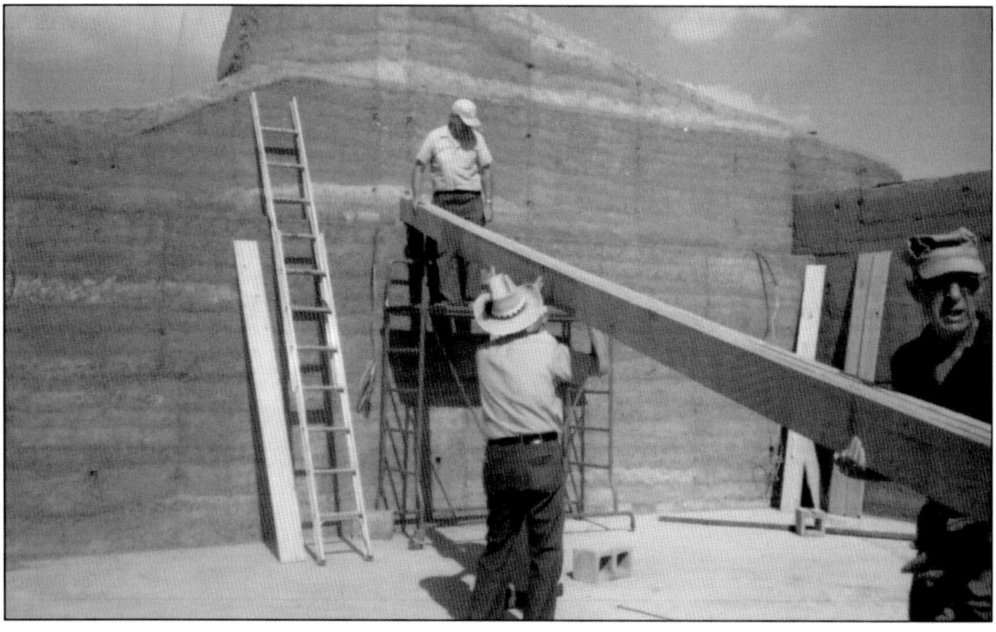

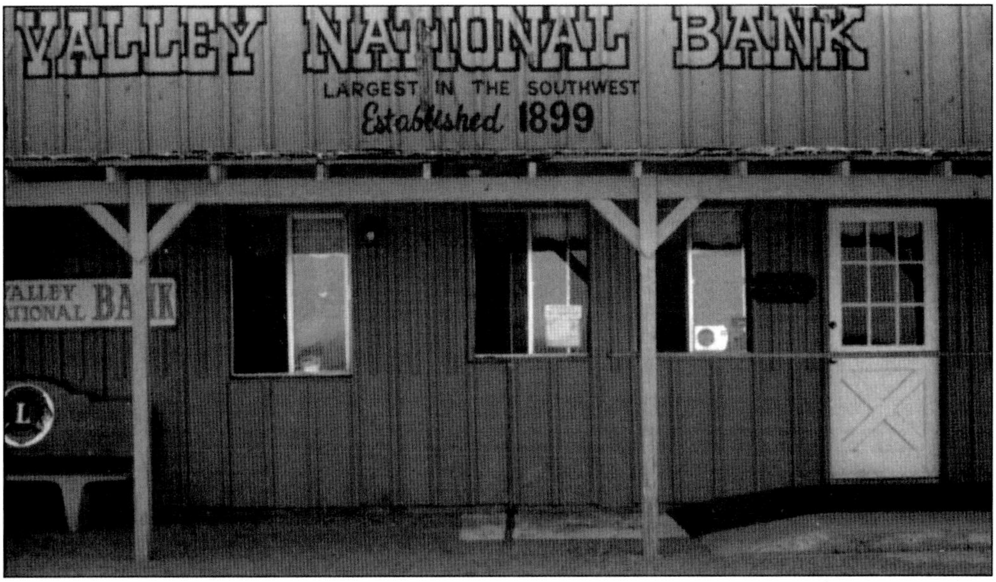

Sunsites residents welcomed a branch of Valley National Bank to the village during an open house on December 9, 1972. The bank had its offices in the building on Frontage Road that had housed the motel during the 1960s. In 1984, they built a new building at the corner of Justin Street and Frontage Road. The bank hosted people from the Sulphur Springs Valley at a festive open house on October 15, 1984. The photograph above shows the exterior of the bank in the 1970s. The photograph below, taken during construction of the new building, shows the Church of Jesus Christ of Latter-day Saints and the newly built library in the background. (Both, Marie Decker Martin.)

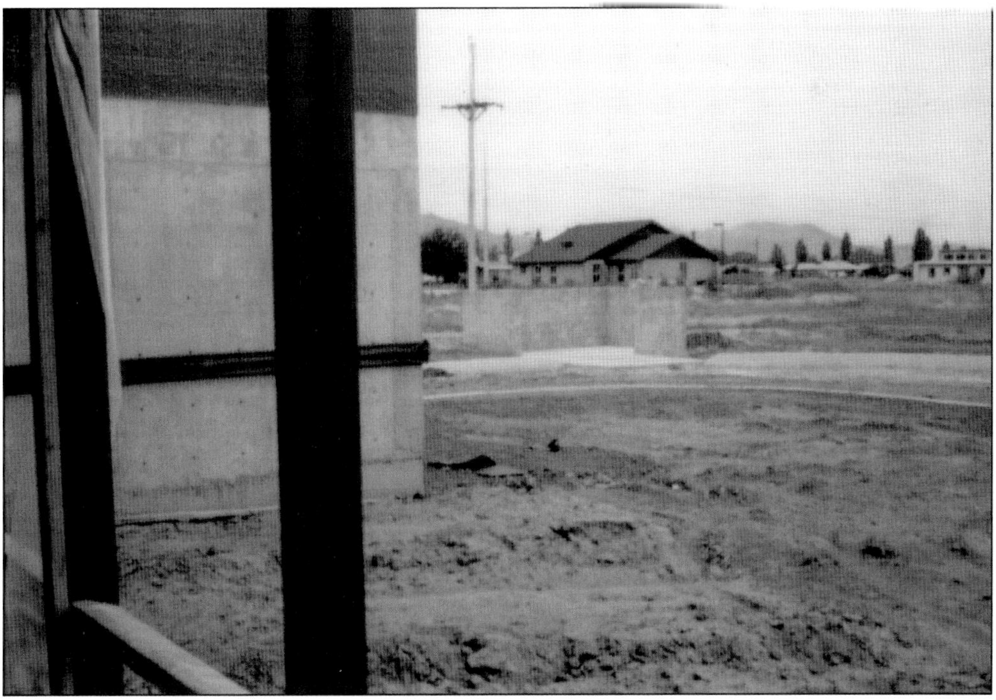

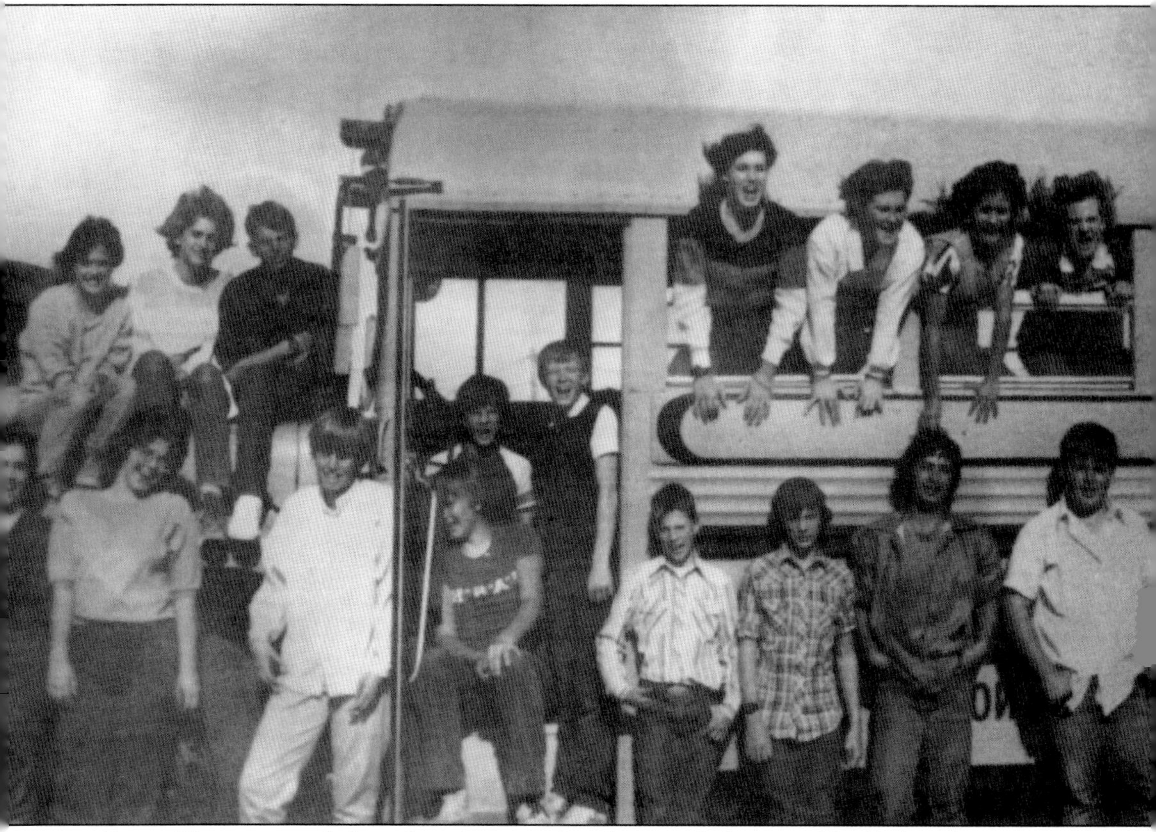

Pearce Elementary eighth graders, shown in this photograph from 1985, had bake sales, a carnival, a raffle, and a walk-a-thon to raise money for their weeklong graduation trip to Disneyland, Knott's Berry Farm, and Marineland in California. The students include Angie Mazzi, Heidi Hughes, Todd Carpenter, Kim Sutcliff, Tia Zoccola, Minnie Spear, Paula Lane, Sherri Hedges, Randi Chess, Marcie Wagner, Eric Michael, Raymond Chapman, Jesse Garrison, Shawn Nyswonger, Chad Culp, Kelly Hernandez, and Dale Bower. (Diana Armsden.)

Sunsites Transportation provided reliable public transportation for Sunsites residents for more than 25 years. The Buzz Stop sold gasoline and snack foods. They ceased operation at the end of September 2005. (Kathy Larsh.)

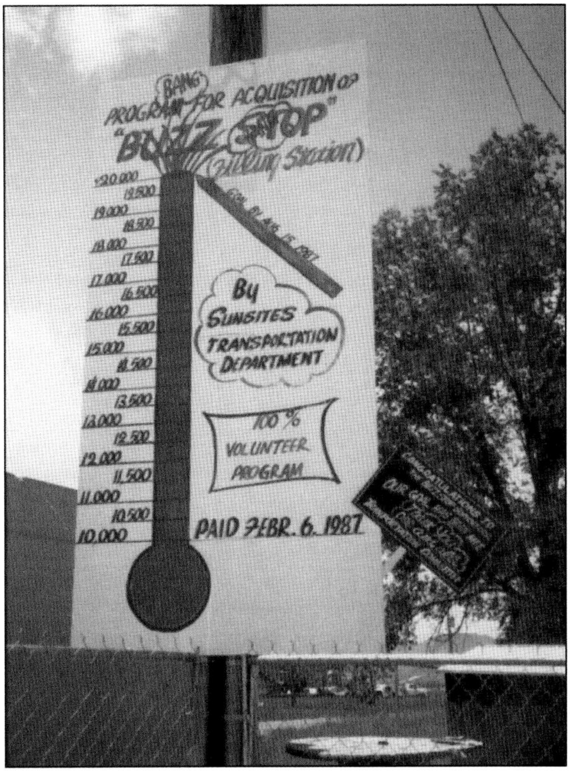

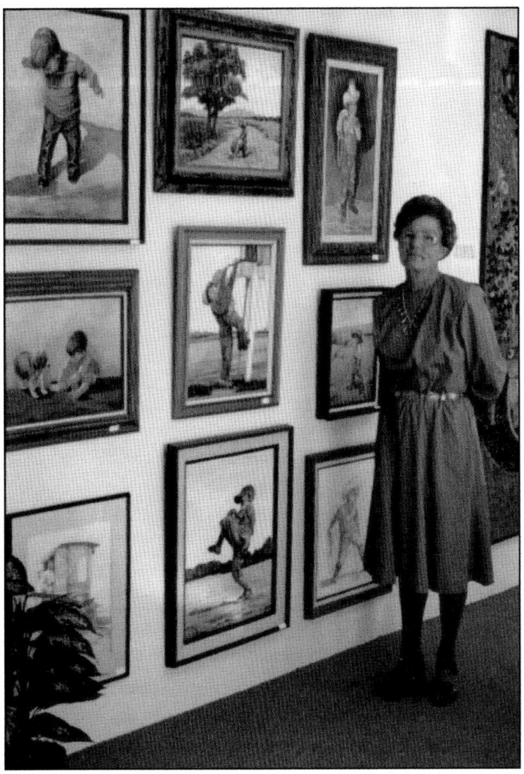

Margaret "Peach" Busenbark had a showing in a Las Vegas art gallery in the mid-1980s. The center painting with two boys working together to get into a mailbox is on display at the Pearce Post Office in Sunsites. Peach and her husband, Jack Busenbark, ranched in the Pearce area. (Mary Appel.)

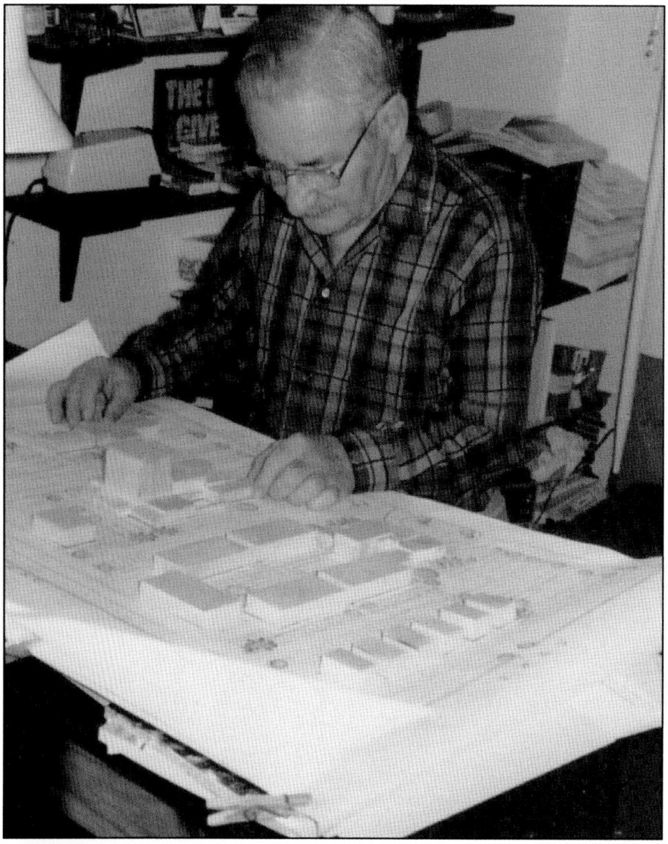

On July 1, 1986, small communities in Arizona took on improvement tasks in an attempt to win cash prizes. Valley National Bank sponsored the Action Arizona project and donated $22,500 for prizes. Glen Hoar built a model to illustrate Sunsites's ambitious plans. (Library Archives.)

Some of the cast of *A Fabulous, Funny, Enchanting, Musical, Magical Review* enjoy their time on stage in 1988. They include, from left to right, Julia "Julie" Pilon, Dori Giehrl, Diana Ganfield, and Florence Larson. The Way Off Broadway Little Theater (located 2,456 miles from New York's famed Broadway) put on the show. (Library Archives.)

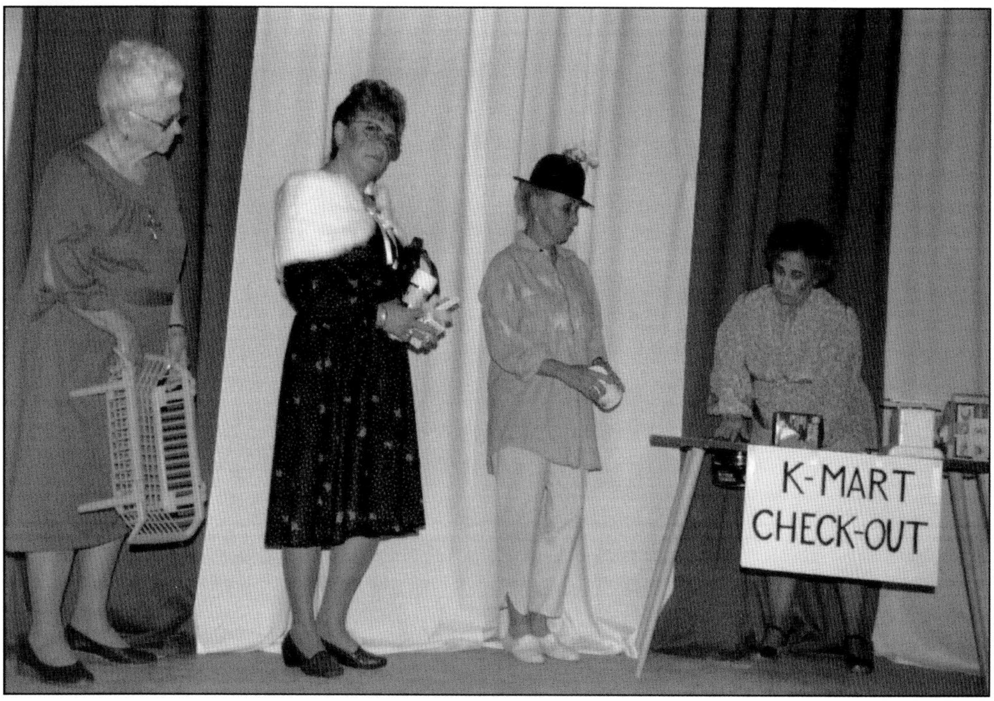

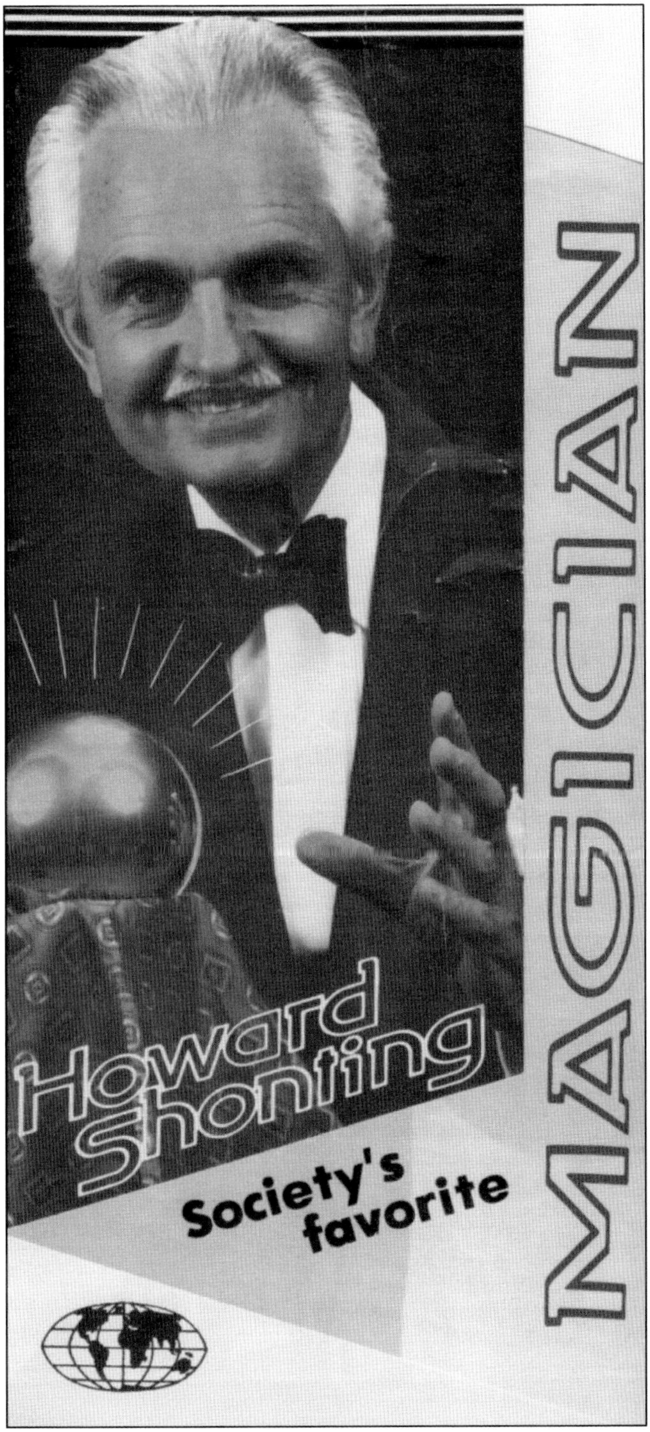

Howard Shonting worked his magic off stage as well as on. In addition to entertaining audiences, he steered Sunsites through Action Arizona competitions, served as president of the chamber of commerce, and took over the *Sunsiter* when Julia Witherspoon retired from her duties. (Library Archives.)

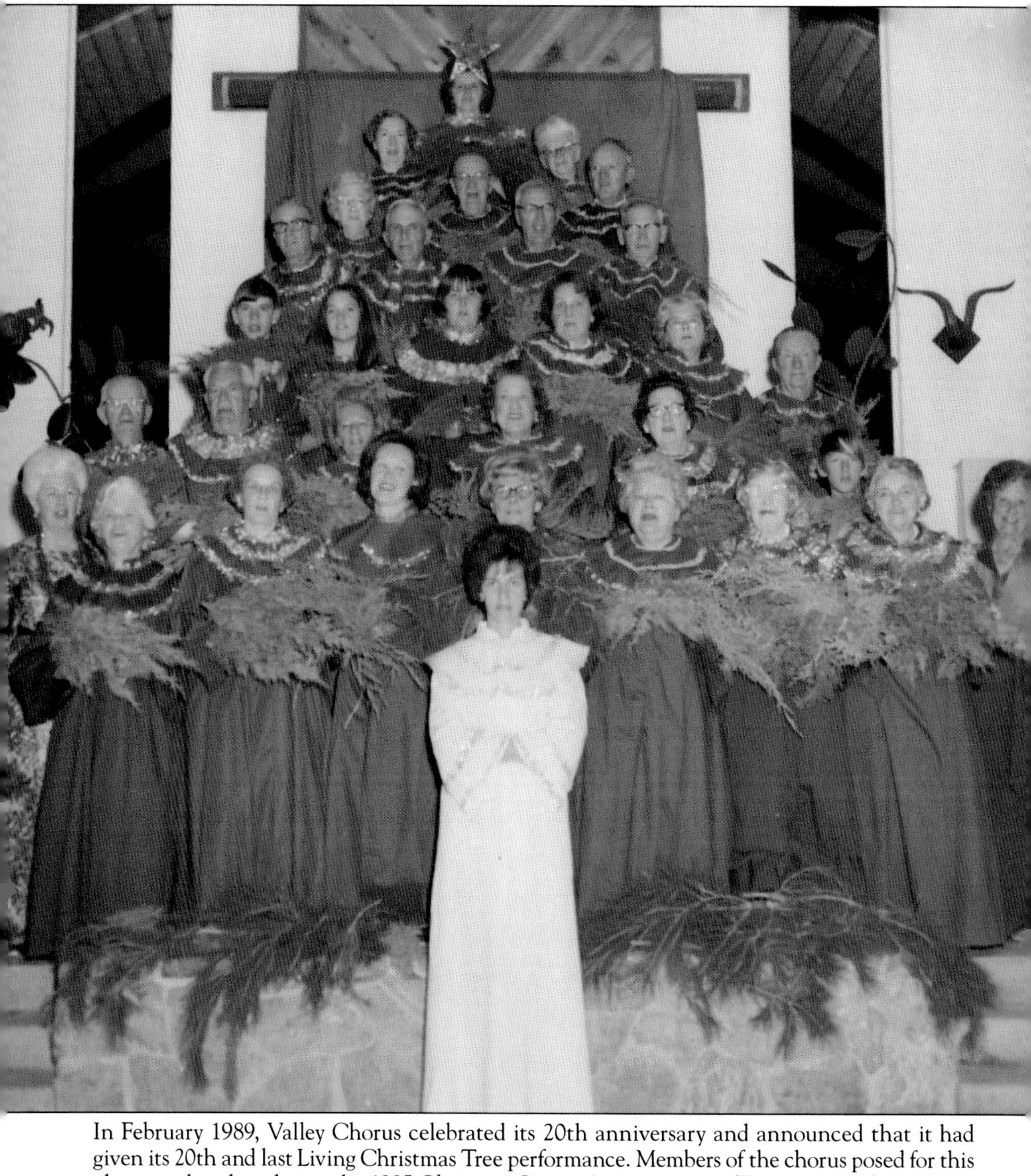

In February 1989, Valley Chorus celebrated its 20th anniversary and announced that it had given its 20th and last Living Christmas Tree performance. Members of the chorus posed for this photograph, taken during the 1985 *Christmas Comes Again* program. (Frances Marx.)

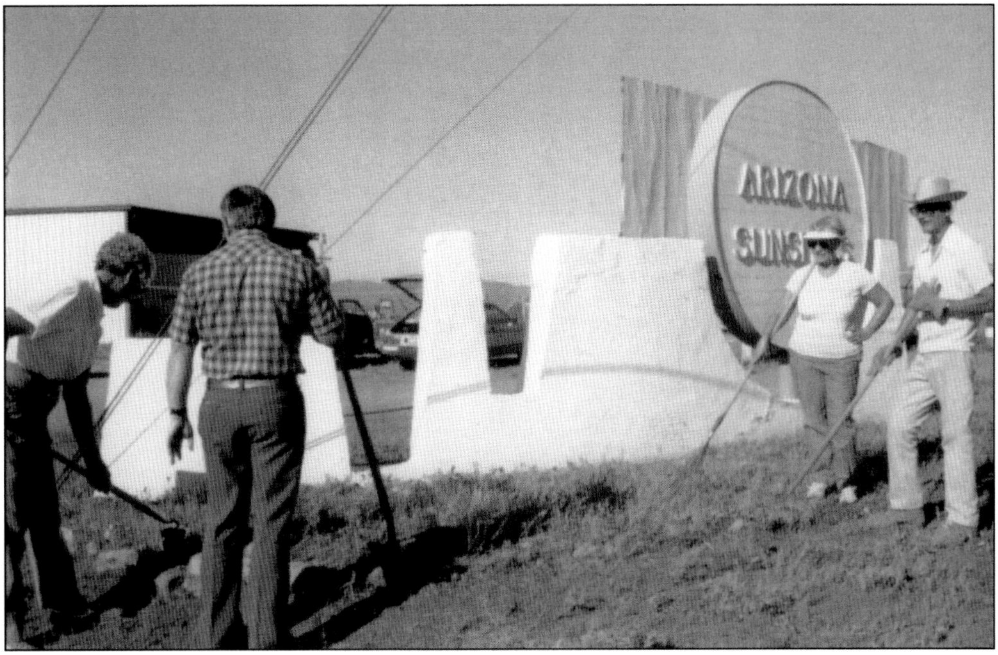

During the Action Arizona competition in 1987, Operation First Impression targeted the entrance signs to Sunsites that had been erected 20 years earlier. In addition to cleaning up around the signs, the competition leaders announced a contest to redesign the signs. Part of the criteria for the contest was to eliminate the word *Arizona* from the sign, but keeping the Sunsites name somewhere on the sign. Shown cleaning up around the sign are, from left to right, Betty Mayo, Duke Vandeyacht, Jane Johnston, and Jack Avedon. (Library Archives)

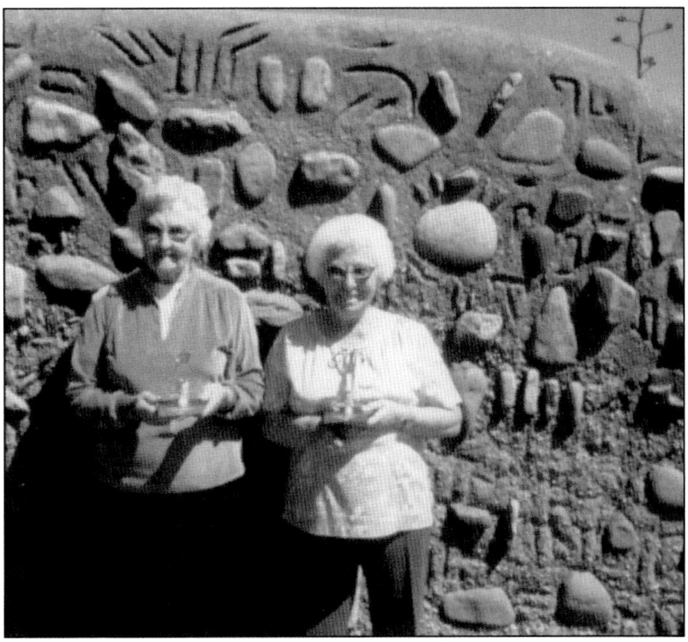

In 1986, golfers Donelda Oaks (left) and Fran Williams show off their trophies while posing in front of the custom adobe and rock wall sculpture built by artist Marilyn Zwak Henson and located adjacent to the restaurant at the intersection of US Highway 666 and Frontage Road. She handpicked the rocks in the Turkey Creek area, and used her fingers and the sides of her hands to add slashing impressions. At the time this photograph was taken, the restaurant was named Cochise Adobe Inn. (Sunsites Ladies Golf Association.)

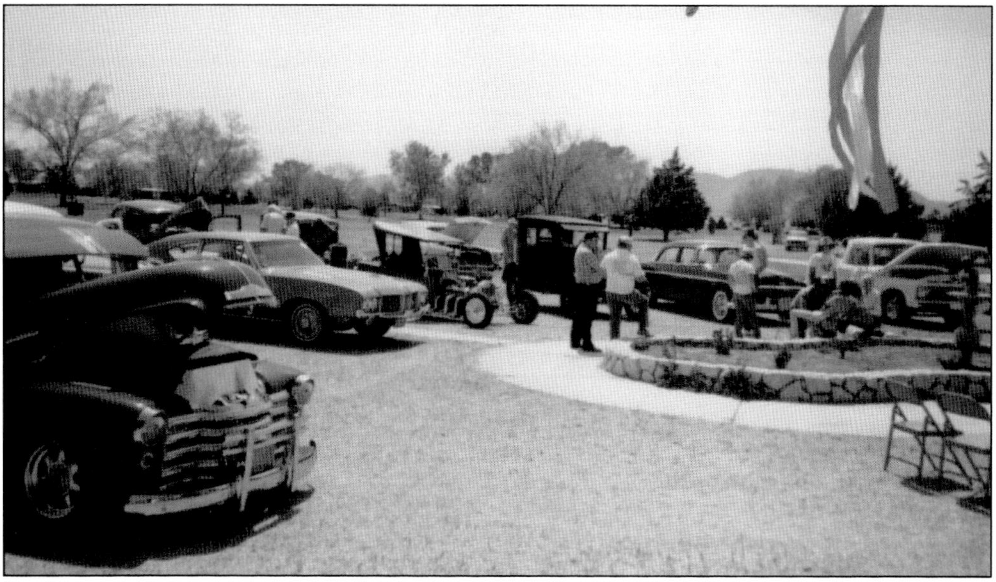

Roadrunner Transportation sponsored antique car shows at the community center, beginning with the first show on April 5, 1987, and continuing into the 1990s. This photograph was taken at the 1988 show. (Edith and Jerry Muir.)

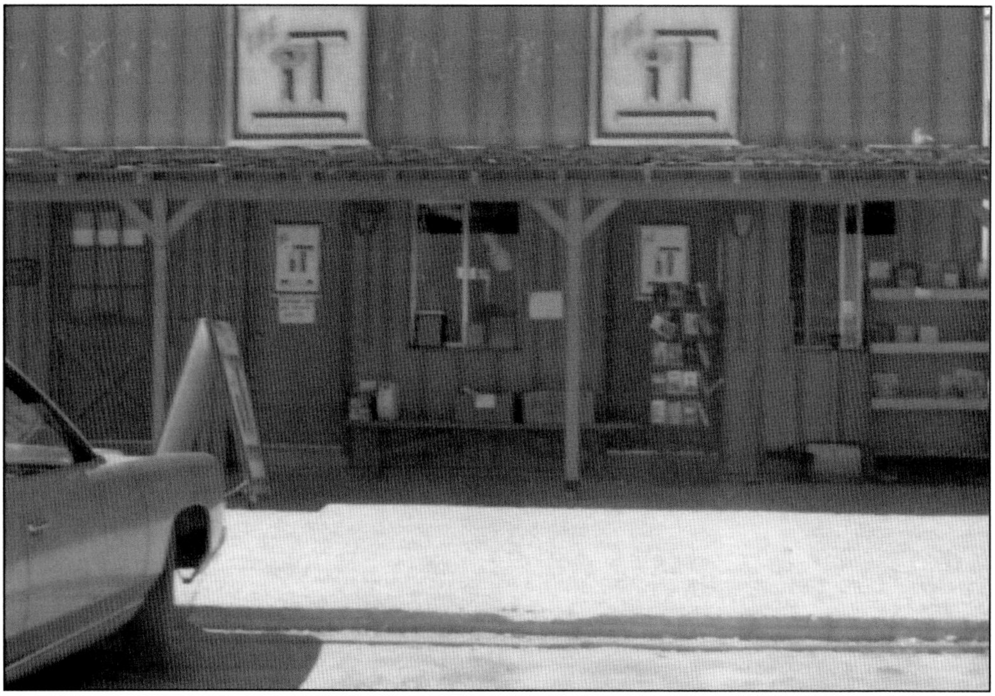

The iT, the business featured on this postcard, set up shop in the building that once housed the motel. Sunsites residents are vague in their recollections about what type of business it actually was and how long it was located on Frontage Road. One of the owners was Dorothy Howard. She was known as "Dot," and she had a business partner also called "Dot." The Dots printed a novelty newsletter, also called *The iT.* (Melanie Pope.)

Eight

Murder, Money, and Hands Up

Mystery, music, and magic characterized the 1970s and 1980s, but murder made headlines on June 29, 1994. On that day, in the Cochise Stronghold near the Broken Arrow Baptist Camp that he founded, Pastor Clyde Thacker stopped his car to offer assistance to two young men who flagged him down. His last words to the local teenaged boys who shot him with a .44 Magnum handgun were, "Boys, you don't have to do this." Pastor Thacker started the Valley Bible Baptist Church in 1971. The congregation first met in the Arts and Crafts Building and later built a church on Ironwood Road. Now known as Broken Arrow Baptist Church, the congregation continues Clyde Thacker's mission from a 13,000-square-foot building on Highway 191. Sunsites celebrated in 1990, when it won $10,000 in the Action Arizona competition. With that joy came the reality that Horizon's presence continued to diminish. After years of staff reductions, Horizon left Sunsites. They donated parkland next to the firehouse to the Sunsites Community Association, and they sold Clear Springs Utility to Buck Lewis Engineering. Horizon Corporation opened and operated three golf courses in Sunsites between 1963 and 1983: the executive par-three course in 1963, the regulation nine-hole course in 1973, and the regulation eighteen-hole course in 1982. March 1993 launched a series of different groups of optimistic investors, coming between 1993 and 2008. Rallying and finding solutions to problems comes naturally to Sunsites residents. In 1994, new golf course owners restricted the use of the community center to golf-related activities and shut down the popular executive course. The restrictions on use of the space that functioned as the hub of social life prompted community leaders to begin planning a new center. On December 1, 1995, Evelyn and Gerald Williams donated land on Treasure Road for a new building. On February 27, 1998, the community gathered for the groundbreaking. After Shadow Mountain LLC purchased the course in 2005 and then floundered, Sunsites residents rallied and organized, creating the Sunsites Community Golf Association in October 2008.

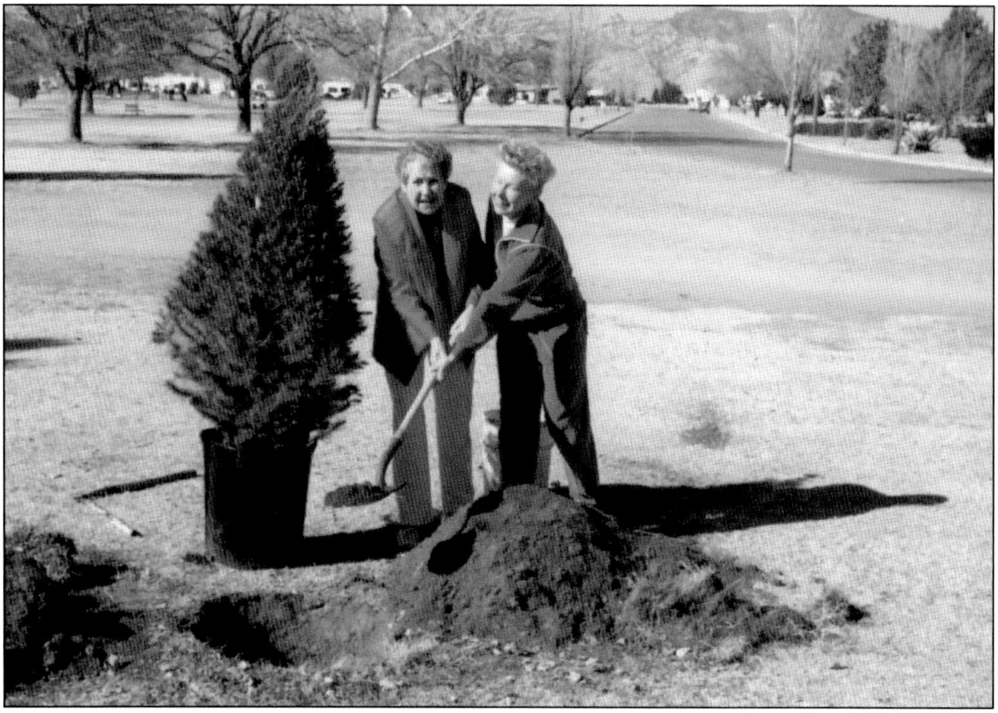

Marie Kobussen (left) and Diana Ganfield, of the Sunsites Ladies Golf Association (SLGA), planted a memorial tree on the par-three executive golf course in January 1990. Planted in memory of Frank Glaser, a longtime resident of Sunsites, the tree replaced two previous trees that had not survived. January 1990 was all about the trees. The community pruned trees, planted trees, and painted tree trunks as part of the beautification of Sunsites's Action Arizona participation. On June 26, 1990, Sunsites received the $10,000 first prize at a ceremony in Tucson, hosted by Valley National Bank. (Sunsites Ladies Golf Association.)

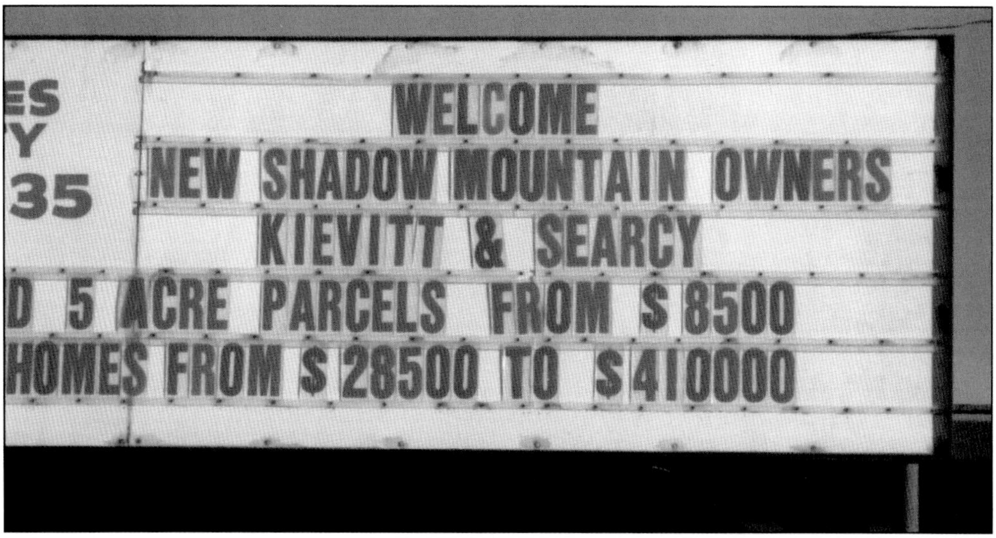

The new owners of Shadow Mountain Golf Course got a great big welcome in the spring of 1999 with this sign displayed by a local real estate office, when August Searcy, his son John, and Frank and Annie Kievitt took over operation of the course. (Annie and Frank Kievitt.)

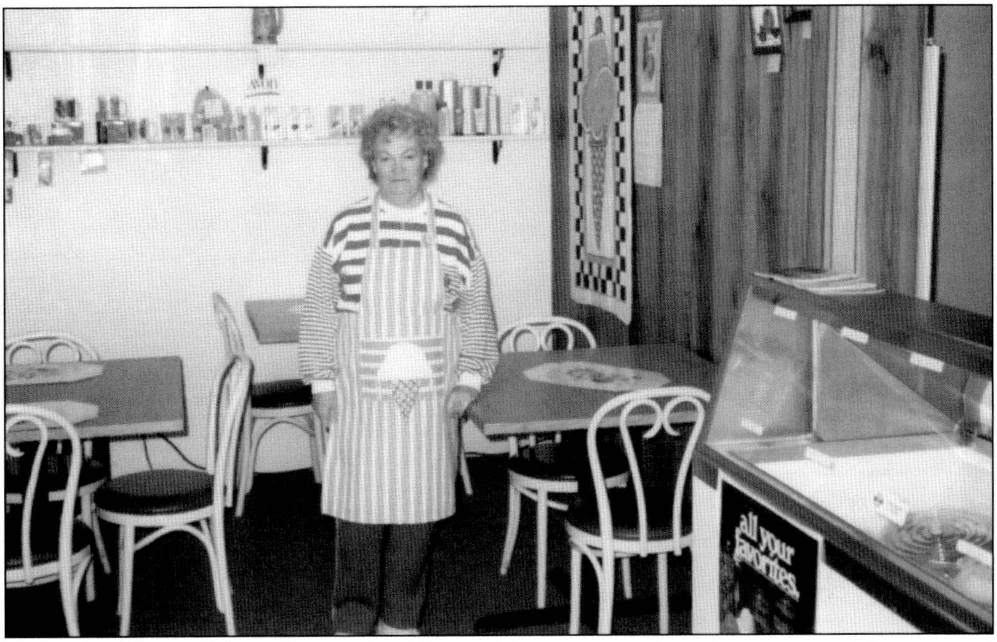

Joan Jenewein stands inside Wayne's Ice Cream and Yogurt, which she and her husband, Wayne, owned in the early 1990s. The Jeneweins moved to Sunsites in 1988. (Joan and Wayne Jenewein.)

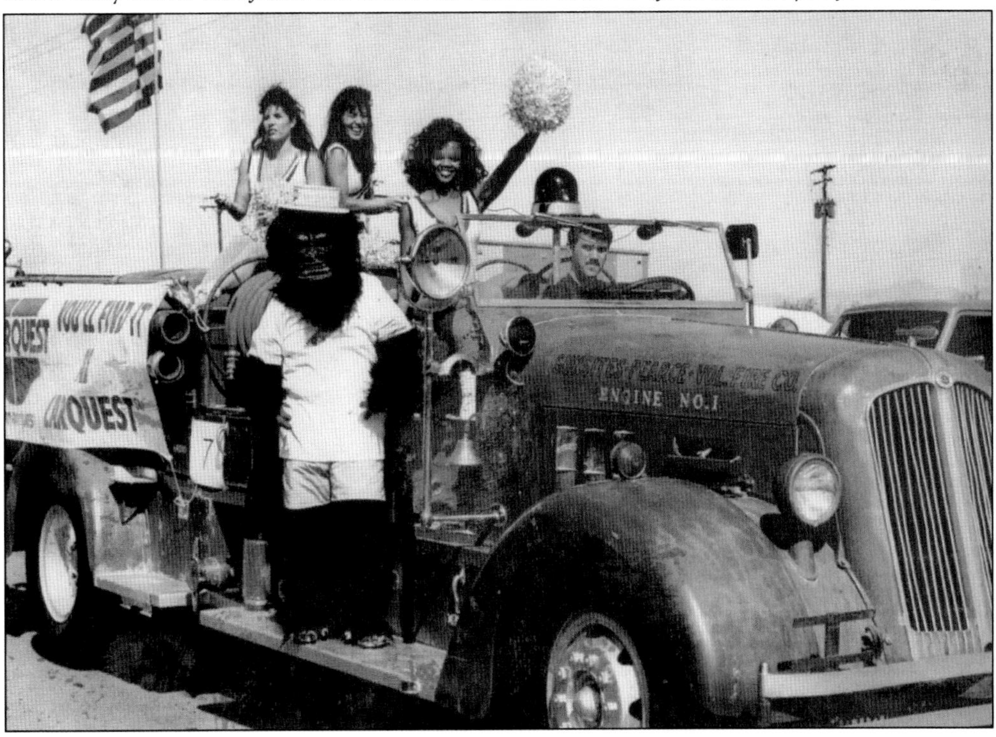

This Seagraves 1930s-era fire truck was the first fire truck used by the Sunsites Fire Department. Rose and Russ Vandeyacht later purchased the truck. Jerry Woodard drove the Vandeyachts' truck in a Cochise Days parade in the mid-1990s. The Phoenix Cardinals cheerleaders and the CARQUEST Auto Parts gorilla rode on the truck with Woodard. (Rose and Russ Vandeyacht.)

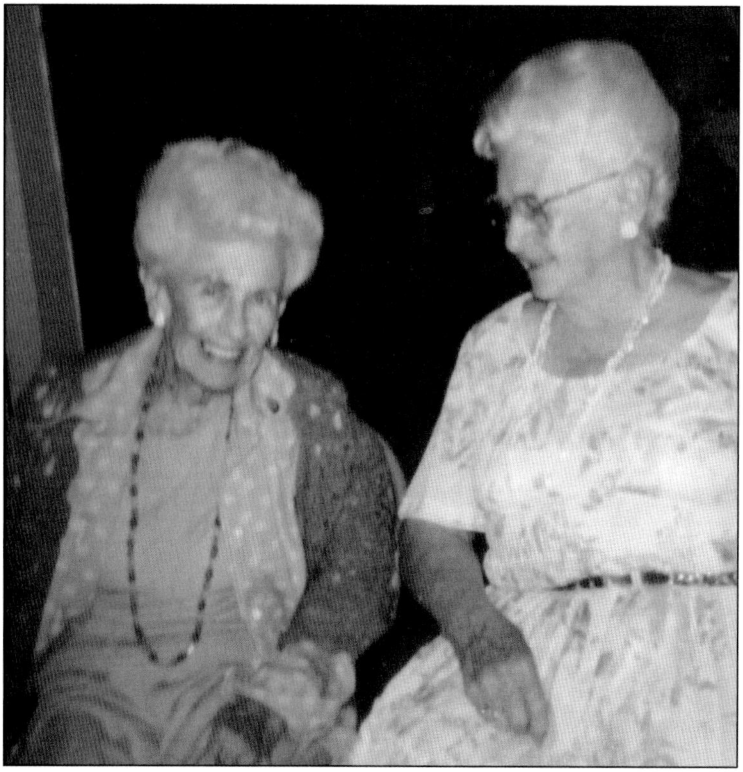

Julia Witherspoon (left) and Julia "Julie" Pilon developed a lifelong friendship in 1968, when they each moved to the same street in Sunsites from the Detroit area. Although they had not known each other before moving to Sunsites, the pair became Sunsites's own version of *Julie & Julia* (a 2009 Sony Pictures movie). Julia Pilon became "Julie" so that she was not confused with Julia Witherspoon. This photograph was taken in 1992 at a Sunsites Squares dance. (Yvonne Lauraitis.)

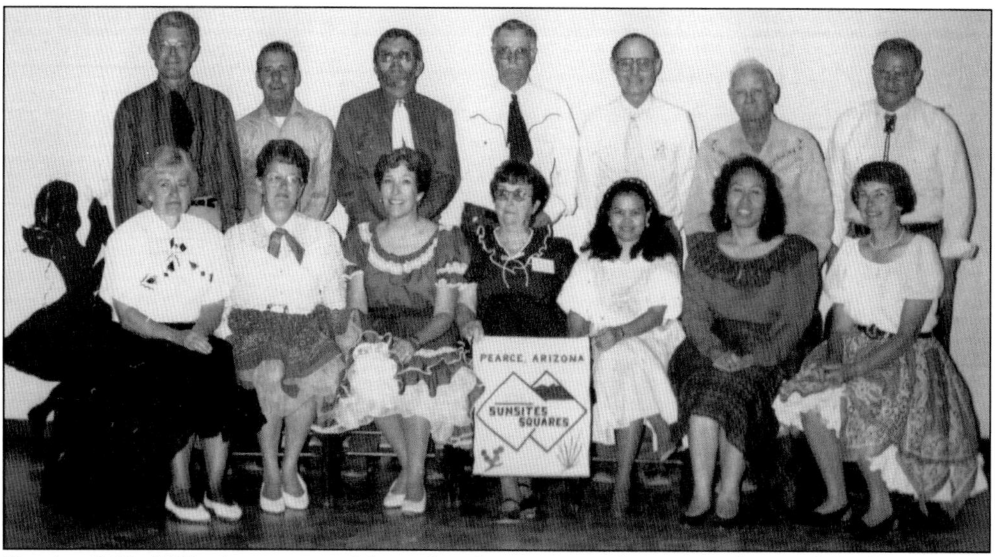

On April 30, 1993, this group celebrated induction into the square dance club, the Sunsites Squares. Members include, from left to right, (first row) Virginia Zuelow, Rita Bommersbach, Sue Gunwall, Bertha Gregory, Lucy Cornforth, Alma Remington, and Joan Brown; (second row) Jim Zuelow, Dick Bommersbach, Lynn Gunwall, Bob Gregory, Dave Cornforth, Steve Remington, and Charles Brown. (Yvonne Lauraitis.)

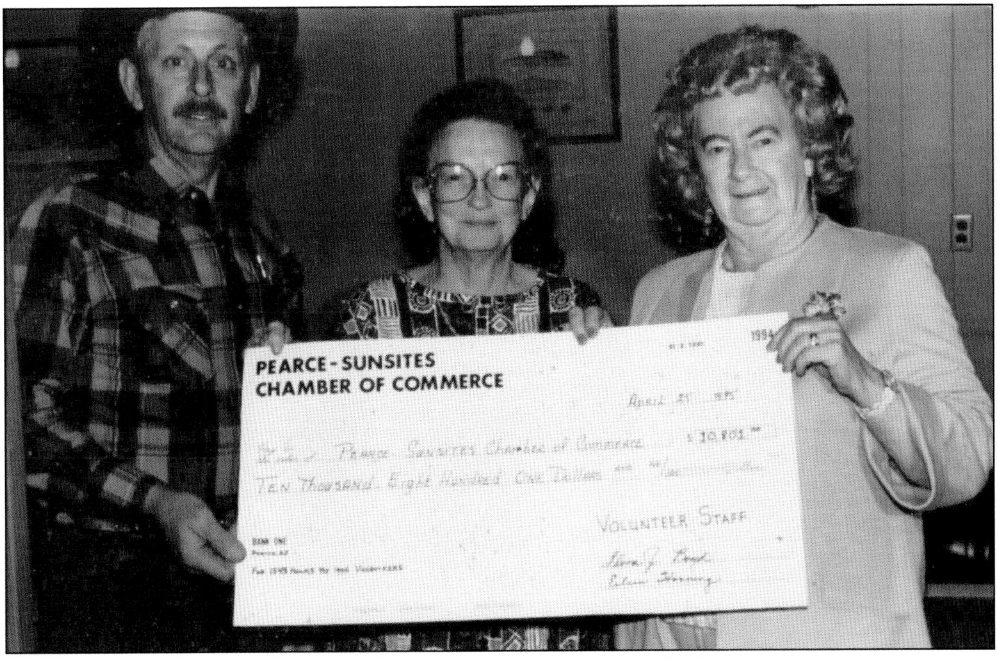

Pearce-Sunsites Chamber of Commerce president Leo Gingras (left) accepts a mock check from volunteers Flo Boyd (center) and Eileen Horning at an appreciation dinner on April 25, 1995. The mock check for $10,801 represented 1,543 hours worked by chamber volunteers in 1994. (Pearce-Sunsites Chamber of Commerce.)

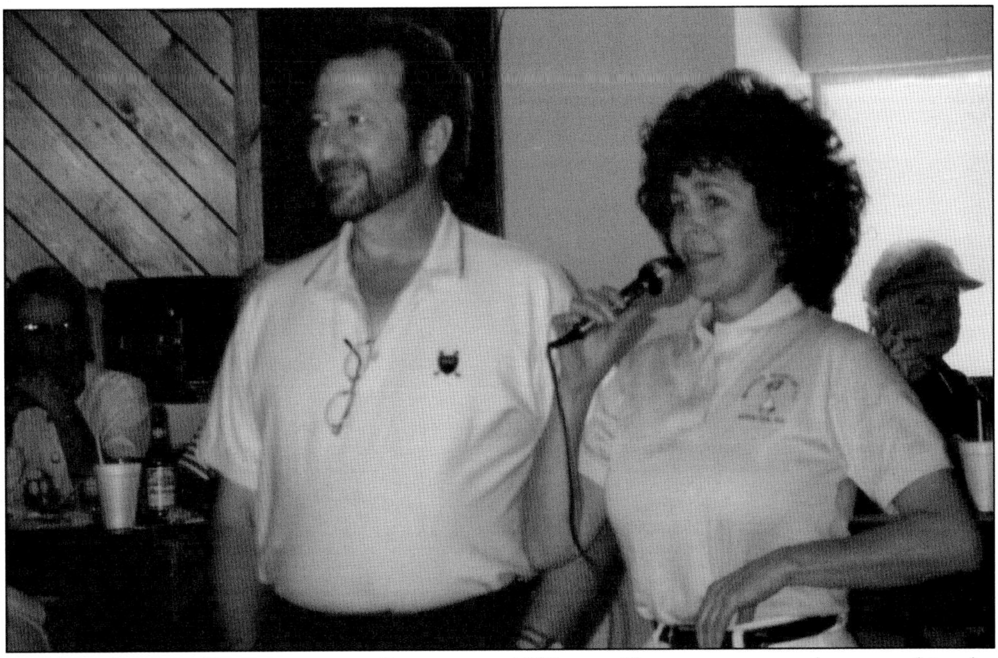

Frank and Annie Kievitt came to Sunsites in 1999 as golf course owners, but stayed in the community after the golf course was sold. The popular entertainers give generously of their time and talent. They are shown performing at a Sunsites Ladies Golf Association event. (Sunsites Ladies Golf Association.)

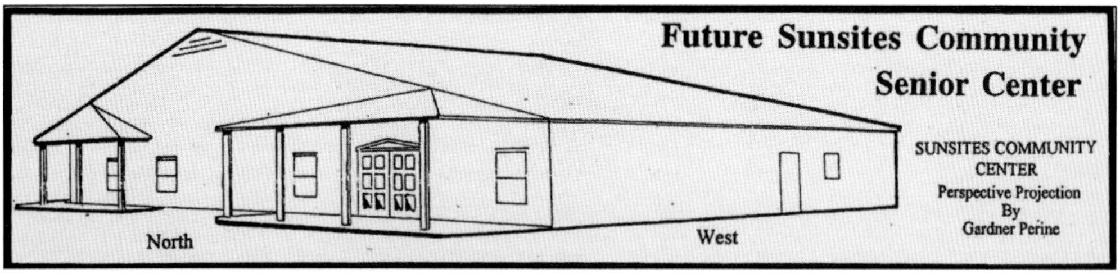

On May 15, 1997, the *Sunsiter* published this perspective by Sunsites artist Gardner Perine. He drew the pictorial of the north elevation during the design phase for a future Sunsites Senior Community Center. After many design changes and construction bids, residents gathered to break ground for the center on February 27, 1998. In early 1998, when the Arizona Sunsites Country Club dissolved, $10,000 was awarded to pay for a kitchen. (Nancy Edmiston.)

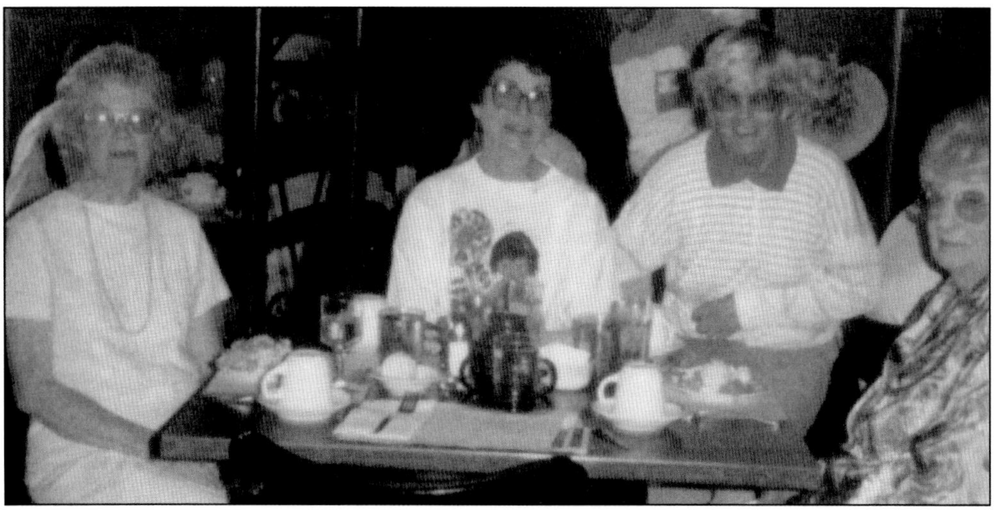

The Sunsites Ladies Golf Association celebrated its 20th anniversary at its 18th Invitational Tournament on September 26, 1992. The four remaining charter members were honored at the event. The charter members are, from left to right, Evelyn Staley, Doris Merritt, Alice "Tommie" Sawyer, and Louise Simmons. (Sunsites Ladies Golf Association.)

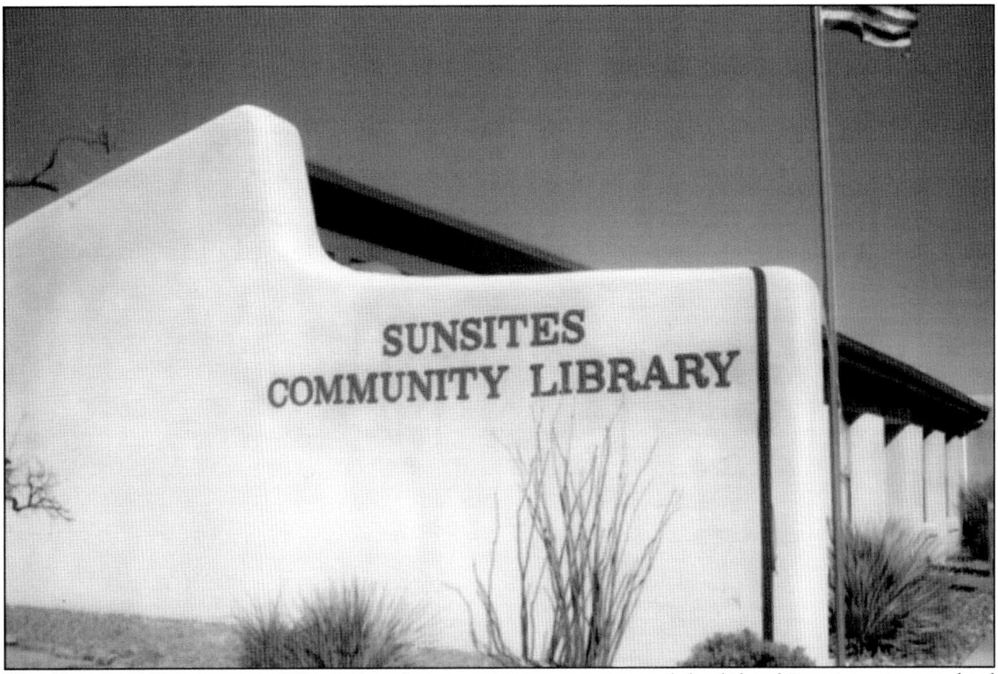

The Sunsites Community Library has been an important part of the life of Sunsites since it had its beginnings in a bookcase on the stage of the Sunsites Community Center, built by Horizon Land Corporation. Horizon donated the land for the attractive rammed-earth building that was erected by volunteers. The Friends of the Library run the popular bookstore adjacent to the library and hold Elegant Dessert Night in December as a way to raise money to maintain the library facilities. The dessert night includes an auction, live music, and desserts prepared by volunteers. (Both, Library Archives.)

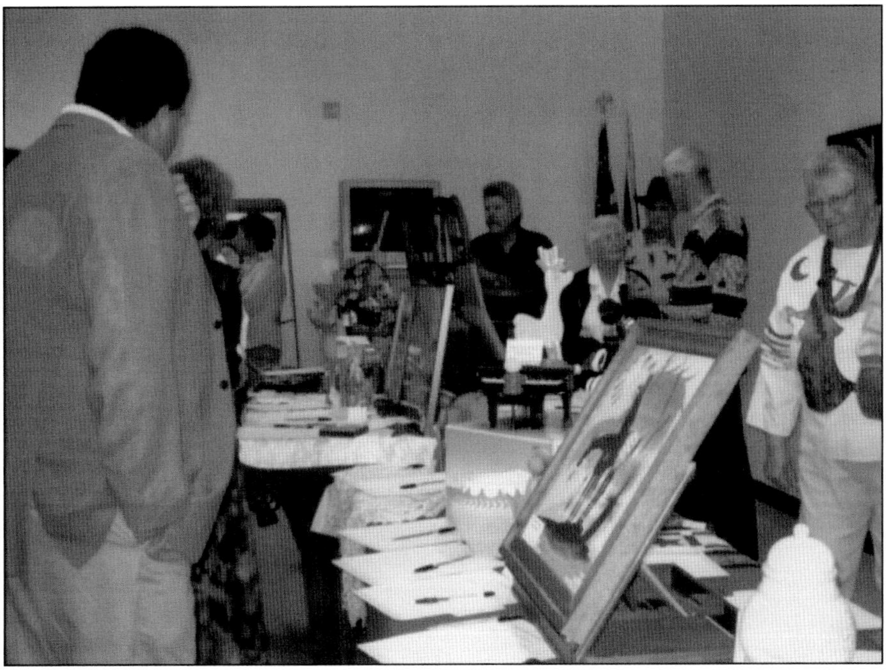

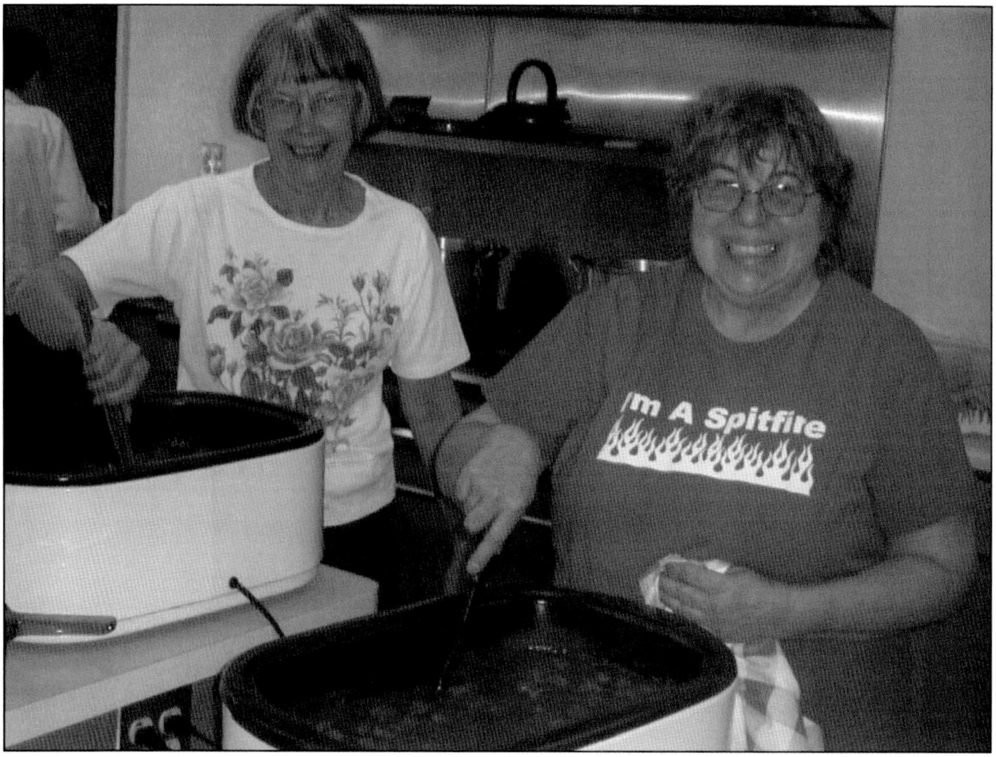

Joan Brown and Andrea Steele work together to prepare the monthly senior lunch served at the Sunsites Community Center. The center stays busy from morning to night with exercise classes, club meetings, and special events. People come from all over the Sulphur Springs Valley for Wednesday-night bingo, sponsored by the Cochise Stronghold Lions Club. (Library Archives.)

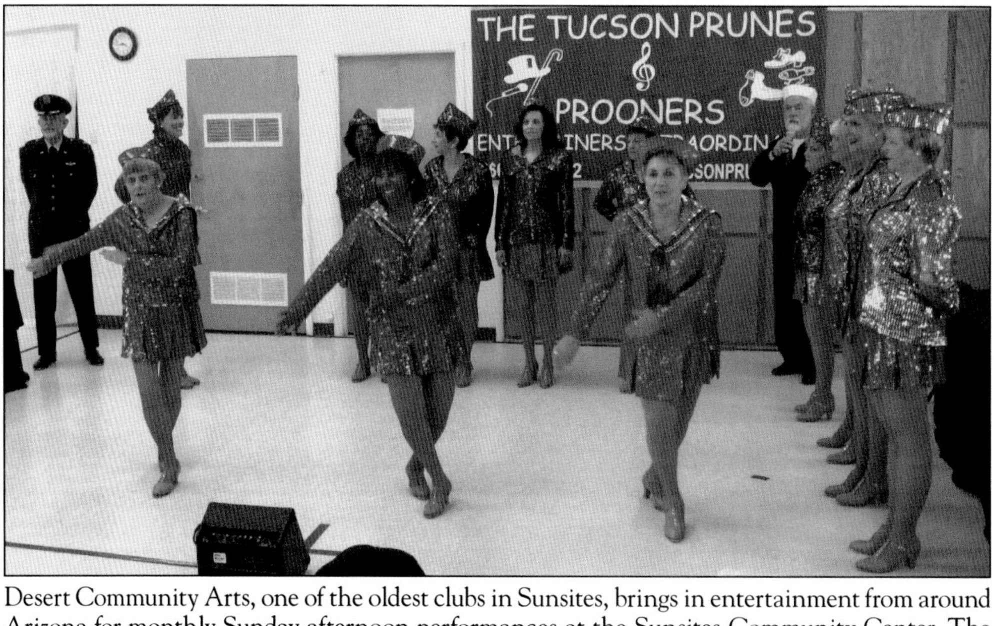

Desert Community Arts, one of the oldest clubs in Sunsites, brings in entertainment from around Arizona for monthly Sunday-afternoon performances at the Sunsites Community Center. The Tucson Prunes put on an entertaining show for the crowd. (Jonathan Williams.)

Joe Fink (left) and Charles Appel, from the Cochise Stronghold Lions Club, take subscriptions for the Sunsites flag program. The Lions place flags at the homes of subscribers on federal holidays. They were participating in the Meet the Clubs event, sponsored by the Sunsites Community Association. (Library Archives.)

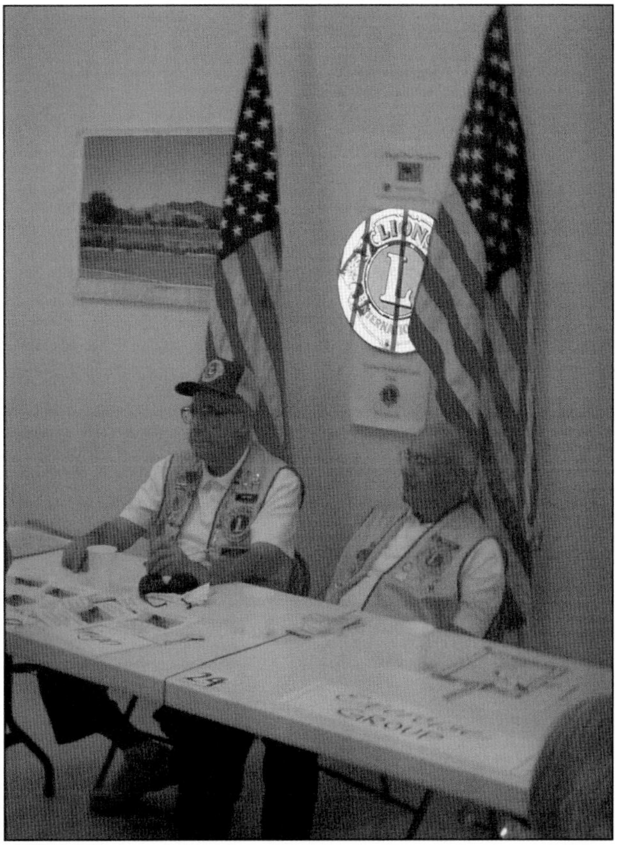

Bob Weston (right), president of the Cochise Stronghold Lions Club, stands with Gardner Perine (left) and Billie Lally, Melvin Jones Memorial Award honorees, in 2009. The prestigious award is named for the founder of the Lions Club. (Bob Weston.)

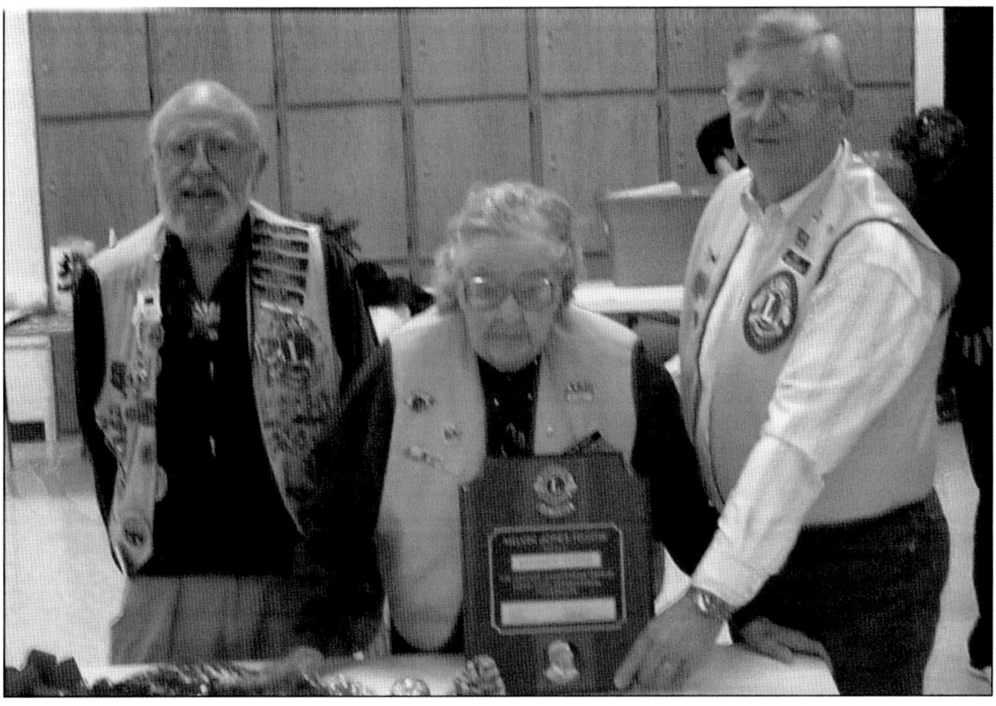

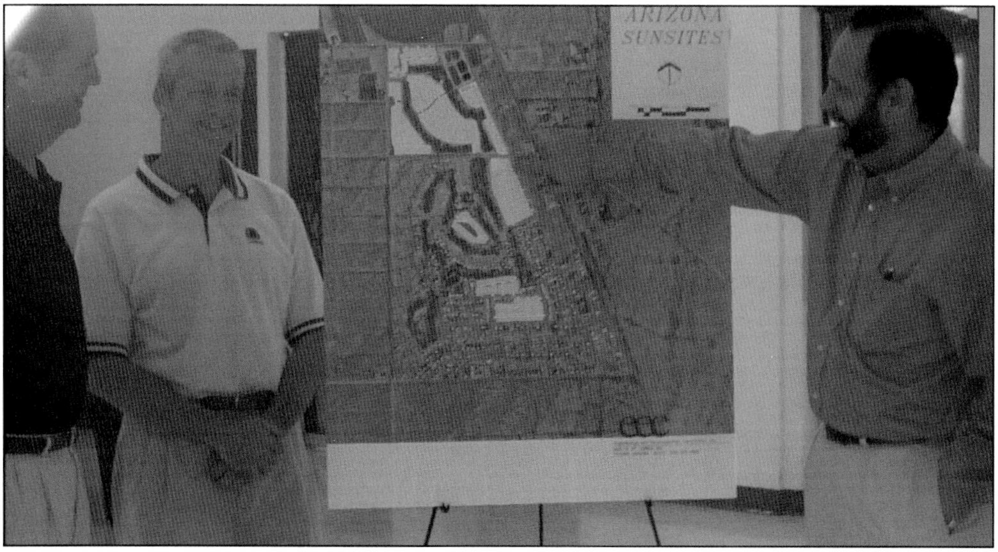

In November 2005, an investment group presented new development plans for Shadow Mountain Golf Course and other Sunsites-area properties. Mark Lundberg (left), Bill Fisher (center), and Bill Carroll discuss extensive updating for the golf course properties and for future residential development on the acreage south of Treasure Road. However, all of their plans fell apart when the real estate market went into a sharp decline. (Library Archives.)

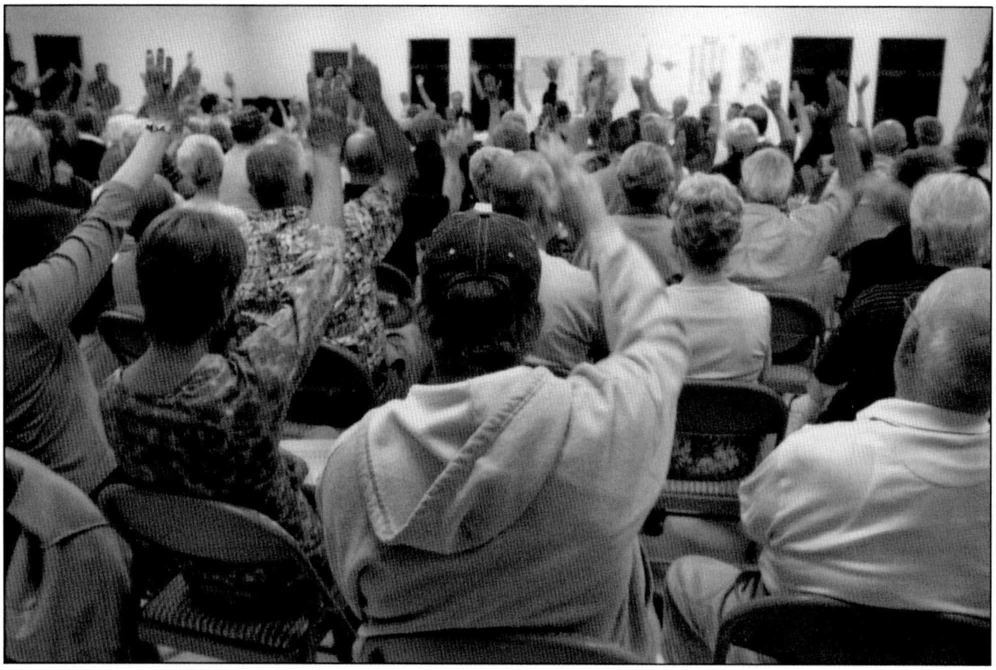

This "hands-up" photograph shows Sunsites-area residents giving virtually unanimous approval for renewing the Shadow Mountain Golf Course Association's lease on the golf course for a year. The association was formed by concerned residents after the golf course owner ordered the course closed in 2008. The course operated under a six-month lease as the association worked to improve the course's finances, operation, and maintenance with the assistance of volunteers. (Denise Eggman.)

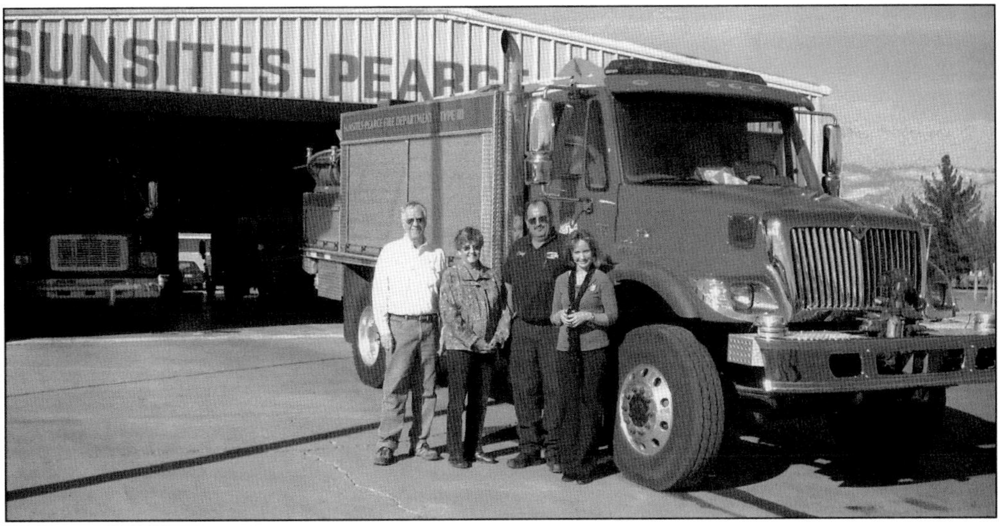

Organizations in Sunsites have joined forces to raise funds to build a permanent heliport for the area, so local residents can be evacuated more easily during a medical emergency. The landing area will be about a quarter mile north of the Old Pearce Jail. Pictured from left to right are Ray Klumb, president of the Sunsites Community Association; Mary Appel, the initiator of the project; Chief Mike Martinez of the Sunsites Pearce Fire Department; and Elaine McIntosh Perry with business development for Air Methods LifeNet Arizona. The company donated $500 to the heliport. (Ray Klumb.)

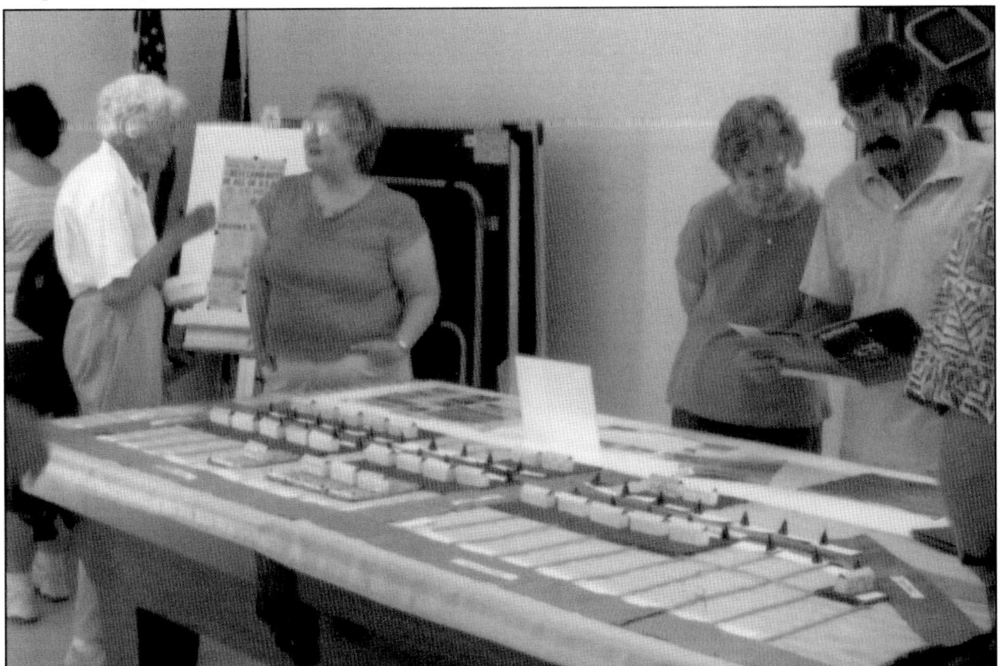

Sunsites residents view a Memory Project display of the early homes of Sunsites, at the Sunsites Community Center during the monthly senior lunch in May 2009. Nina Peterson (left) talks to Frances Marx, while on the right, Celia and John Skeeles read Horizon Corporation marketing literature. (Library Archives.)

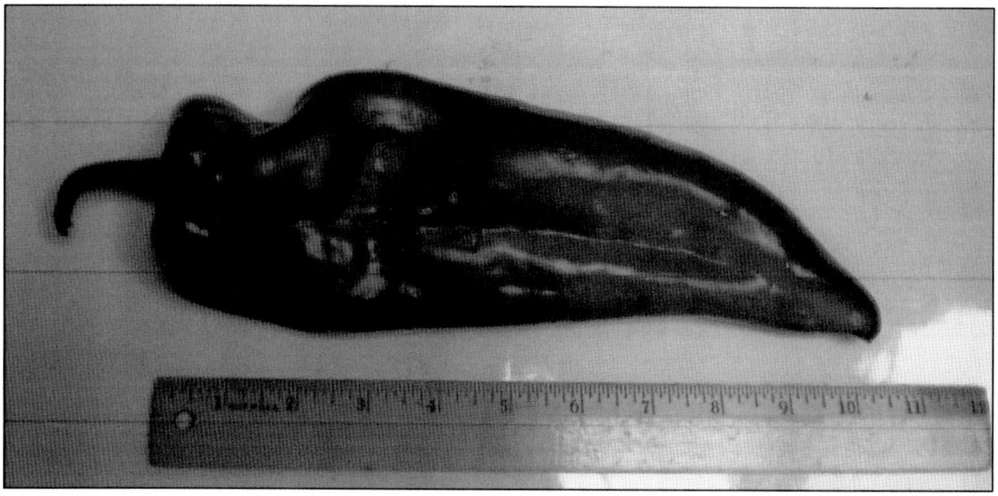

This chili pepper won a certificate from the Guinness World Records for heaviest pepper. Weighing in at 0.63 pounds, the 10.25-inch-long-by-3.76-inch-wide pepper was grown by Edward Curry, at Curry Farms, adjacent to Sunsites. (Edward Curry and Curry Farms.)

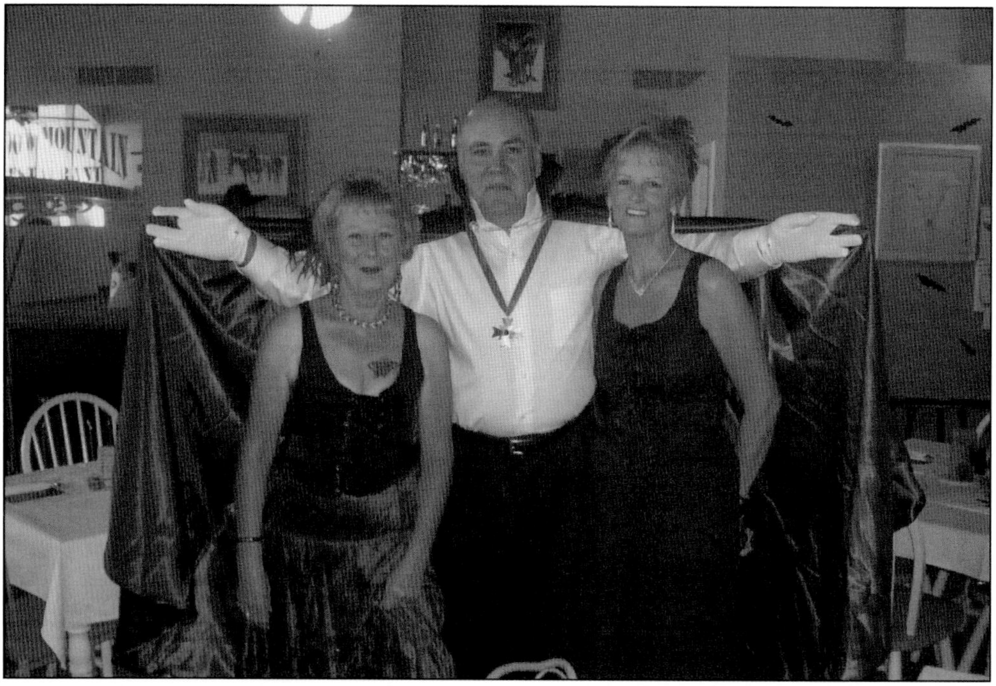

Cindy Weller (left) and Bette Greene pose with David Knecht (dressed as Dracula) at the Halloween Guest Chef night at Shadow Mountain Golf Course, Recreation, and Event Center in 2010. The Shadow Mountain Golf Course, Recreation, and Event Center has sell-out crowds for the Guest Chef series dinners. (Linda Gorton.)

Nine

Pearce Today

While it will never relive its glory days, 2011 finds Pearce alive and well. A handful of residents are still here. Besides the school, there are two businesses in town. And while many of the older occupied buildings are still in great shape, others have fallen prey to age and the elements. In 2008, the Old Pearce Preservation Association (OPPA) was formed, not only to preserve the history of Pearce, but to also tell its story. Their efforts have paid off with the erection of several educational signs and the fencing of the Old Pearce Jail property. With work, perseverance, and support, the group hopes to continue its efforts to keep Pearce alive.

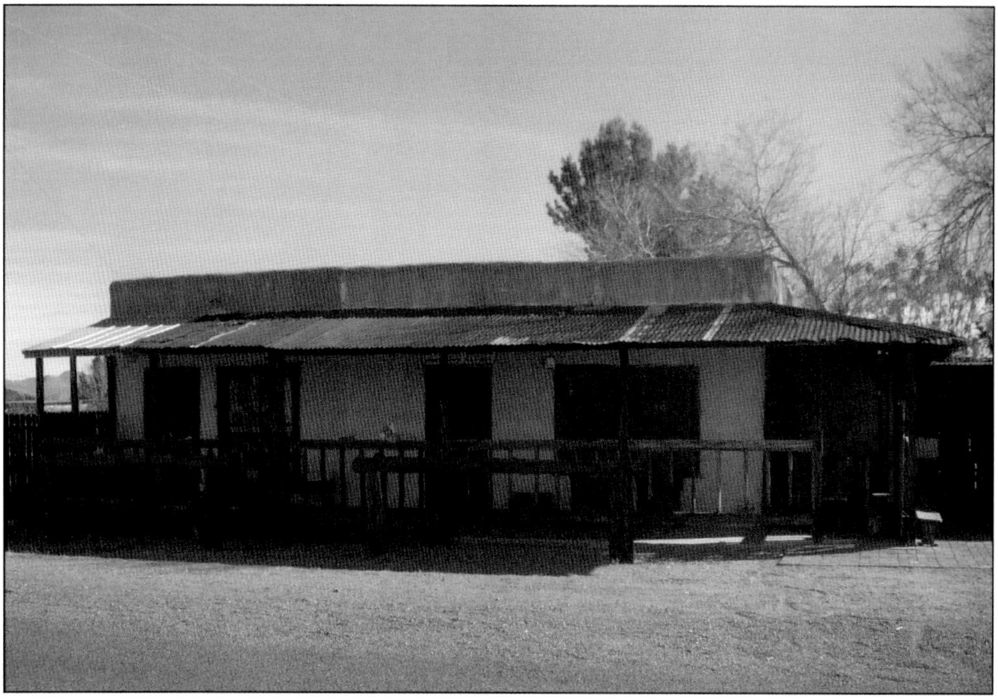

The post office building is now a private residence. The Old Pearce Pottery (pictured below), one of two businesses in town, opened in 1995 and continues to serve locals and visitors alike. The *Ghost Town Trail News*, a monthly newspaper combining history and local events in equal measure, is printed in the shop. (Both, Old Pearce Preservation Association.)

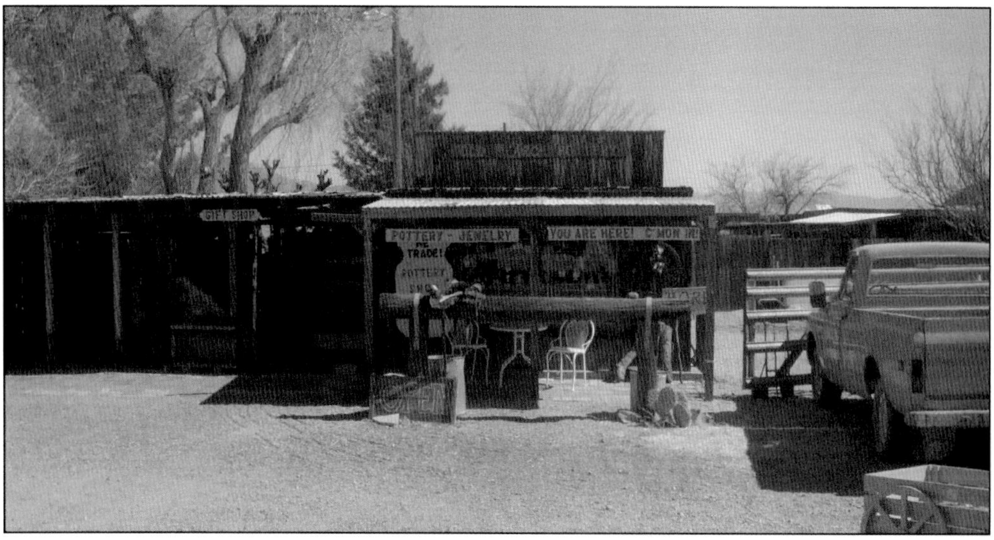

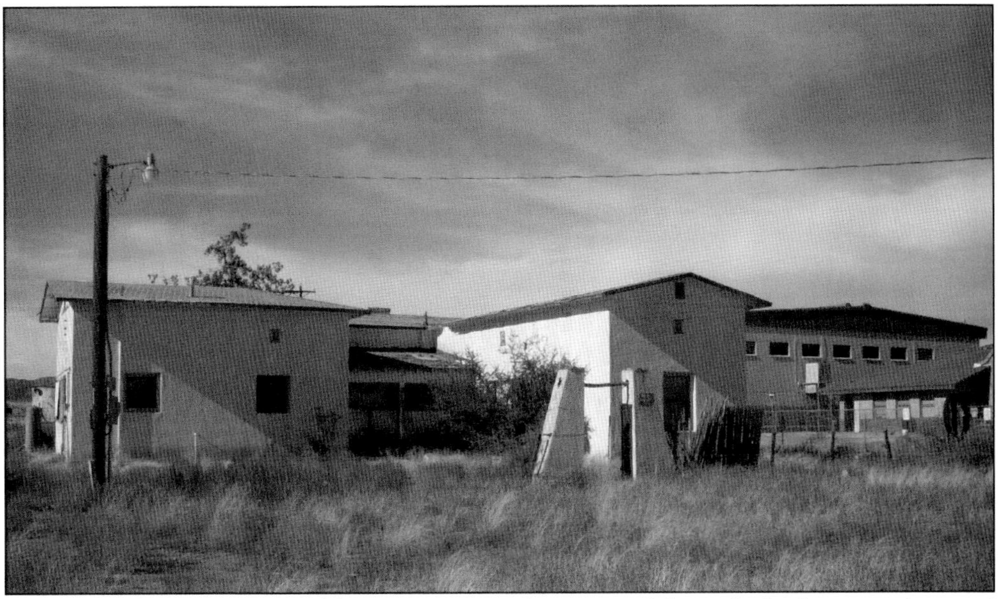

Still part of the Common-Wealth Mine property, the manager's house looks the same; the metal roof is the one thing that has changed over the years. Used sporadically, the house has fallen into disrepair because of weather and vandals. To the right, in the background, is the school gymnasium and part of the school administration building. (Old Pearce Preservation Association.)

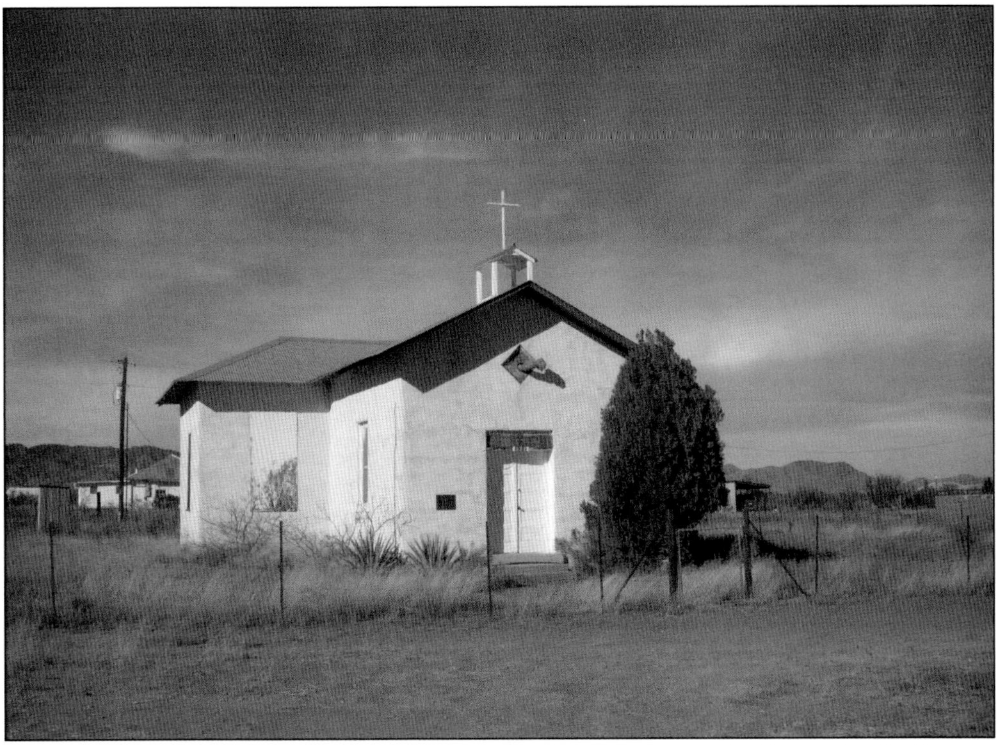

Today, the church looks very different than in its early years. Gone is the flat roof and bell tower. The stained-glass front piece is missing, and the building is now privately owned. In 2004, the church was listed in the National Register of Historic Places. (Old Pearce Preservation Association.)

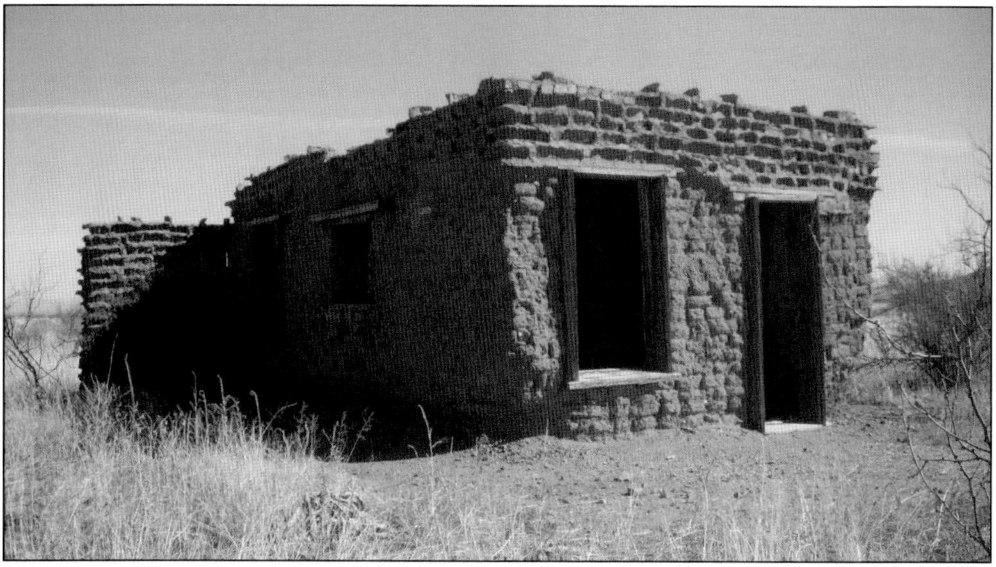

This building stands northeast of the Renaud House and for whatever reason—whether because of luck, its proximity to the often-occupied Renaud House, or because of a lack of interest by vandals—it remains relatively solid to this day. The heavy wooden beams supporting the flat wood roof are intact, as are the door and window frames. However, it is evident the weather has wrecked havoc with the exposed adobe blocks, and it is only a matter of time before this house, like most of the other adobe buildings in Pearce, falls victim to neglect. (Both, Old Pearce Preservation Association.)

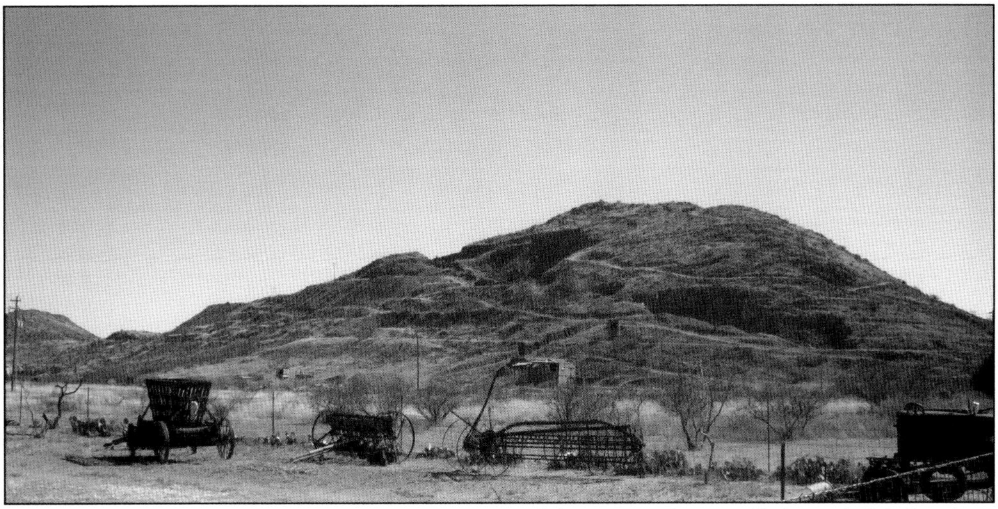

The buildings of the Common-Wealth Mine have all been torn down. All that is left behind are the remnants and scars visible today—a reminder of what happened on the hill all those years ago. (Old Pearce Preservation Association.)

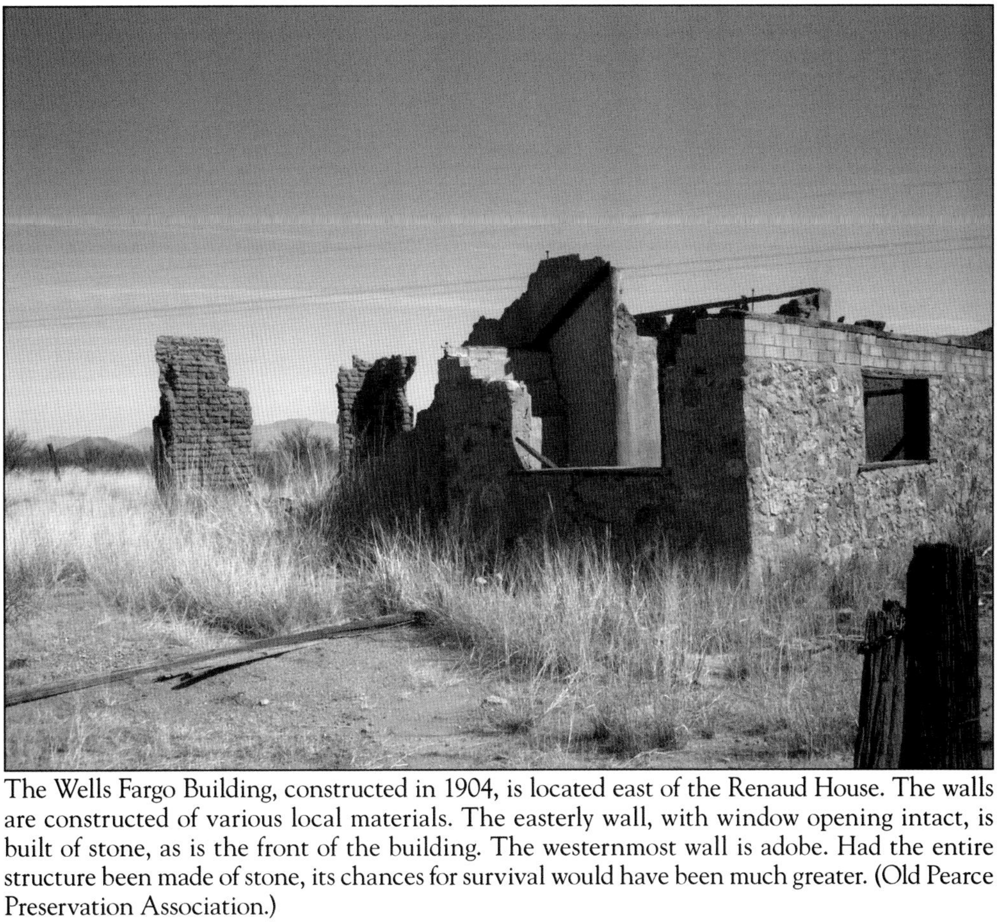

The Wells Fargo Building, constructed in 1904, is located east of the Renaud House. The walls are constructed of various local materials. The easterly wall, with window opening intact, is built of stone, as is the front of the building. The westernmost wall is adobe. Had the entire structure been made of stone, its chances for survival would have been much greater. (Old Pearce Preservation Association.)

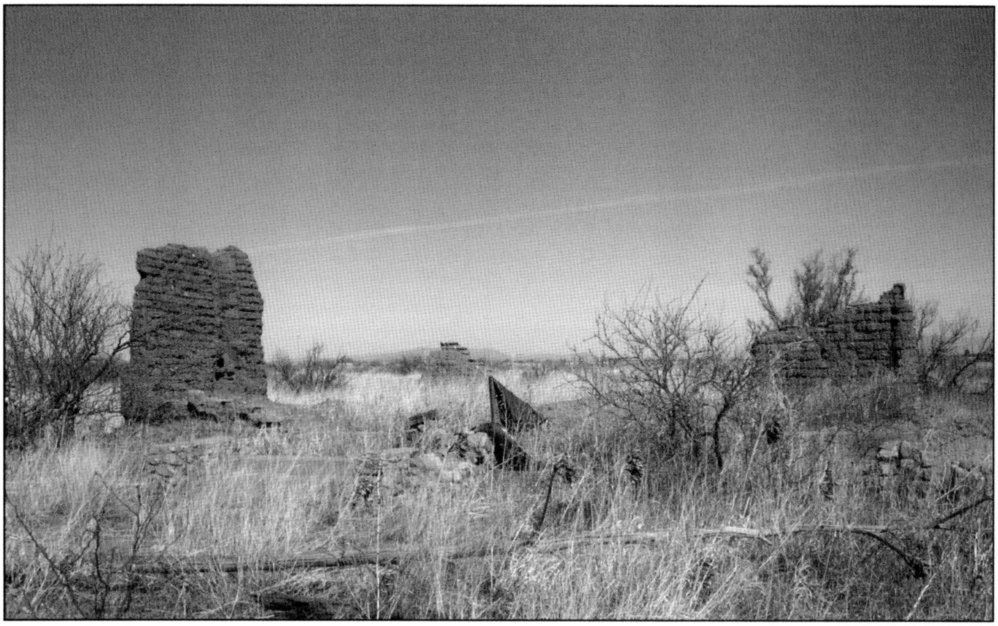

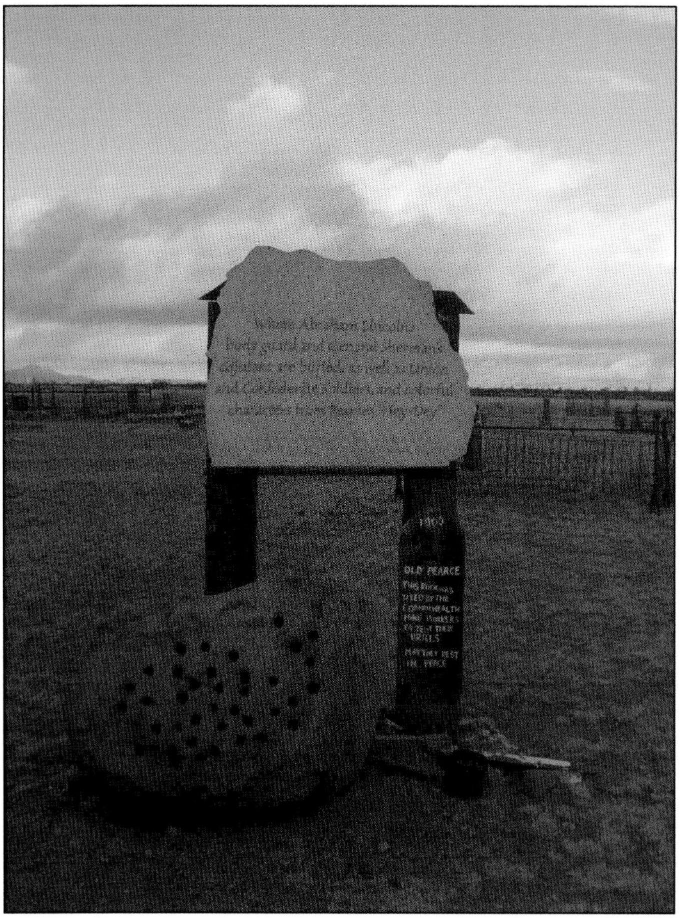

The consequences of neglect, weather, and vandalism are apparent in this image of what is left of a once-opulent Pearce home. As late as the 1960s, buildings remained erect, their roofs and beams in place, supporting the adobe walls. Once vandals stole the wooden substructures and roofs, it was only a matter of time, wind, rain, and snow before the adobe melted down into the earth from which it originated. (Old Pearce Preservation Association.)

The Pearce Cemetery continues to serve the area at large. The acreage acted as a burial ground before it officially became a cemetery in 1916. Many of the older gravestones are gone. The cemetery is in the care of a nonprofit organization. (Old Pearce Preservation Association.)

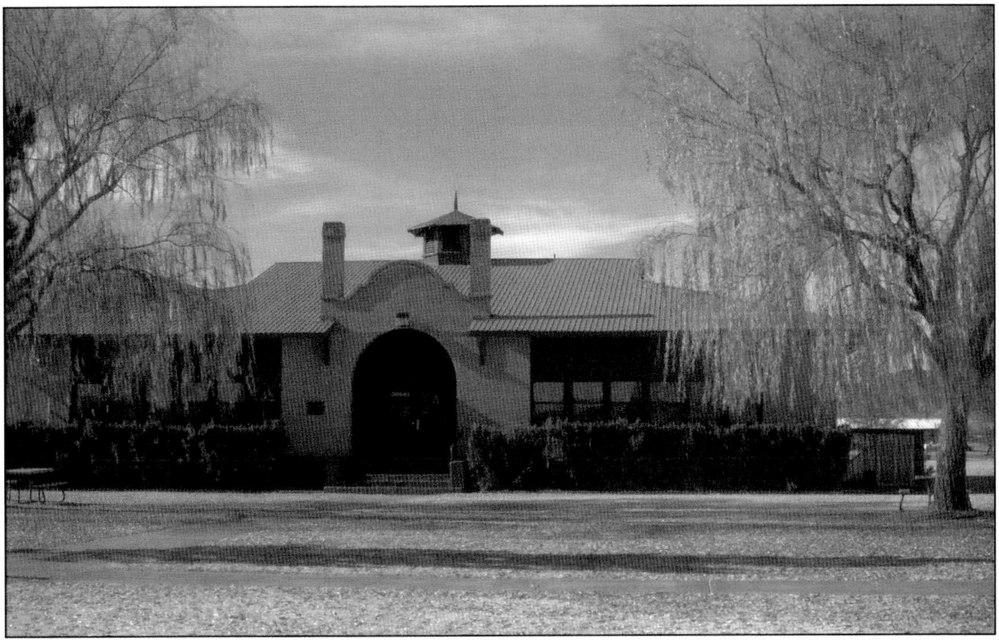

Following the 1960s, the school added many new buildings, including a gymnasium and an administration building. In 2011, the school attendance was 93. The 1912 building still stands in the center of the school grounds; in 2007, the building was dedicated to Mary Magoffin, who was involved in many community organizations, including the Cochise County Historical Society and the Old-Timer Reunion, a meeting of past Pearce School alumni. (Above, Old Pearce Preservation Association; below, *Ghost Town Trail News*.)

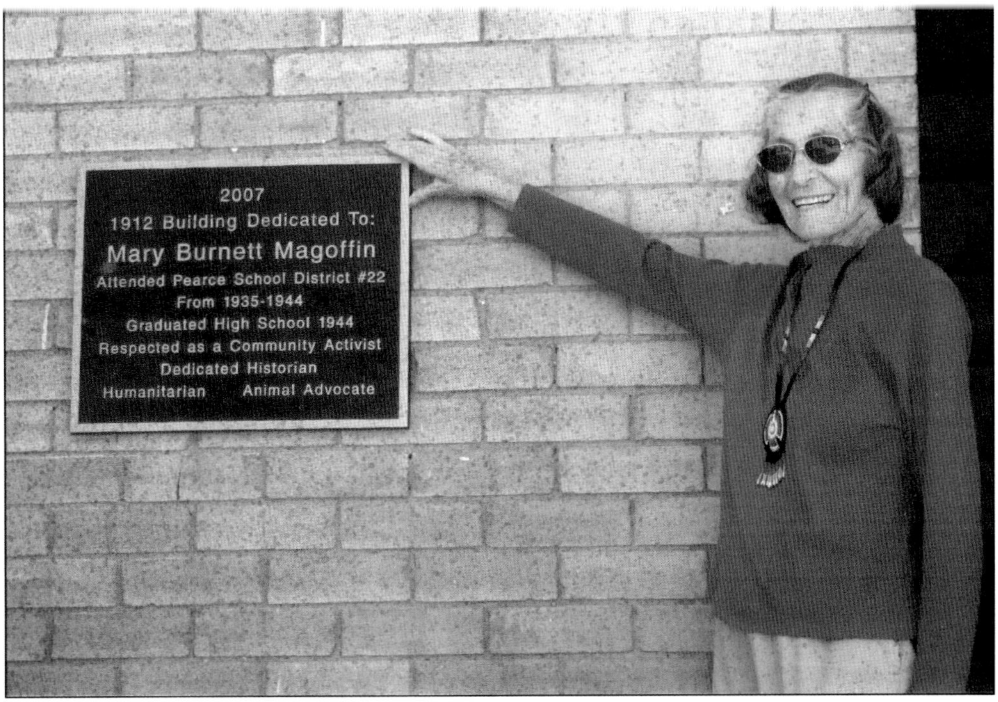

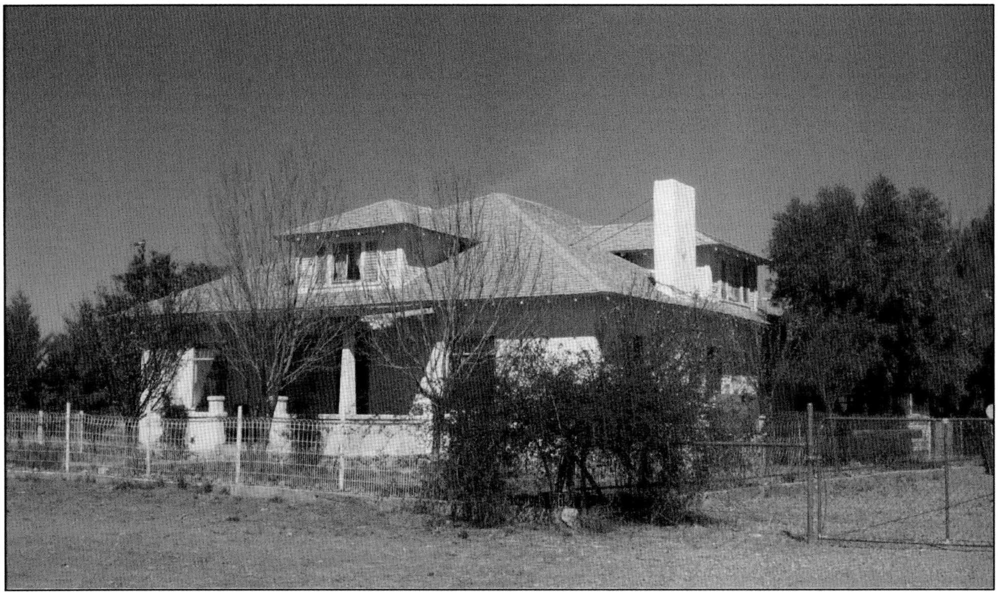

The original Charles M. Renaud home burned in June 1915, the fire not only taking the house and outbuildings, but also Renaud's Studebaker automobile. This Prairie-style adobe structure was built soon after the conflagration and is unusual in that the interior walls continue through the wood floors to the ground below. In this way, Renaud believed another fire could be prevented from spreading and destroying his second home. (Old Pearce Preservation Association.)

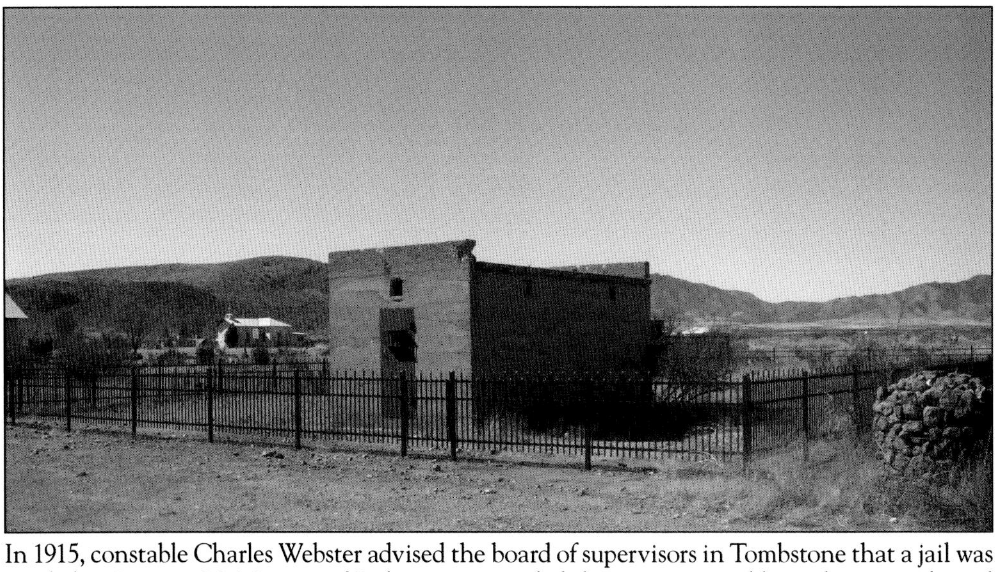

In 1915, constable Charles Webster advised the board of supervisors in Tombstone that a jail was needed in Pearce. G.M. Porter, of Bisbee, was awarded the contract, and later that year, the jail was completed at a cost of $615.45. Constructed of layers of poured concrete reinforced by rebar and with a flat roof, the jail has two cells. The walls are 10 inches thick, and the two doors are iron. (Old Pearce Preservation Association.)

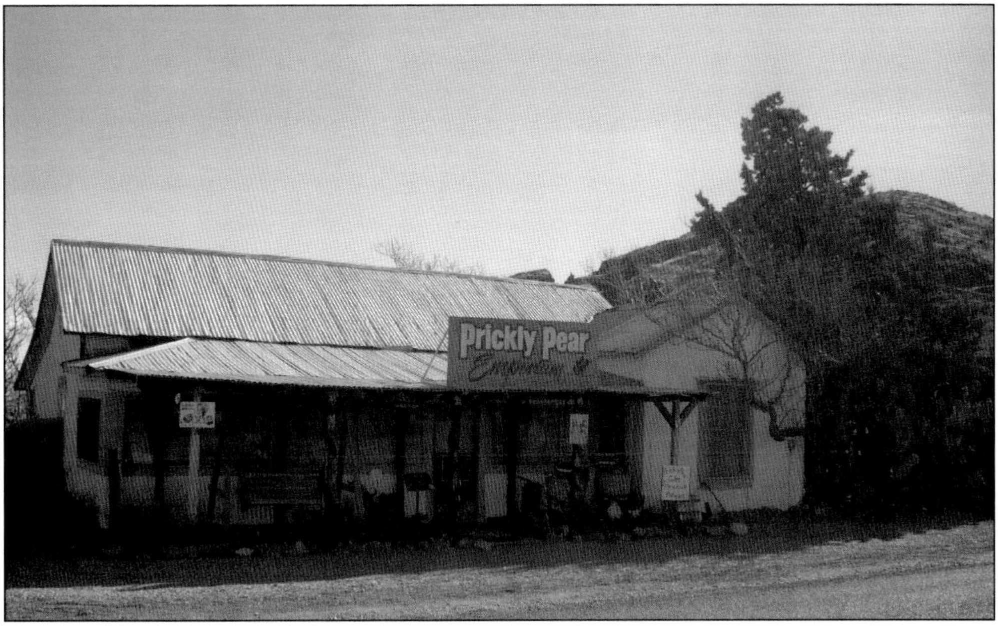

In 2002, sisters Kay Harris and Dianne McElhaney opened the Prickly Pear Emporium gift shop. The building is one that was transported from elsewhere during the rush to Pearce. In June 2010, the Old Pearce Preservation Association installed its first historic marker sign in front of the building. Seen below are past OPPA president Ruth Wilcoxson and current president Brian Ballard. (Both, Old Pearce Preservation Association.)

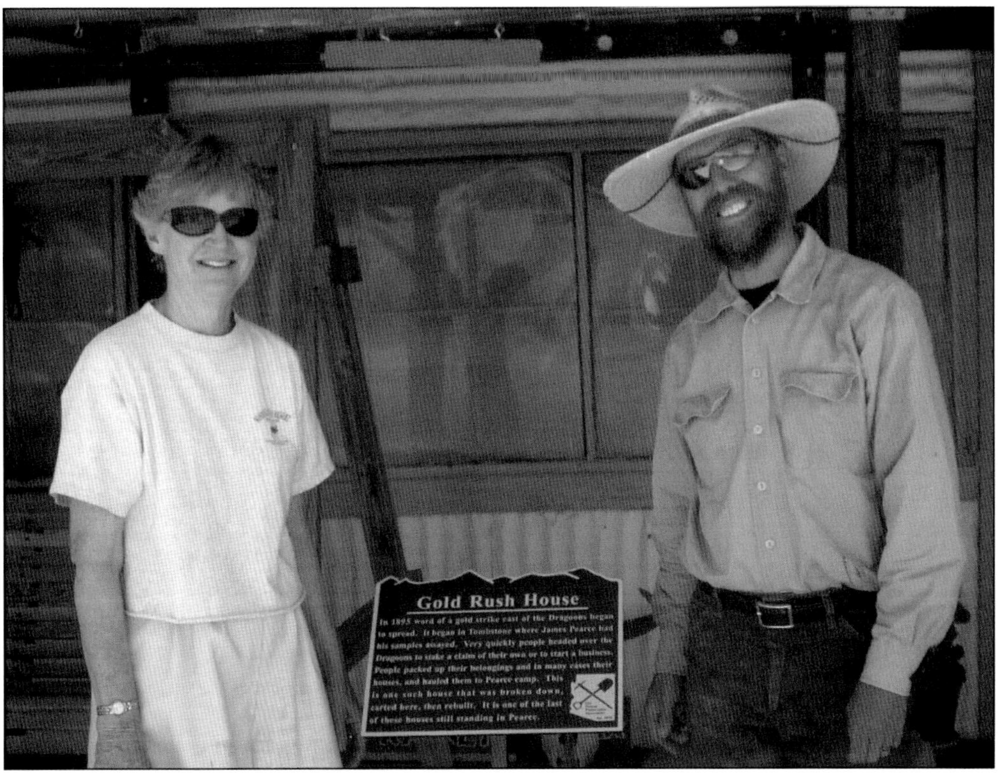

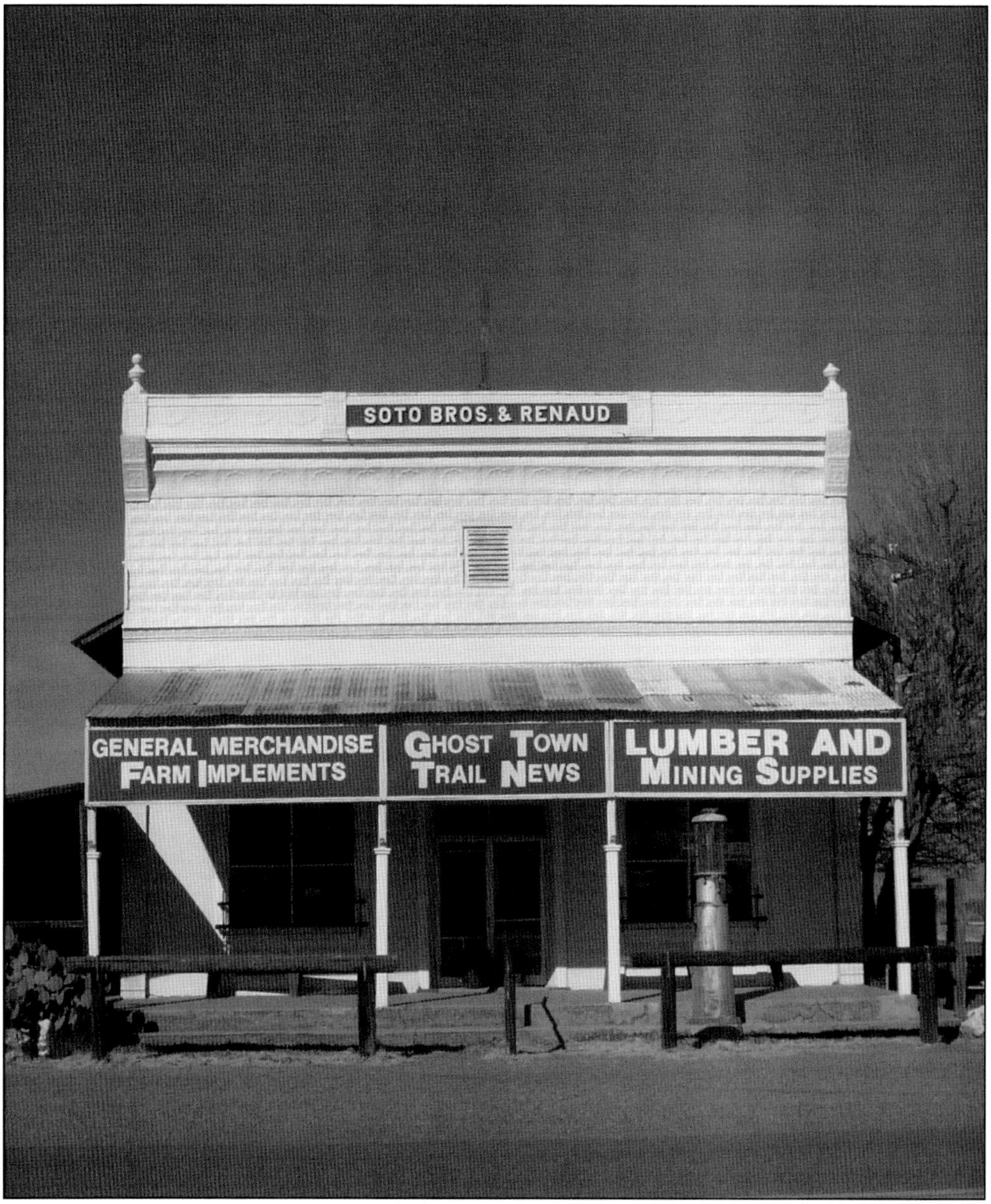

The Soto Bros. and Renaud store is one of the largest adobe structures still standing in Cochise County. Today, the privately owned building is a museum, shared with the community by appointment for tours and parties, and enjoyed by all during the annual two-day Old Pearce Heritage Days festival. (Old Pearce Preservation Association.)

Ten

ATTRACTIONS

Stargazers find the clear skies irresistible. Hikers and horseback riders appreciate the trails. History-lovers find more than they hoped. Adventurers seek the treasures hidden in the mountains and the desert lands. The Sulphur Springs Valley attracts people from all over the world. They come first for just a look, and then they come again and again. The mild winters bring more than just snowbirds. The climate and the grain fields draw many specimens of birds and, in particular, thousands of large sandhill cranes. Visitors go home and tell their friends and family about the friendly people they meet, the laid-back lifestyle, and the natural, unspoiled beauty of Cochise County and the Pearce-Sunsites area. Permanent residents enjoy a simple and self-reliant lifestyle. Willcox has Wings Over Willcox; Sunsites has Cochise Days; Pearce has Old Pearce Heritage Days. Visitors plan their trips to the area so that they can enjoy these events. Bed and breakfasts and guest ranches cater to travelers looking for unique experiences. Film crews find ideal locations, far from traffic and crowds. Residents of Pearce and Sunsites take special pride in sharing the exceptional beauty they experience daily.

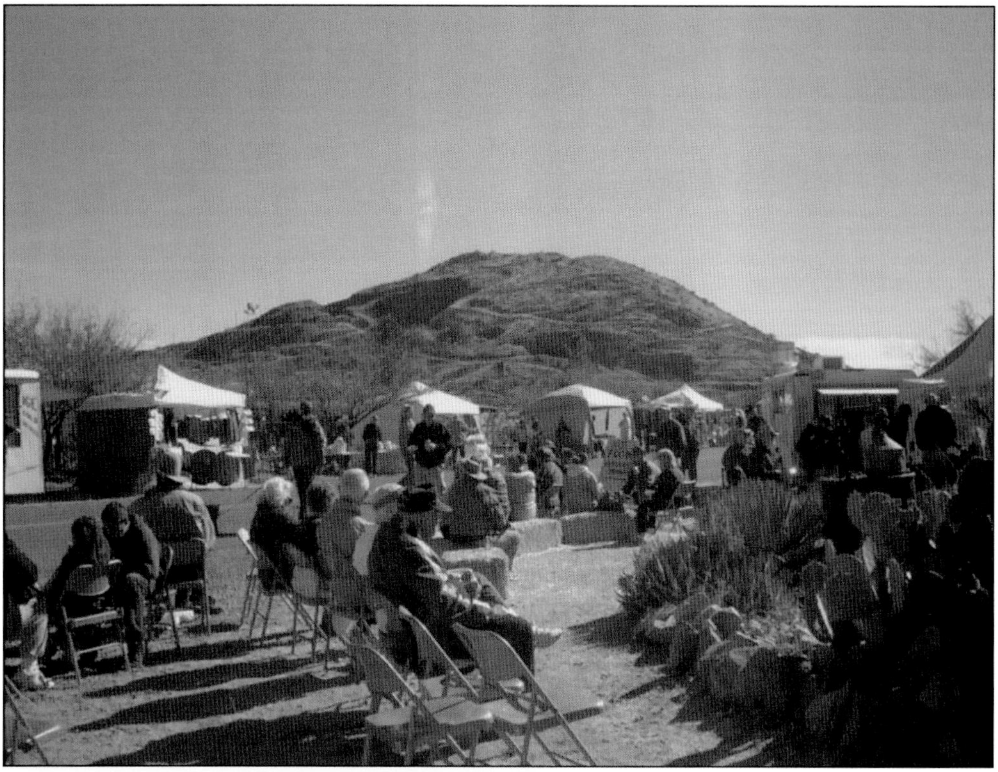

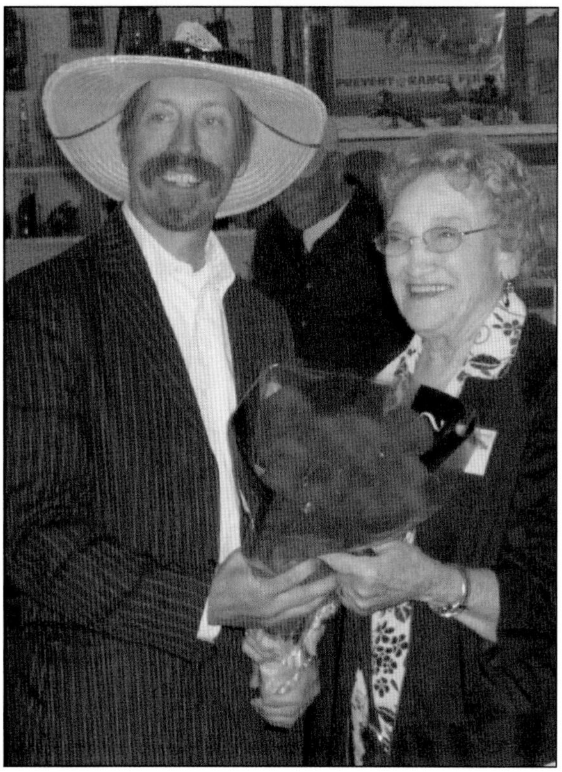

The Old Pearce Heritage Days event takes place on the Friday and Saturday after Thanksgiving. Since its inception 10 years ago, when it was called the Old Pearce Holiday Festival, it has been a celebration of Pearce's history. Local arts and crafts, music, food, and displays of area history liven up the event, and for those two days, the Old Pearce Mercantile is open free to the public. (Ballard collection.)

As part of Old Pearce Heritage Days in 2008, the OPPA invited past Pearce residents and students of Pearce School to recount some of their Pearce history. Jean Newman-Watkins came from Oklahoma. It was her first time back in the old store since the 1930s. For two hours, she recounted her life in Pearce. Pictured here, OPPA treasurer Brian Ballard presents Jean with a bouquet of roses. (Old Pearce Preservation Association.)

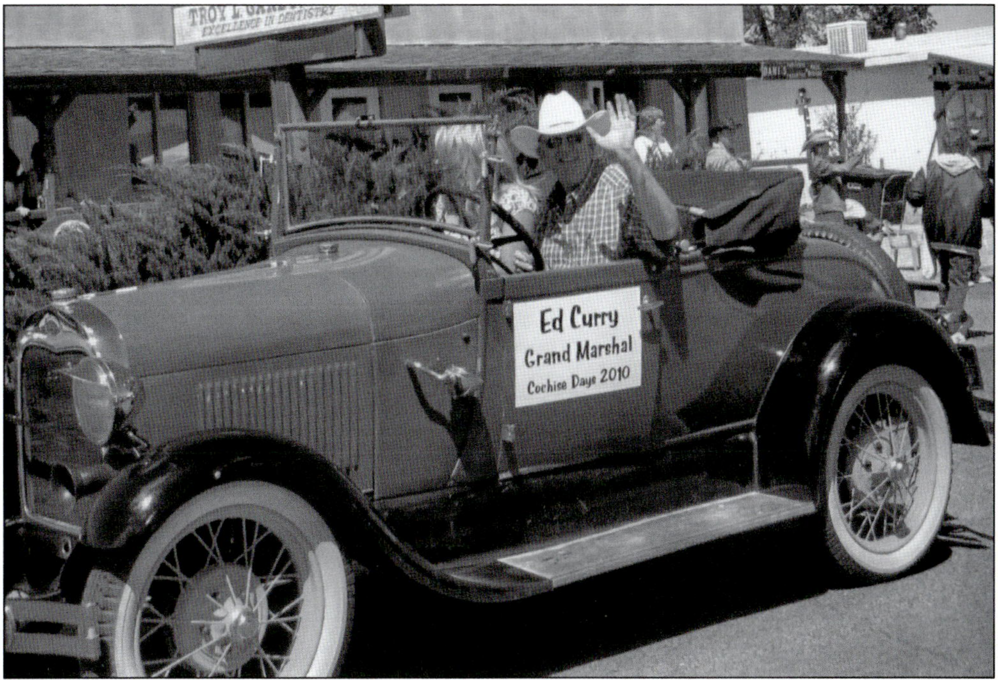

Ed Curry was grand marshal for the 2010 Cochise Days celebration. The Pearce-Sunsites Chamber of Commerce sponsors the yearly gathering, which attracts enthusiastic crowds for family-friendly events and activities. (Above, Pearce-Sunsites Chamber of Commerce; below, Ed Borgnaes.)

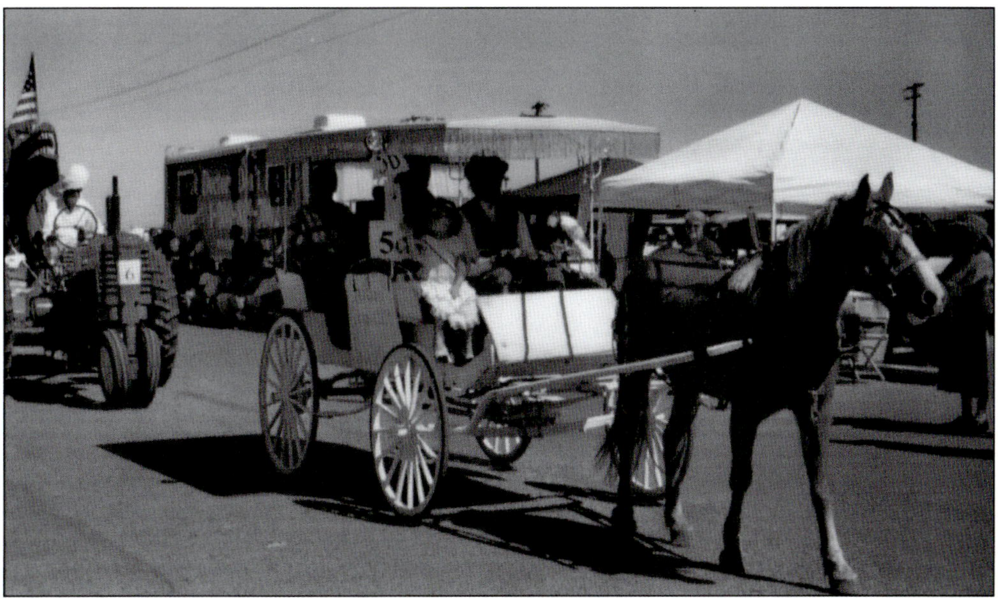

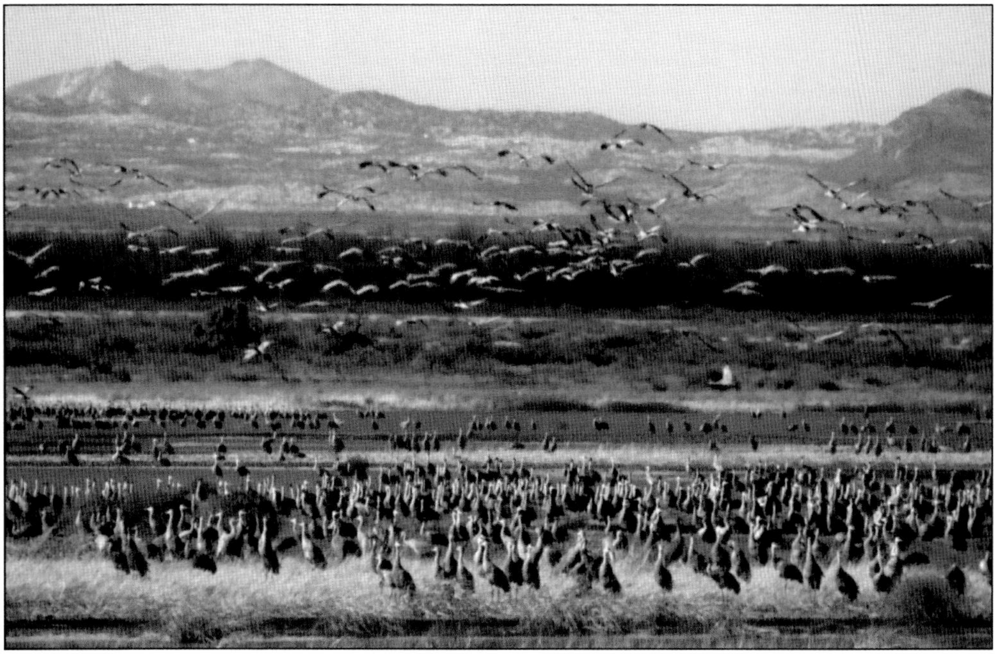

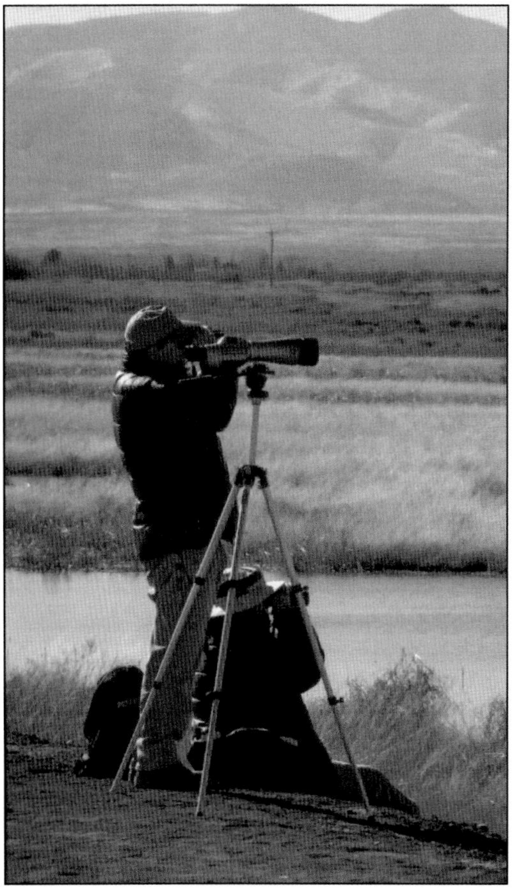

During the winter months, birds and birdwatchers migrate to the Sulphur Springs Valley. In 2010, the Arizona Game and Fish Department counted 40,499 wintering sandhill cranes in southern Arizona. Sandhill cranes have a wingspan of six to eight feet. (Both, Jonathan Williams.)

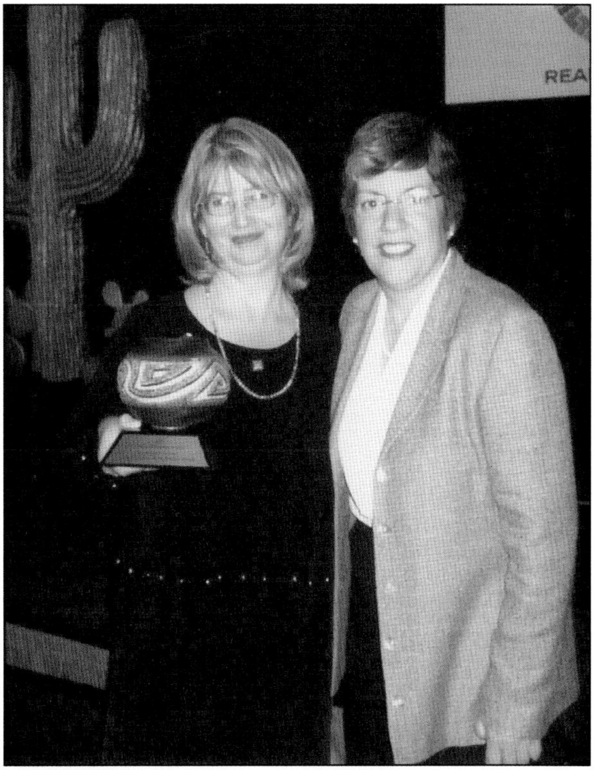

Nancy Yates (left), owner of Cochise Stronghold, a canyon nature retreat, received the Best Practices in Technology award in 2009. Janet Napolitano, governor of Arizona, presented the award to John and Nancy Yates in recognition of their well designed website. The Cochise Stronghold has special appeal for visitors and for film crews from abroad. Nancy Yates took the photograph below of an Italian film crew working on the Yates property in the Stronghold. (Above, John Yates; below, Nancy Yates.)

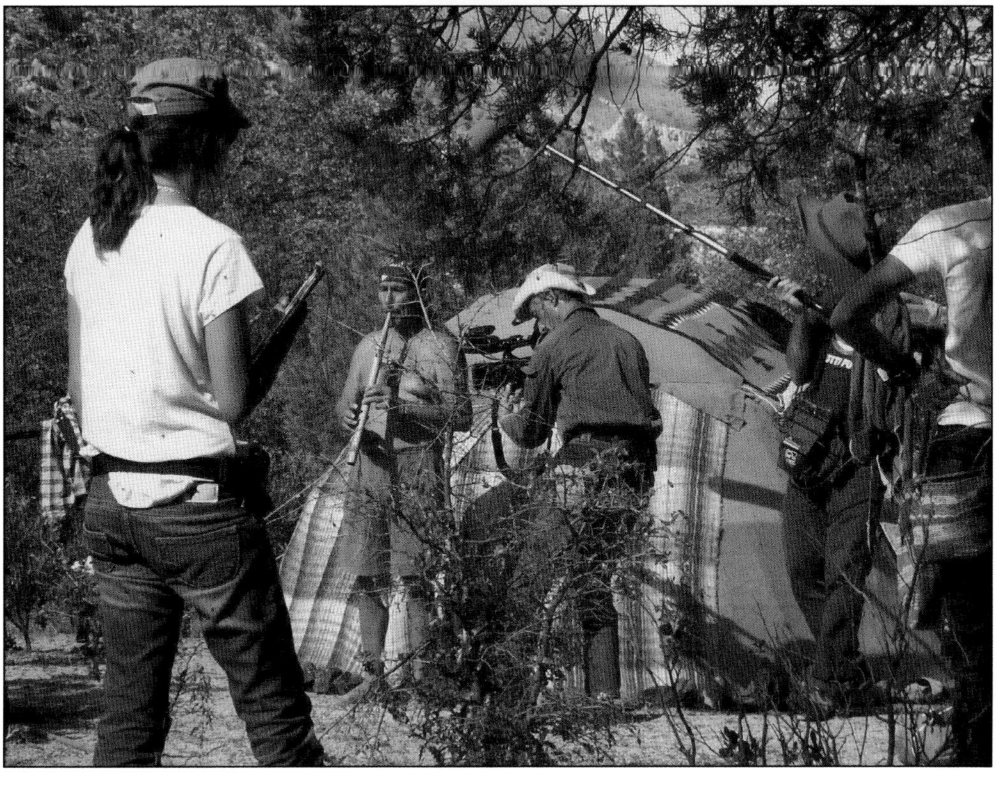

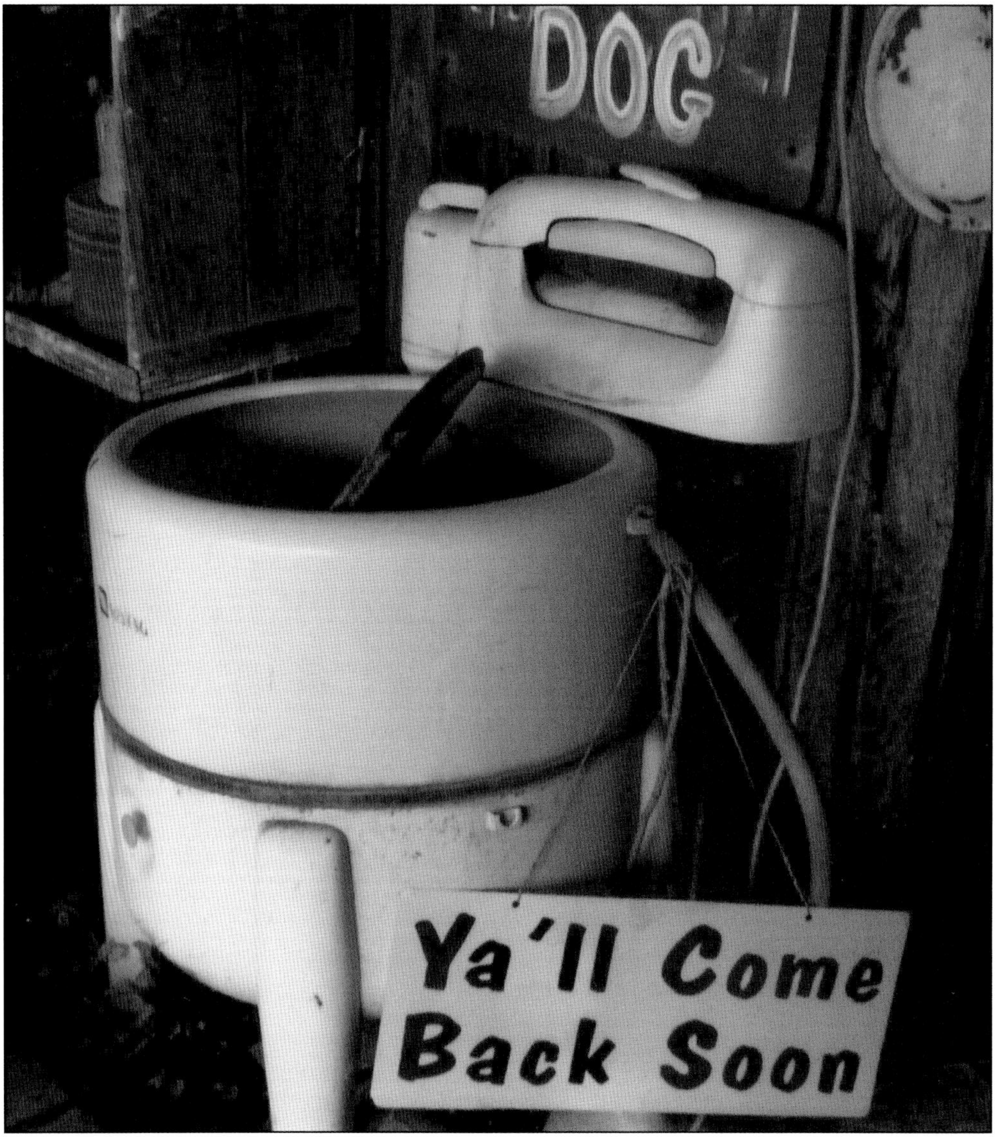

The authors thank the reader for visiting Pearce and Sunsites and learning more about the area. "Y'all come back soon!" (Jonathan Williams.)

About the Organizations

Old Pearce Preservation Association

The Old Pearce Preservation Association (OPPA), a non-profit organization, was founded in January 2008 by a small group of concerned individuals willing to give the time and effort it would take to preserve the town of Pearce, its history, its buildings, and its heritage. Since its inception, OPPA has been successful in obtaining county signage, calling attention to the significance of the town of Pearce (one of three ghost towns located along the Ghost Town Trail). It has erected the first of many signs designating important buildings in the town and has obtained funding to fence in the Old Pearce Jail and its companion edifice, the generator building, protecting both from vandalism and further deterioration, while keeping the public safe. Utilizing its major fundraising event, Old Pearce Heritage Days, which occurs on the Friday and Saturday following Thanksgiving, and the Classy Closet monthly rummage sales, OPPA hopes to fund many future projects. The ultimate goal is to open a museum with displays, photographs, and artifacts from Pearce, preserving the memories from a bygone era for generations to come. Operated by volunteers and funded by memberships and donations, OPPA can be contacted via mail at PO Box 776, Pearce, AZ 85625, and by email at saveoldpearce@yahoo.com.

Sulphur Springs Valley Historical Society

Founded in 1974 to preserve the heritage of Willcox and the surrounding area, the Sulphur Springs Valley Historical Society (SSVHS) was successful in getting the original business buildings and homes listed in the National Register of Historic Places and creating a historic district. They began to document the history of these buildings and applied for grants and raised funds to help in their preservation. After renovating the 1880s Schwertner family home and the Southern Pacific Railroad depot, the society opened the Chiricahua Regional Museum and Research Center in 1999. Located at 127 East Maley Street, the museum features the history of the Chiricahua Apache people, plus ranching, mining, and the history of Willcox and the surrounding towns. The research center archives include books, photographs, newspapers dating from 1894, family histories, displays from the Toggery store, and the Judge Edward R. Monk family collection. Operated completely by volunteers with funding by donations and memberships, the museum is open Monday through Saturday. The research library is open Wednesdays and Thursdays and by appointment. For more information, the museum can be reached by telephone at 520-384-3971.

Sunsites Memory Project

The Sunsites Memory Project is a collaborative community effort sponsored by the Sunsites Community Library, the Sunsites Community Association, and the Pearce-Sunsites Chamber of Commerce. The organizations work together to gather historic information and to plan events to celebrate the 50th anniversary of Sunsites in 2012.